Inviting Transformation

Fourth Edition

Inviting Transformation

Presentational Speaking for a Changing World

Fourth Edition

Sonja K. Foss
University of Colorado Denver

Karen A. Foss
University of New Mexico

WAVELAND
PRESS, INC.
Long Grove, Illinois

For information about this book, contact:
Waveland Press, Inc.
4180 IL Route 83, Suite 101
Long Grove, IL 60047-9580
(847) 634-0081
info@waveland.com
www.waveland.com

Contents

Discovering Knowledge and Belief

Acknowledgments

We never intended to write a public speaking book. In fact, for years, we steadfastly refused even to consider the possibility because we did not believe the world needed another public speaking textbook. There came a time, however, when we felt we had something to say about public speaking that had not been said before and that maybe needed to be said. We decided that we wanted to write a book on the subject so that we no longer would have the experience of lecturing on a concept in a public speaking class, turning to write it on the board, and finding ourselves thinking, "I don't believe this anymore; this doesn't fit my experience." The result is *Inviting Transformation*. Our primary intent with this book is to expand the options for public speaking—or what we prefer to call *presentational speaking*—so that all of us are better prepared for the changing world in which we live.

Once we decided we wanted to write a book on presentational speaking, the writing was helped along by many others. Our publishers, Carol Rowe and Neil Rowe, have been extremely patient and supportive through all four editions of this book. Thank you for trusting us and our vision for this book. Special thanks to Sally Miller Gearhart and Sonia Johnson for sharing with us their notions of transformation that are at the heart of this book. Ongoing conversations with several others about these ideas also were invaluable: Karen Carlton, Deborah Fort, Cindy Griffin, Josina Makau, Steve Moore, and Ann Skinner-Jones. Sonja's advisees at Ohio State University supplied valuable insights about translating theory into practice: Kimberly Barnett Gibson, Gail Chryslee, Debra Greene, D. Lynn O'Brien Hallstein, Cristina Lopez, Helene Shugart, and Catherine Egley Waggoner.

Special thanks to Susana Rinderle and Fahed Al-Sumait for their willingness to prepare and deliver the videotaped presentations. We appreciate your creativity in developing the presentations and your perseverance during the taping process.

Our thanks also go to those who read the book in manuscript form and offered honest feedback and valuable ideas: Robert Trapp, Gail Chryslee, Judith Hendry, Ann Skinner-Jones, Stephen Littlejohn, Melissa McCalla Manassee, and Barbara Walkosz.

We tried out versions of this book on students at Ohio State University, Humboldt State University, the University of Colorado Denver, and the University of New Mexico. Our students provided important feedback and allowed us to use their speaking plans and presentations as models. Teaching assistants and instructors in presentational speaking at the University of New Mexico and the University of Colorado Denver—Carmen Lowry, Kristy Frie, Mary Domenico, and Elizabeth Brunner—provided syllabi, exercises, exams, sample presentations, and insights. Instructors using the book at the International College Beijing of the University of Colorado Denver—Victoria DeFrancisco, Jennifer Gruenewald, Laura Hahn, Cheris Kramarae, and Sharon Varallo—were helpful in addressing multicultural dimensions. We are especially grateful for the confirmation all of you offered that we were on the right track.

Others helped behind the scenes in various ways. Kelly O'Connor Mendoza served as a research assistant, and Marcel Allbritton, Joseph Milan, and M. Rosie Russo helped with the instructor's manual. Rachael Shaff and Kellie Marin produced a YouTube video about invitational rhetoric and the writing of the book. Leah Charney, Christina Villa, Adrianne Devereux, and Anthony Radich allowed us to tape a discussion at the Western States Arts Federation (WESTAF) to use as a sample presentation, and Kendis Paris transcribed two of the presentations at the end of the book. Amy Hasinoff reviewed the section on PowerPoint for us, and Leilani Norman supplied an example for us for chapter 9. Eric Berson provided companion passes on United Airlines to make the process of getting together to write the first edition of the book easier.

Finally, as always, our thanks to Anthony Radich and Stephen Littlejohn for enduring yet another book with patience, good humor, and love.

1

Inviting Transformation

Not that long ago, most people in the United States were raised in homogeneous communities. They grew up, went to school, attended church, and worked with people who were pretty much like they were and who agreed with them on basic issues and values. They rarely met people who were very different from them. But recent changes in the world make such communities a rarity. People are now able to connect easily with people around the world and thus come into contact almost daily with people who are significantly different from them.

THE CHANGING WORLD: ENCOUNTERING DIFFERENCE

What is responsible for the changes that have connected diverse people? You might be surprised to hear that the fall of the Berlin Wall in 1989 was one of the primary causes of such changes. The Wall, which separated West Germany from East Germany, represented a struggle between the two economic systems of capitalism and communism. The fall of the Wall encouraged a view of the world as a single community because "there was only one system left and everyone had to orient . . . to it one way or another."[1]

Developments in transportation that allow for ease of travel also have caused increased exposure to difference. Because of these developments, you are able to leave your home community and venture out into the world. The beginning of regular transatlantic jet service in 1958 was a major catalyst for such travel. "In one fell swoop," boasted Juan Trippe of Pan American World Airways, "we have shrunken the earth."[2] The increased mobility that characterizes the world also means that not only can you leave your community to travel but you can also relocate to new places for school or work, to live in areas you enjoy, or to be with people you love.

The most important change that has increased exposure to difference was the development of new communication technologies such as cell phones, email, social networking, and search engines such as Google. All of these allow you to communicate almost instantaneously with people all over the world. As a result, you can interact with people who live in other countries and whose lives are substantially different from yours. You have access to information and resources you would not have had the opportunity to encounter even a few decades ago. As a result, according to author, reporter, and columnist Thomas Friedman, the world has "flattened."[3] What he means by this is that "all the knowledge centers on the planet" are now connected "into a single global network."[4] As a result, "it is now possible for more people than ever to collaborate and compete in real time with more other people on more different kinds of work from more different corners of the planet and on a more equal footing than at any previous time in the history of the world."[5]

Friedman contrasts current changes in the world with those that came before and concludes that the recent changes have gone "to a whole new level."[6] What he calls *Globalization 1.0* began when Columbus sailed from Spain in 1492, and it lasted until about 1800. This period of globalization, which opened trade between the Old World and the New World, focused on "how much brawn—how much muscle, how much horsepower, wind power, or, later, steam power—your country had and how creatively you could deploy it."[7] In Globalization 1.0, the primary question that characterized the era was: "How can I go global and collaborate with others through my *country*?"[8] Globalization 1.0, Friedman explains, "shrank the world from a size large to a size medium."[9]

The second period of globalization, Globalization 2.0, lasted from 1800 to 2000 and was marked by the creation of a global market and a global economy. Multinational companies looked globally for markets and labor, and, with the dawn of the Industrial Revolution, began producing goods to sell on multiple continents. The major forces driving this era of globalization were "breakthroughs in hardware—from steamships and railroads in the beginning of the period to telephones and mainframe computers toward the end."[10] The big question that characterized this period was: "How can I go global and collaborate with others through my *company*?"[11] This era, Friedman asserts, "shrank the world from a size medium to a size small."[12]

Globalization 3.0 began in about 2000 and was characterized by the power of "*individuals* to collaborate and compete globally."[13] New developments in software and the creation of a global fiber-optic network have enabled individuals and groups to go global easily and seamlessly. In the era of Globalization 3.0, virtually everyone is exposed to difference: "Globalization 3.0 is going to be more and more driven not only by individuals but also by a much more diverse—non-Western, nonwhite—group of individuals. Individuals from every corner of the flat world are being empowered."[14] Individuals in this era ask: "Where do *I* fit into the global competition and opportunities of the day, and how can *I*, on my own, collaborate with others globally?"[15] Globalization 3.0 is "shrinking the world," Friedman says, "from a size small to a size tiny."[16]

Although Friedman himself has not defined Globalization 4.0, others have suggested that globalization is at the beginning of another major evolution.[17] Globalization may seem to be in jeopardy with the rise of isolationism and protectionism that are evident in, for example, new tariffs, the withdrawal of the United States from the Trans-Pacific Partnership trade agreement, and the struggles of many countries to deal with immigration. New developments, however, continue to increase the connections among the world's peoples. The number of global travelers was 1.32 billion in 2017,[18] and the number of Internet users now exceeds four billion.[19] Technological innovations such as file sharing and the outsourcing of activities such as designing, programming, and analysis allow individuals across the world to be connected by work, research, and interests. Virtual currencies like bitcoin promise to make international transactions more secure, thus encouraging even more global interaction. New digital retail platforms—Amazon, Etsy, and Airbnb—allow individuals and small businesses to sell their products and services globally and individual consumers to access them easily with their cell phones and computers.

As possibilities for connection increase, you undoubtedly are discovering differences among the people you encounter in terms of political perspectives, ethnicity and race, gender, religious and spiritual traditions, occupations, economic class, learning styles, dress, educational levels, and values, to name a few. Individuals the world over have the opportunity to experience difference in ways that were not possible only a few years ago. Along with the others with whom you share the planet, you probably are realizing, at the dawn of Globalization 4.0, that the universe is not homogeneous. In fact, it might more appropriately be called a *multiverse* instead of a *universe*.[20]

RESPONDING TO DIFFERENCE

The question of how to live with difference has never been more important than it is now. Encountering different worldviews, value systems, beliefs, and practices (as frequently happens in the era of Globalization 3.0 and in the emerging era of Globalization 4.0) can be challenging and even scary. Several options are available for responding to such difference: (1) isolating yourself; (2) criticizing others; (3) attempting to change others; and (4) welcoming difference.

Isolating Yourself

One way in which you might choose to respond to diversity is by iso-lating yourself and trying to protect your beliefs and values from chal-lenge. Internet programs and sites that present one perspective—Townhall, Breitbart News, and Gateway Pundit on the conservative side or their liberal counterparts Slate, The Young Turks, and Democracy Now!, for example—are comfortable and affirming because they align with your worldview. But they are also examples of isolationism because you are exposing yourself to only one viewpoint. You isolate yourself as well when you don't reach out to new people you encounter on campus, hanging out instead with your friends from high school. In both of these instances, the response to encountering difference is to isolate and pro-tect your worldview from perspectives that differ.

Criticizing Others

A second response you may choose when you encounter diverse world-views is to criticize different perspectives. When you choose this response, you expose yourself to differences, but you scrutinize them and then evalu-ate or judge those differences to be stupid, silly, incorrect, immoral, or bad. Criticizing others who differ from you can range from condemning and attacking your sister because of her choice of clothing to blaming a racial group for rising crime in your neighborhood to accusing all individuals from the Middle East of terrorism. Stereotyping is often part of this process—attributing characteristics to an entire group of people. You might decide, for example, that all members of one ethnic group or all people from one coun-try or all adherents to a particular religion are somehow inferior and wrong.

Attempting to Change Others

Another common response to difference is to try to change those who are different from you. When you select this stance toward differ-ence, you seek uniformity among those you encounter and try to get them to become more like you—to believe and act as you do. If you can get others to change to be like you, your own beliefs are affirmed. You also are likely to feel a sense of power or increased self-worth if your efforts to change someone are successful.

When you try to change others, you do so using four primary modes of rhetoric or approaches to communication: (1) conquest rhetoric; (2) conversion rhetoric; (3) benevolent rhetoric; and (4) advisory rhetoric.[21] The way we are using the term *rhetoric* here may be unfamiliar to you. *Rhetoric* is an ancient term for what is now called *communication*. The term comes from the classical Greeks, who were the first in the Western tradi-tion to study rhetoric in a systematic and formal way. Both terms—*rheto-ric* and *communication*—mean the same thing: the study of how humans use symbols to communicate.

Conquest Rhetoric

The goal of conquest rhetoric is winning. In this kind of rhetoric, you are successful if you win the argument, your view prevails, or you get your way. The purpose of this mode of interaction is to establish your idea, claim, or argument as the best among competing positions. Conquest interactions follow one basic rule: *"Every disagreement has to end with a winner and a loser."*[22]

Conquest rhetoric is a very common form of rhetoric in US culture. It is an inherent part of many cherished American political, legislative, and judicial systems of public communication and decision making. These systems are designed to uphold the rights of individuals, to discover the truth about a situation, and to arrive at judgments concerning controversial issues. In other words, they provide mechanisms that allow individuals to live together in civil ways, despite differences, by creating a means for one perspective to win over another.

In political, legislative, and judicial systems, conquest rhetoric is directed at determining the correct position and rejecting opposing ideas or positions. Conquest rhetoric is used in the political context, for example, when presidential candidates debate. Determining a winner and a loser is an important part of the process. The election itself constitutes conquest rhetoric in that one candidate wins, and the other loses. In Congress, passage of a bill means that supporters of the bill have won, and opponents have lost. A decision by a jury that finds a defendant guilty or not guilty is another example of conquest rhetoric. One side—either the defense or the prosecution—is victorious, and the other is the loser. In more personal realms, conquest rhetoric is apparent as well. In authoritarian families, a father might dictate rules for behavior, and children must comply or be punished.

The #MeToo Movement, designed to raise awareness about the prevalence of sexual harassment and assault, functions as a protest against conquest rhetoric. Those in power in the workplace have been able to engage in sexual harassment and sexual assault, and their victims often felt they had no choice but to acquiesce and remain silent. Although individuals or groups submit to the other in conquest rhetoric, they usually do not change their minds. Their perspective has not been heard or has not prevailed. They go along—they acquiesce on the surface—because they perceive they do not have a choice.

Conversion Rhetoric

Conversion rhetoric is communication designed to change others' perspectives on an issue or to change behavior in some way. It is designed not to defeat an opponent or a position but to convince others of the rightness or superiority of a perspective. Persuasion is the primary method involved in conversion rhetoric. Advertising, marketing, and sales are examples of conversion rhetoric. Religious groups engage in conversion rhetoric when they try to persuade others to believe as they do. Activists in groups such as Idle No More, a group of Native activists fighting the rollback of environmental protections in Canada, or the Silent No More Awareness Campaign, designed to reach out to those hurt by abortion, engage in conversion rhetoric when they direct their efforts toward persuading the public to adopt their views. When you and a friend are planning to see a movie, your friend uses conversion rhetoric when he tries to persuade you to see a romantic comedy rather than the action film you want to see.

Benevolent Rhetoric

Benevolent rhetoric is designed to provide assistance to individuals out of a genuine desire to make their lives better. In this type of communication, the speaker attempts to get audience members to change their beliefs and/or actions out of a concern for their well-being. Benevolent rhetoric usually assumes the form of providing information to others that they can use in their lives in some way. The primary goal in this mode is to benefit others, in contrast to conquest and conversion rhetoric, in which the primary goal is to benefit the speaker in some way.

Health and public safety campaigns are examples of benevolent communication. The Ad Council's Texting and Driving Prevention campaign, featuring the slogan "Stop the texts, stop the wrecks," is designed to discourage individuals from texting while driving. A campaign that encourages workers in outdoor settings to use sunscreen is designed to alert individuals to the dangers of skin cancer and to suggest health practices that will reduce the likelihood of developing it. In an interpersonal context, when you see someone doing a task in a way that seems inefficient and suggest another way to accomplish it, you are using benevolent rhetoric. The individual may or may not choose to adopt your suggestion, but the communication is created from your genuine desire to make life easier or better for your friend or family member.

Advisory Rhetoric

Advisory rhetoric is communication designed to provide requested assistance. In contrast to benevolent rhetoric, in which information is given that was not requested, advisory rhetoric is offered in response to an implicit or explicit request from others for advice or information. Individuals who request advisory rhetoric are interested in learning, growing, and changing, and they deliberately seek out interactions with or information from individuals who can help them accomplish these goals. In advisory rhetoric, individuals with special information and resources provide guidance to others designed to broaden their understanding in some way.

Counseling and education are the paradigm cases of advisory communication. Individuals who choose to go to counseling or therapy to work through difficulties in the hope of leading happier lives or who choose to develop themselves through education deliberately expose themselves to new perspectives they believe will be useful to them. You benefit from advisory rhetoric when you ask a friend who is highly knowledgeable about cars for her advice on what kind of car to buy. Advisory rhetoric is also taking place when you ask a clerk in a department of motor vehicles how to obtain a driver's license, and you follow the instructions given.

Welcoming Difference

When you encounter difference, you have options other than isolating yourself, criticizing, or trying to change those who are different from you. You can stay open to diversity, embracing challenges to your thinking as opportunities for growth and change. In this option, you deliberately look for difference, approaching it in an open and inquiring way and delighting in the exploration of new ways of thinking and being.

We believe that being open to diversity is the best way to respond to difference because it allows you to experience multiple interpretations of an issue. People do not simply observe the world and absorb what is there. Rather, everyone has a distinctive interpretation of what is happening because people are different. Individuals have filters in their heads—what Kenneth Burke calls *terministic screens*—that frame their understanding of a situation.[23] Anything that occupies time, efforts, and energy can serve as a screen or filter for perceptions—professions, hobbies, and education or training are among the most common. Identifying as a vegan, a Christian, a gamer, or as unlovable, for example, is a filter, just as being an engineer, a musician, or a barista is. Thus, there will be as many different interpretations of what is going on as there are people observing. Unless you reach out to and deliberately seek to understand other perspectives, you will only have access to one interpretation of any situation—yours!

Because every perspective is necessarily partial, alternative viewpoints enhance your understanding. When you observe or experience a situation, you get part of it, and someone else gets another part. Together, these parts contribute to a fuller understanding of the whole. When more and more people are included in the process of observing what is going on and contributing their unique interpretations, understanding grows. According to leadership consultant Margaret Wheatley, "the more participants we engage in this participative universe, the more we can access its potentials and the wiser we can become."[24]

The story of the blind men trying to understand an elephant by feeling different parts of the animal is an example of the wider resources available when you actively seek diverse perspectives. One man decides an elephant is long, slim, and flexible because he feels the trunk. Another thinks an elephant is flat and wide because he feels an ear. Another concludes that an elephant is a round and stout creature because he feels a leg. An openness to diverse perspectives allows you to connect your pieces of reality with others who see things differently: "Instead of labeling 'us' as right and 'them' as crazy, blind to the obvious, or refusing to see, we find out that they know something we don't. When we collaborate, we can see the whole elephant."[25]

The awareness that diverse perspectives can serve as resources for understanding requires that you approach difference with genuine appreciation rather than tolerance. The connotations of the term *tolerance* convey a judgmental attitude toward difference. Tolerance implicitly suggests that you are willing to put up with individuals who hold different views, but you still disapprove of them and wish their perspectives aligned with yours. Canadian Prime Minister Justin Trudeau provides a good rationale for rejecting tolerance as a goal:

> I think we can aim a little higher than mere tolerance. Think about it: Saying "I tolerate you" actually means something like, "OK, I grudgingly admit that you have a right to exist, just don't get in my face about it, and oh, don't date my sister." There's not a religion in the world that asks you to "tolerate they neighbor." So let's try for something a little more like acceptance, respect, friendship, and yes, even love.[26]

Openness to diversity means that you actively and even joyfully allow another person to be different from you—celebrating and appreciating those differences. You are delighted with those who hold different perspectives because those differences offer new ways of looking at, understanding, and enriching your world.

Max Hawkins, a Google engineer, provides an example of someone who deliberately decided to embrace difference. Realizing he was in a rut—he went to the same places, did the same things, and saw the same people—he designed a Facebook app that randomly selected an activity for him in the San Francisco Bay area. Every Friday, he headed out to experience what his app had found for him to do. He tried salsa dancing and acroyoga, got drunk with some Russians, and attended a pancake breakfast at a community center. He even used the app to choose where he would celebrate Christmas; the app selected a party at a couple's home in Fresno. He now lets the app select his music, the restaurants where he eats, and where he goes on vacation. Max appreciates how much bigger his world is and how many new subjects and perspectives he has had a chance to explore because of his deliberate effort to seek out new experiences.[27]

When you encounter someone with a different vision and understanding of the world, you have an opportunity to gain a more complete and comprehensive perspective. You may begin to think or act differently. As your exposure to difference transforms you, so, too, is the world changed. A change in your perspective can have an impact on external material conditions in a number of ways.

One way in which your own transformation creates changes in the external world is that something you once saw as a problem no longer is. When you gain a new perspective, you might find that something you once thought was troublesome no longer requires your time and energy. This is the case even with things we often believe are fixed—like physical pain. An elderly man who had severe pain in his feet had a hard time focusing on anything else; he enrolled in a program of meditation to address the pain. He told the class the pain was so bad he wanted to cut off his feet. At the end of the program, he offered a different assessment, even though the pain was about the same. He said that "the pain hadn't changed much but that his attitude toward his pain had changed a lot. . . . His feet were less of a problem."[28] Perhaps your father left your family when you were young, and you have always seen his departure as a problem. You can reframe that perspective and choose not to see it as a problem by appreciating how well your mother provided for your family and how much you were loved by (and not abandoned by) your mother and your siblings. You also can try to understand why leaving made sense to your father.

The Dalai Lama provides an explanation for why a change in interpretation can diminish the perceived severity of a problem:

> It seems that often when problems arise, your outlook becomes narrow. All of your attention may be focused on worrying about the problem, and you may have a sense that you're the only one that is going through such difficulties. This can lead to a kind of self-absorption that can make the problem seem very intense. . . . But if you can make comparisons, view your situation from a different perspective, somehow something happens.[29]

Choosing to interpret something differently encourages you to be open to new possibilities and ways of solving a problem.

The opportunity to discover resources for innovating that were not evident to you before is another way your transformation may alter conditions in the outside world. When you change yourself by adopting a new vantage point, you see the resources out in the world as more abundant than you did previously. You might discover people in your environment who direct you to resources you didn't know existed, or you might come up with a solution to a problem that you could not see before. Perhaps you don't get the job you thought was your dream job, for example, but the interview gives you an idea for a niche market that you hadn't heard about before where you can make excellent use of your skills. Your perception of the availability of a greater number of resources provides more options for you to use to alter your conditions: "When your mind changes, new possibilities tend to arise. . . . Your thinking expands in scope."[30]

Asset-Based Community Development (ABCD) is an example of the process of discovering and employing resources that were not initially conceptualized as resources. ABCD is a worldwide movement designed to reframe conditions that typically are seen as problems—abandoned storefronts and blighted neighborhoods, for example—into assets. It uses the skills of a community's citizens—young people, disabled people, artists, and thriving professionals—as well as the resources of its formal institutions—businesses, schools, libraries, parks, and social service agencies—to construct community assets in imaginative ways.[31] An example of how ABCD works can be seen in the Hillside Court neighborhood of Richmond, Virginia. Because it was the site of several murders and drive-by shootings, the neighbors of Hillside Court got together to see what could be done to make the neighborhood a safe place. Eventually, nine different initiatives were started that serve the entire community, including a job program, a cheerleading team, a football league, a senior women's sports team, a food pantry, and a cooking class.[32] A change in interpretation, prompted by ABCD, allowed the community to recognize and make use of resources it had not previously perceived as assets.

There's another explanation for how changes in the outer world can result from small individual acts. It's the phenomenon known as the *butterfly effect*—the idea that a "small effect can have significant consequences."[33] Meteorologist Edward Lorenz, who identified the butterfly effect, discovered in his modeling of the weather that "a nearly imperceptible change in a constant will produce a qualitative change in the system's behavior" and that "small initial differences will amplify until they are no longer small."[34] Thus, "the flap of a butterfly's wings in Brazil today may make the difference between calm weather and a tornado in Texas next month."[35] Theoretical physicist and cosmologist Stephen Hawking provides another example of the butterfly effect:

> If the density of the universe one second after the big bang had been greater by one part in a thousand billion, the universe would have recollapsed after ten years. On the other hand, if the density of the universe at that time had been less by the same amount, the universe would have been essentially empty since it was about ten years old.[36]

On a smaller scale, the decision to walk a different way home from school or to stop and talk to a neighbor may have consequences that you cannot see in the moment. These small changes may enable you to encounter a job opportunity or to discover some information you have been seeking for a long time. A very small change, then, can drastically alter an outcome—suggesting that, as you change, the world itself may change.

Former *Washington Post* reporter and staff writer for *The New Yorker* Malcolm Gladwell offers yet another explanation for how individual change creates larger societal changes. He discovered that a "small number of people" in a "small number of situations" start behaving very differently, and that behavior spreads to others in similar situations. Each transformation, no matter how small, gains strength because it is connected to other changes. Gladwell gives the label the *tipping point* to "that one dramatic moment . . . when everything can change all at once."[37] The rapid legalization of gay marriage in the United States and many countries around the world is an example of the tipping point in operation.

Same-sex marriage had been prohibited and, indeed, unthinkable for centuries. Then, suddenly, individual states in the United States began legalizing gay marriage. In 2015, the Supreme Court ruled that the Fourteenth Amendment requires all states to recognize same-sex marriage. Other countries did the same, including Ireland, which became the first country to approve gay marriage by popular vote.

Welcoming the input that divergent perspectives provide and allowing those perspectives to transform you can result in a better and more expanded understanding of the world. We call this option *invitational rhetoric*. Invitational rhetoric involves a deliberate exposure to and consideration of diverse voices as beneficial rather than detrimental. The different perspectives that exist all around you constitute an invitation for you to reconsider and expand your perspectives, growing and changing in the process.

DEFINITION OF INVITATIONAL RHETORIC

An invitation is a request for the presence or participation of someone. When you issue an invitation, you ask someone to engage in some activity with you.[38] In invitational rhetoric, you invite your audience members to see the world as you do and to seriously consider your perspective. The object of invitational rhetoric is understanding, reached as communicators engage in a "sharing of worlds through words."[39] The goal is not to win or to prove superiority. Instead, the goal is to clarify ideas and to achieve understanding for all participants involved in the interaction. In invitational rhetoric, the speaker and audience jointly consider and contribute to thinking about an issue so that everyone involved gains a greater understanding of the subtlety, richness, and complexity of that issue. As diverse perspectives are considered, those involved do their best to value the perspectives of others, even if they disagree with them.

The result of invitational rhetoric is often more than an understanding of an issue. Because of the nonjudgmental and nonadversarial framework in which the interaction takes place, the participants themselves understand one another better. For example, using invitational rhetoric, you might explain to a friend why you are a supporter of President Donald Trump. You then would listen carefully to your friend's explanation of why he thinks Trump is a poor president. Both of you would better understand the reasons for the other's views, but you also would understand one another better because you would have a clearer idea of the motivation and rationale for your various perspectives.

Invitational rhetoric brings benefits to both the speaker and the audience. When you initiate communication with others using this mode, you are inviting the audience to see and experience the world in new and more comprehensive ways. At the same time, as you engage with others, you are open to learning from their perspectives. You enter an interaction seeking to share your perspective with others, and you compare it with the perspectives that audience members offer you. You may choose, as a result, to engage in a process of questioning and rethinking your own viewpoint, perhaps changing in some way as a result.

Why would you want to be changed or transformed? What are the benefits to changing your mind about something or deciding to adopt some new way of behaving? For one, you cannot not change. Although you might want constancy in your life and want to stick with familiar environments, habits, and beliefs, you can't because everything is always changing—the only things that are not changing are dead. But we are asking you not only to recognize the constancy of change but to embrace and welcome it. People who regularly seek out fresh experiences and perspectives tend to be more mentally agile, creative, and emotionally resilient than those who don't. When you adopt new perspectives and allow yourself to act in new ways, you have the opportunity to live your best life because you have access to many more possibilities, resources, and opportunities from which to draw for crafting your life.

ASSUMPTIONS OF INVITATIONAL RHETORIC

Six key assumptions characterize invitational rhetoric, all of which help you use this mode of rhetoric to approach difference as a resource: (1) understanding is the purpose of communication in invitational rhetoric; (2) participants in invitational rhetoric listen with openness; (3) in invitational rhetoric, speaker and audience are viewed as equals; (4) participants enter invitational rhetoric willing to be changed; (5) invitational rhetoric creates a world of appreciation for difference; and (6) invitational rhetoric is one of many options in your communication toolbox.[40]

Understanding is the purpose of communication in invitational rhetoric.

The purpose of invitational rhetoric is understanding. Both you and your audience enter an interaction seeking to understand the ideas and attitudes of the other. You adopt the frame of reference of the other concerning the issue under discussion. As psychotherapist Carl Rogers explains, "To be with another in this way means that for the time being, you lay aside your own views and values in order to enter another's world without prejudice."[41] The goal of understanding in invitational rhetoric encourages both the speaker and the audience to "venture outside the walls that normally protect them from hearing things that don't fit their worldview. . . . They feel a new curiosity about the words and beliefs of people who see things differently. . . . It is more than hearing another's point of view—it is making room for that point of view."[42]

The Public Conversations Project (PCP) is a group designed to seek understanding rather than change. Formed to deal with intractable social conflicts, the group is best known for its conversations between pro-choice and antiabortion activists in 1994, following the murder of two abortion-clinic staff members. To help the community heal, the PCP invited six activists in the abortion debate—three from each side—to come together for a different kind of conversation than is typical for highly charged issues. Over dinner the first night, participants shared the life experiences that brought them to their particular views on abortion. During the hours of conversation that followed, participants came to better understand the other side of the issue and why someone might have a different perspective about abortion. The conversations, designed to last for four sessions, continued for almost seven years. None of the participants changed their minds on abortion, but they became fast friends in spite of their strong differences of opinion on the issue.[43]

There are multiple terms for the focus on understanding that characterizes invitational rhetoric. Philosopher Martha Nussbaum uses the term *narrative imagination* to characterize the communicator's stance in this kind of interaction. Narrative imagination involves the "ability to think what it might be like to be in the shoes of a person different from oneself, to be an intelligent reader of that person's story, and to understand the emotions and wishes and desires that someone so placed might have."[44] Other terms for this kind of understanding are *trial empathy, trial identification,* and *transient identification.*[45] In invitational rhetoric, you try on another person's perspective to experience how it feels and to discover how it makes sense to that person. At the end of an invitational interaction—if you have genuinely worked to understand someone else's perspective—you should be able to express that person's perspective "so clearly, vividly, and fairly" that the other person could say, "'Thanks, I wish I'd thought of putting it that way.'"[46]

Trying to understand someone is very different from what we usually do when we interact with others, which is to try to change them. But have you ever noticed how hard it is to change other people, especially on issues about which they care deeply? Many approaches to persuasion implicitly suggest that changing another person is possible and almost easy, even when the targeted beliefs are deeply held. According to these theories, individuals gladly embrace a new way of believing or acting when they are presented with, for example, logical or emotional appeals, vibrant metaphors, or dynamic modes of delivery. Persuasion is seen as a natural outcome of the use of these kinds of appeals.

Our experience of trying to persuade others is different from what these theories describe, and we suspect yours is, too. Think about what happens when someone tells you what you should do or how you should think. What is your likely response? If you are like most people, you get defensive and even angry and suggest all sorts of reasons why what you are doing or thinking works just fine for you. You usually "dig in your heels" and maintain your position with greater commitment than before.

Myles Horton, founder of the Highlander Folk School for community-based organizing, describes what often happens when people try to change others: "If people have a position on something and you try to argue them into changing it, you're going to strengthen that position."[47]

Because our society provides very few examples of people who try to understand instead of trying to change one another when they disagree, engaging in invitational rhetoric can seem strange at first. This kind of interaction exercises an entirely different set of communication muscles from what you are probably used to using. But once you try it a few times, you will learn that you can talk about issues without trying to get others to change their minds, and you will learn how to approach others in ways that help you understand them and their perspectives.

Participants in invitational rhetoric listen with openness.

When you listen to other people talk, you may find yourself listening in various ways, but many of them involve listening to win. You may listen, for example, to formulate a good comeback to what the other person is saying. You may listen only for what you already know or for what you expect to hear. Maybe you have a tendency to interrupt the other person so you don't even hear the entire explanation. You are listening, in other words, to have your perspective prevail.

In invitational rhetoric, listening is different. It is done with openness and with the intent to understand. Listening is "an invitation—a hosting. This hosting of the other is as a guest, as a not-me."[48] One way to think about listening with openness is to invert the two parts of the word *understand* so that listening becomes *standing under*—consciously standing under "the other's perspective, letting it wash over, through, and around" you, letting it inform and even challenge your thinking. By standing under the perspective of another, you turn listening for mastery or control of others—for winning—into listening for receptivity and openness.[49] As psychologist Michael P. Nichols suggests, "To listen is to pay attention, take an interest, care about, take to heart, validate, acknowledge, be moved . . . appreciate."[50]

Listening in invitational rhetoric requires a certain degree of detachment. Communication professor Lisbeth Lipari calls this kind of detachment *listening being*:

> I come to the conversation empty—not empty of my experience or
> history—but empty of the belief that my experience or history defines
> the limits of possible meaning and experience. Thereby, in *listening
> being* I am being empty of possession and of all intentions other than
> the intention of engagement with you and of the what-will-happen.[51]

She elaborates: "I need to be fully present to the ongoing expression of you. Letting go of my ideas about who you are, who I am, what 'should' be. I let all that go, and stay present, attending, aware."[52] Invitational lis-

teners' emptiness is a form of inner silence that suspends the noise of dis-
cursive thought and facilitates a focus on and attention to the other that
enables them to really absorb the other's words. Listening being is not
unlike the philosophy of dialogue explored by philosopher Abraham
Kaplan: "If I am really talking with you, I *have* nothing to say; what I say
arises as you and I genuinely relate to one another. I do not know before-
hand *who* I will be, because I am open to you just as you are open to me."[53]

Listening in invitational rhetoric looks different, then, from the listening you might be inclined to do. Invitational listening means you do not
interrupt others but give them time to say what they want. You make an
effort to think from the perspective of the other, trying to make that new
perspective vivid in your own mind. You don't argue mentally, you finish
listening before you speak, and you don't assume you know what the
speaker is going to say next. You do not assume the speaker is using particular words in the same way that you do, and you paraphrase or restate
the speaker's message to test your understanding of what you heard. As
you listen, you are asking yourself questions such as: "How attentive am I
to the speaker?," "How are my experiences and values affecting what I am
hearing?," and "What can I say to show I understand?"[54]

In invitational rhetoric, speaker and audience are viewed as equals.

In traditional models of speaking, you as the speaker take center
stage; all eyes are on you, and you generally are assumed to be the expert
on your topic. Such a privileged stance typically characterizes speaking in
the conquest and conversion modes and sometimes in the benevolent
and advisory modes. The speaker is viewed as superior to the audience—
as having more knowledge, experience, or resources than others do.

Audiences also are viewed in a particular way in traditional models of
speaking. Audience members are seen as uninformed, misguided, or
naïve. The belief systems and behaviors they have created for living in
the world are devalued and considered to be inadequate or inappropriate
simply because their views differ from those of the speaker. The speaker
approaches the audience with an attitude of "let me help you, let me
enlighten you, let me show you the way."[55] Even if an audience member
is someone you love and respect, when you use traditional models of
speaking, you unintentionally reduce that person to someone who is less
able than you are to think through an issue or to make an informed and
appropriate decision without your input.

The relationship between the communicator and the audience is different in invitational rhetoric. The speaker and the audience are regarded
as equal peers; the speaker is a facilitator rather than an all-knowing
expert. As a communicator in invitational rhetoric, you encourage others
to contribute equally to the interaction with you. You may have access to
helpful knowledge or resources that those with whom you are interacting

do not, but you do not claim that your experiences or your perspectives are superior to theirs. This view is summarized by writer Ursula Le Guin, who asks how can one experience "deny, negate, disprove, another experience? Even if I've had a lot more of it, *your* experience is your truth. How can one being prove another being wrong? Even if you're a lot younger and smarter than me, *my* being is my truth."[56]

In invitational rhetoric, audience members are seen as having experiences and holding perspectives that are valuable and legitimate. You conceptualize audience members as authorities on their own lives who hold the beliefs they do and act as they do for reasons that make good sense to them. Self-determination, then, is part of an invitational worldview. Grounded in a respect for others, self-determination allows individuals to make their own decisions about how they wish to live their lives. As activist Sonia Johnson explains, the principle of self-determination involves a trust that others are doing the best they can at the moment and simply need "to be unconditionally accepted as the experts on their own lives."[57]

But what if someone has more power than another in an interaction? How can the individuals involved be seen as equals? This is a very common situation—maybe someone has more authority, physical power, access to resources that others don't have, or interpersonal power because of personal charisma. When power differentials are present, seeing and valuing all interactants equally can seem difficult if not impossible.

Keeping the objective of the interaction in mind is key to the negotiation of power differences in an invitational exchange. The participants are engaged in interaction because they want to understand—they want to learn about other perspectives. The goal is to separate the power other people have from the value assigned to their perspective. Focus on the perspectives that participants offer in the interaction, and remember that they all have the power of their unique perspectives. Enter interactions acknowledging the various kinds of powers of the interactants and the influence such powers may have on perspectives. Once those perspectives are articulated and offered, they lie on the table side by side—equal in value, all being considered fully by everyone involved.

The power you enact in invitational rhetoric is power-with, where power to create knowledge and make decisions is shared between the speaker and the audience. The resources, ideas, and creativity of all participants are accessed and valued as everyone works together to solve a problem or make a decision. In power-with, decisions are made not because one person suggests an option or persuades others but because the group, as a collective, comes to believe a certain idea or plan is good.[58] Power-with is "dependent on personal responsibility, on . . . creativity and daring, and on the willingness of others to respond."[59] Power is not a quality to exercise over others but is something that can be employed by all participants in the interaction so that it energizes, facilitates, and enables everyone involved to contribute to and learn from the interaction.

Participants enter invitational rhetoric willing to be changed.

According to the field of physics, molecules necessarily shift and change when individuals interact with each other. The change that is common to all communication can be conceptualized as a kind of disruption of the integrity of participants. *Integrity* is a vision of yourself marked by a sense of continuity and coherence of your perspectives, developed from your particular experiences and how you have chosen to respond to those experiences. Any new perspective that you encounter disrupts or interrupts the settled integrity you have created for yourself. Exposure to new perspectives inevitably unsettles and disorients you, at least temporarily.

Such a disruption in integrity, which occurs in both persuasive and invitational encounters, happens in different ways in the two kinds of interactions. In persuasion, communicators deliberately seek to disrupt the integrity of others—to challenge and change the ways of thinking, believing, and acting that others have created for themselves. In this approach to change, arguments often harm or damage another person's belief system and disrupt that person's integrity. This approach can feel like an intrusion—harsh, painful, and unwelcome.

In contrast, individuals in an invitational exchange interrupt their own integrity and welcome the disruption. They willingly assume the standpoint of the other by engaging that person's perspective. One metaphor to describe this access to new ideas and understanding is a journey to new places—change feels light, anticipatory, and welcomed. The change can also feel like a lightning bolt if understanding and accepting another's perspective shatter previously held beliefs.

The process of transformation more readily happens in invitational rhetoric than with the other modes of rhetoric because participants in invitational rhetoric enter communication situations willing to be changed. In contrast to conquest or conversion rhetoric, the risk involved in invitational rhetoric "is not that you may lose but rather that you may change."[60] As Rogers notes, "if you are willing to enter [another's] private world and see the way life appears to him . . . you run the risk of being changed yourself."[61] Because you are open to new ways of understanding, you are willing to yield your perspective or to change your mind about what you believe. A willingness to change is not compromising your beliefs or surrendering your values. Instead, it is a genuine shift in perspective that results from a consideration of another's views. Another way to think about change in invitational rhetoric is that it is much like the "I-Thou" relationship described by philosopher Martin Buber—a turning toward the other. Invitational rhetoric involves meeting another's position "in its uniqueness, letting it have its impact."[62] You enter the communication situation willing to dismantle your point of view, willing to revise yourself.

In invitational rhetoric, change is the result of inner motivation and readiness to change. Rhetorical theorist Sally Miller Gearhart explains the process as follows:

> No one can change an egg into a chicken. If, however, there is the potential in the egg to be a chicken . . . the "internal basis for change"—then there is the likelihood that in the right environment (moisture, temperature, the "external conditions for change") the egg will hatch. A stone, on the other hand, has no internal basis for hatching into a chicken and an eternity of sitting in the proper conditions of moisture and temperature will not make possible its transformation into a chicken.[63]

Change happens when an environment is created in which individuals decide to change themselves. At most, as a speaker, you are able to create an environment in which audience members are willing to consider changing. As a result, they may or may not decide to make a change. Perhaps they choose not to change immediately, but your presentation might plant an idea they will continue to think about, with change coming months or even years later.

To be willing to change violates a very strong tenet of human nature: "Human beings like to be right. It is programmed into us as a survival mechanism. If you were to question everything, you wouldn't survive."[64] When the things you know to be true and right are challenged, you often find that you are very uncomfortable. In an invitational interaction, you may be asked to call into question the things that are most important to you, which can be a frightening process. As consultant and author Annette Simmons points out, "There is always a risk when you engage in the process of learning. Even though you can be assured that this mental redesign will incorporate a higher level of understanding than you have right now, the potential disruption is daunting. Like renovating a house, it can be inconvenient to add that new wing."[65]

Gearhart offers an example of this willingness to change in her life. She is strongly opposed to the hunting of animals, but she deliberately leaves open the possibility that hunting is acceptable: "And that means that I've got to risk believing that hunting . . . may be in some cases a viable thing for human beings to do. And that's scary."[66]

Invitational rhetoric creates a world of appreciation for difference.

You have a choice about the kind of rhetoric in which to engage— conquest, conversion, benevolent, advisory, or invitational. Different choices create different worlds in which to live. By the choices you make in your use of communication, you create your reality. Communication isn't just words and sounds and gestures that reflect your world—it is the means through which you create that world. This relationship may sound backwards from how you think of the relationship between communication and reality. You may assume that reality is outside of you in the external world, and you use communication to name and talk about that reality. But reality or knowledge is the *result* of the process of communication. Reality is not fixed; it changes according to the symbols or the communication you use to talk about it. Linguist Deborah Tannen explains that often when we think we are using language, language is using us. The terms with which we talk about something shape the way we see it and the way we think about it: "This is how language works. It invisibly molds our way of thinking about people, actions, and the world around us."[67]

Some examples will clarify the relationship between the symbols you choose and the reality you experience. How you choose to name or label a situation determines how you respond to it. If you call a person a *friend,* for example, that is different from calling the person an *acquaintance* or a *lover.* Each label orients you in a different way to that person, and you treat that person accordingly. You experience and treat a rambunctious child differently depending on whether you call her *gifted, spoiled,* or *obnoxious.* Similarly, you experience a colleague differently if you describe him as *ambitious* and *motivated* or *pushy* and *aggressive.* You've also probably had the experience of deciding you were not going to have a good time at a party, and then you had exactly the lousy time you predicted through your self-talk.

Each of the types of rhetoric creates different kinds of worlds. For example, the use of conquest and conversion rhetorics creates an adversarial and contentious world. Tannen uses the term *argument culture* to describe the nature of this world and suggests that it is marked by "a pervasive warlike atmosphere that makes us approach public dialogue, and just about anything you need to accomplish, as if it were a fight."[68] The argument culture tends to be a world of negative emotions because conquest and conversion rhetorics often produce feelings of inadequacy, humiliation, guilt, or angry submission for some and feelings of superiority and domination for others.

Examples of the adversarial world that conquest and conversion rhetorics have created are readily apparent. Negative political advertisements distort candidates' records and predict catastrophic consequences if the opposing candidate is elected. Road rage consumes drivers, who try to get revenge through words, gestures, or worse. Children experience the harassing behavior of bullies in their schools, and at the college level, bullying becomes hazing. People rant and rave on the Internet, television, and radio—intimidating, demonizing, insulting, and humiliating others who are different from them or who hold perspectives different from theirs. Her description is harsh, but linguist Suzette Haden Elgin describes the world that conquest and conversion rhetorics have created in this way: "Everybody bickering and bad-mouthing and putting each other down; everybody nagging and griping and sneering, whining and carping and bellyaching."[69]

Another outcome of an adversarial world is that it continually creates the conditions for the next conflict. When positions are polarized and entrenched, conquest and conversion modes of communication persist, and additional conflict is the inevitable outcome. Most important, however, the adversarial world created by conquest and conversion rhetorics tends to shut down opportunities for transformation. Acts of power-over practically guarantee another cycle of disagreement and conflict because no one likes to lose. People resent the imposition of power and resist it, using whatever means are available to them. In the adversarial world, different perspectives are not seen as opportunities for growth but as perspectives to be squashed and squelched.

In contrast, if you choose invitational rhetoric, you are creating a different kind of world through your communication—a world of appreciation for difference. You are grateful for the different perspectives that others have because they provide you with new information about the world—information that helps you understand something better. Because invitational rhetoric is designed to open up ways of being in the world by making room for multiple viewpoints, invitational rhetors value and, in fact, seek variety, newness, difference, surprise, and even discomfort as they are open to a variety of perspectives. Tension dissipates as you let others believe and act as they choose, delighting in how different their choices are from yours. In this world, people feel safe, are valued, and have the freedom to make their own decisions about their lives. The outcome is a civil exchange of ideas and appreciation for the diversity those ideas provide.

Invitational rhetoric is one of many options in your communication toolbox.

You may be thinking that an invitational mode of communication is not practical if you wish to be successful in your personal and professional life. Because conquest and conversion rhetorics are prominent features of the contemporary world, you may believe you need to employ them to accomplish your goals. We want to make clear that invitational rhetoric cannot and should not be used in all situations. We are not asking you to forego the other modes of rhetoric and to use invitational rhetoric exclusively.

Conquest, conversion, benevolent, and advisory rhetorics have their place, and they are the appropriate modes to use in certain situations. In systems based on modes of rhetoric such as conquest and conversion, you may find that you must operate according to the conventions of those systems. In a legal context, for example, argumentative rather than invitational methods are necessary for pleading criminal and civil cases. On the job, you will encounter situations where, in order to be effective, you need to use persuasion to convince someone to adopt your proposal. In situations of crisis, when time is short and decisions must be made quickly, conquest rhetoric may be your only feasible choice. There also are times when you must argue against offensive or dangerous ideas, as Yugoslavian poet Charles Simic suggests: "There are moments in life when true invective is called for, when it becomes an absolute necessity, out of a deep sense of justice, to denounce, mock, vituperate, lash out, in the strongest possible language."[70] Conquest and conversion rhetorics are legitimate and valuable options that help achieve particular communication goals in many situations.

You may discover, however, that there are opportunities for invitational rhetoric in contexts that are predominately conquest or conversion in nature. Even in environments such as the legal context, opportunities for using invitational rhetoric exist as speakers engage in pretrial conferences and negotiations. There are also increasing opportunities to resolve disputes outside of the legal system using mediation. You are likely to be more successful in all aspects of your life if you are able to take in new information and seriously consider its application and relevance to an issue. Recognizing that others may legitimately believe differently from you and genuinely trying to understand what others think and believe are valuable skills. As philosopher Janice Moulton notes, "A friendly, warm, nonadversarial manner surely does not interfere with persuading customers to buy, getting employees to carry out directions conscientiously, convincing juries, teaching students, getting help and cooperation from coworkers, and promotions from the boss."[71]

To summarize, the world today exposes you to differences of all kinds. You can respond to the differences you encounter by isolating yourself, criticizing, trying to change others, or welcoming and appreciating differences. If you choose the last option, you are engaging in invitational rhetoric, a mode of communicating in which your goal is to invite others to understand your perspective just as you try to understand theirs. In invitational rhetoric, you listen to the other person with openness. You and the audience are equal as you each explore the other's perspective, and the kind of power is power-with. You issue an invitation for others to participate in your world rather than seeking to change those with whom you come into contact, and you yourself are willing to be changed by what happens in the interaction. Invitational rhetoric creates a more respectful, appreciative world in which to live, especially in situations when you encounter difference.

The six assumptions about invitational rhetoric describe an ideal interaction. You hope, as you enter a communication situation, that others will want to participate in an invitational exchange with you. You invite them to engage with you around a topic and to exchange perspectives about it. But they may refuse your invitation. They may not want to hear your perspective, they may choose not to share their perspectives with you, or they may listen to your perspective only to figure out how to counter it. You have to be all right with any of these responses. People do not have to accept invitations. Remember, too, that one of the values inherent in invitational rhetoric is self-determination. Just as you want to think and act in ways that you choose, you want to give that same right to others—they get to do what they choose. If your invitation to communicate in invitational ways is refused, you want to thank the audience members for their time and exit the situation in a civil and professional way.

Communicating within an invitational frame is not simply a particular kind of communication practice. It constitutes a unique worldview. To engage in invitational rhetoric is not simply to choose to employ a particular set of communicative forms. It is to enter into a very different worldview and to adopt a different ideological stance from the one that characterizes persuasion. As a result, to be an invitational communicator is not an easy task. You might have difficulty articulating your perspective fully, accurately, and clearly. You might wrestle with the effort to listen to new or different perspectives. You may not know how to ask for clarification, or you simply may be unfamiliar with the act of listening to a perspective that is profoundly different from your own. At other times, you may have difficulty genuinely viewing someone as a legitimate participant in an interaction if that person is someone who frustrates, irritates, or angers you. In other instances, even though you recognize that you are unlikely to be successful in persuading someone, you will have trouble refraining from engaging in persuasive discourse with those you care deeply about. Sometimes, you will grow weary of the commitment to welcoming diverse perspectives and simply want to hold onto yours unchallenged by others for at least a little while.

But there are times when working hard to communicate with someone and to accomplish understanding is worthwhile and important. At these times, you are willing to do the work required for an invitational interaction—to be uncomfortable, to listen to things with which you might not agree, and to have your own beliefs and thoughts challenged in major ways. We turn now to how to enact invitational rhetoric in your daily communication practices.

PRESENTATIONAL SPEAKING

We hope the speaking you do will often take place within an invitational frame. The standard image of giving a speech or making a presentation is not particularly invitational. The image that probably comes to mind is one person speaking from behind a lectern, looking out at an audience of many people. In this conception of public speaking, the speaker does all the talking, and any participation by the audience is limited to asking questions at the end of the speech. You probably associate this kind of speaking event with public settings such as lecture halls, classrooms, workplaces, senate chambers, courts of law, churches, and campaign rallies.

Perhaps the thought of engaging in this kind of speaking terrifies you. You imagine yourself as that speaker, and you immediately get anxious, recalling those times in the past when you had to give a speech. If you are using this book in a public speaking class that is required for graduation from college, you may be worried that you will not pass the course if stage fright overtakes you when you have to give a speech. Your knees, hands, and voice shake; your mouth goes dry, and you may even feel like you are about to throw up. What you are feeling is best described as *public freaking* rather than *public speaking*.

Most of your communication, however, does not take the form of formal public speeches. In fact, most people give those kinds of speeches relatively infrequently. If you develop communication skills that only enable you to speak at events that traditionally are defined as *public speaking*, you will be ill equipped to communicate in the variety of situations you encounter every day. In this book, then, we do not limit our discussion of communication principles and strategies only to those speaking situations in which one person speaks to an audience in a formal speaking context. In general, we believe that every time you speak, you are making a presentation, and you make many presentations in the course of a day, most of which do not take place in formal public settings. This is why we prefer the term *presentational speaking* rather than *public speaking* to encompass the kind of communication that is the focus of this book. Many of these other kinds of presentations are also more likely to allow you to communicate invitationally.

Presentational speaking encompasses all of the kinds of communication in which you engage as you move through your day. You are giving a presentation when people ask your views on something and you offer your opinion, when you raise your hand in class or at a meeting to answer a question, when you converse with a friend about the movie you just saw, or when you give advice about something to your teenaged son or daughter. Similarly, presentational speaking includes the communication used by a coach who gives a pep talk to a wrestling team, a new manager who introduces herself at her first staff meeting, a sales representative who meets with a client, a student who prepares a video introduction for an online class, and a homeowner who interviews a contractor in preparation for remodeling the kitchen. In all of these situations, communicators are engaged in presentational speaking.

Sometimes you will have considerable time to plan your presentation; at other times, you will have little or no time for advance preparation. Whatever form your presentation takes, the basic process of communicating is essentially the same. The tools for constructing presentations offered in this book are designed to be useful across all of your communication encounters. They apply across the continuum of speaking contexts and formats—from casual, informal, one-to-one presentations to formal situations in which you address a large audience.

Not only do we believe that conceptualizing your communication as a series of minipresentations is a more realistic way to think about presentational speaking, but we also believe that thinking about your communication in this way can help with the fear of speaking mentioned earlier. Realizing that you are communicating constantly and that you have considerable practice giving presentations should help you feel more comfortable. If you can transfer the comfort you feel in everyday contexts when you have an audience of one or two to larger audiences, you will discover that such audiences are not as problematic as you might think. (We talk more about speech anxiety in chapter 9, so check out that chapter if this is a problem for you.)

We hope this book makes the process of presentational speaking easier by providing a toolkit you can use to craft the presentations that will be ever present in your life. We hope, too, that you will consider, try out, and come to appreciate invitational approaches as you interact with all those who make up an increasingly diverse world. Finally, we hope you come to enjoy the process of communicating for the opportunities it offers for you to learn about others' perspectives and to share your own about the issues important in your life.

2

Selecting Interactional Goals

You communicate all the time, and you have various reasons for giving the presentations you do. Each reason is an interactional goal—what you hope to accomplish as a result of your decision to speak. You never speak without a reason, so figuring out the reason—the interactional goal—is a crucial first step in developing your presentation.

The particular goal you select depends on the context or situation in which you are speaking. Rhetorical theorist Lloyd Bitzer labels the context for speaking the *rhetorical situation*.[1] In any context in which you choose to speak, you are responding to an exigence. An exigence, according to Bitzer, is a need, problem, or defect in a situation. When you speak, your discourse comes into existence because of some situation to which you want to respond. Kenneth Burke, another rhetorical theorist, talks about communication in a similar way as "answers to questions posed by the situation in which they arose."[2] In other words, when you give a presentation, you do so because you believe you can contribute to a particular situation. Your interactional goal is the strategy you choose for responding to the exigence of that situation.

The idea of invitation introduced in chapter 1 is a good starting place for understanding how interactional goals function. When you host a party, you generally have a reason for doing so. Maybe you want to celebrate a birthday or have friends over to watch the Super Bowl or play Rocket League. You decide which friends you want to invite; when you call, text, or send them an evite, you let them know the purpose for the gathering. An interactional goal functions the same way. It helps you understand, in advance of your presentation, why you are speaking, and it communicates that reason to your audience in the course of your presentation. To return to the party analogy, you communicate with your friends so that they will know that they will be coming over for a birthday party, for example, rather than to play video games.

INTERACTIONAL GOALS

There are five major interactional goals or purposes for speaking: (1) to assert individuality; (2) to articulate a perspective; (3) to build community; (4) to seek adherence; and (5) to discover knowledge and belief.

To Assert Individuality

As a speaker, you continually engage in communication that reveals who you are as an individual. You reveal your identity and your uniqueness, for example, through your clothing, your friends, the kinds of music you like, where you live, your major, and your choice of occupation. In some instances, however, asserting individuality is your main reason for communicating, so this interactional goal becomes the focus of your presentation. In a presentation designed to assert individuality, you emphasize who you are as a unique individual. You reveal something about your values, beliefs, attributes, roles, and/or experiences to help your audience members come to a better understanding of your perspectives, your personality, and your worldview.

Presentations to assert individuality are used in a variety of situations. The workplace is one of the most common contexts for these presentations. In a job interview, for example, asserting individuality is your primary goal. You want the interviewer to recognize your abilities and how you would fit within the organization. You want to make such a good impression that you stand out from the other candidates being interviewed. Every aspect of your presentation is geared toward achieving this end, including how you answer questions, the questions you ask, your attitude, and how you dress. Once hired, the process of asserting individuality continues. When you introduce yourself to your new coworkers, you are asserting individuality. You have opportunities daily to let others learn more about you through your interpersonal communication, formal presentations, reports, memos, and emails.

Conversations with acquaintances, friends, and family members also can be presentations of self-assertion. When you are introduced to someone you do not know, you are asserting individuality when you engage in small talk with that person. When you create a video to introduce yourself to your classmates for an online course, you are asserting individuality. When you want to impress your future mother-in-law, communicate that you are a bright student to the faculty of the department where you hope to attend graduate school, or be noticed by the cute guy on the floor above you in your residence hall, asserting individuality is your goal.

You cannot possibly communicate every facet of yourself to everyone you encounter—and probably would not want to if you could. Asserting individuality involves a selection process, and you continuously make choices about what and how much to reveal about yourself. You disclose different kinds of information when you come out as gay to your parents than you do in a medical school interview, for example. Choices about how to assert your individuality depend on what you expect from the interaction, your audience, and the setting in which the interaction takes place.

Your choices in a presentation focused on asserting individuality also depend on the larger cultural context in which it occurs. Asserting individuality is a very Western notion grounded in individualism—the privileging of the self over the collective or the group. In the United States, where autonomy and independence are highly valued, presentations to assert individuality are common. In cultures in which the collective is valued over the individual self, however, efforts to preserve the consensus and harmony of the group are valued more than the assertion of individuality. In Japan, for instance, communicators tend to seek agreement or consensus on an issue, and preservation of the collective harmony of the group is privileged over individual expressions of difference or individuality. In some cultures, asserting individuality is discouraged for other reasons. Among Native children in Alaska, speaking up and asserting individuality is undesirable because it is considered boasting.[3]

The goal of asserting individuality also must be balanced against the interests and needs of others. Individuals who talk only about themselves or who believe that everything they have to say is so important that they must share their perspectives on every subject are examples of assertion of individuality taken to extremes. Similarly, the speaker who is asked to speak to an organization for half an hour but goes on and on, convinced that what she has to say is more important than what anyone else might contribute, is asserting individuality at the expense of the contributions of others. Both of these examples serve as reminders that, to be effective, the goal of asserting individuality must reflect a balance between the assertion of self and concern for and interest in others. Your desire to assert your individuality should not be valued at the expense of others and their interests.

We have been discussing self-assertion as if what others learn about you is largely under your control. However, social networking sites and ever-growing amounts of information on the Internet allow others to learn all kinds of things about you very quickly. Important to remember is that you cannot control your presentation of self to the degree that you could in pre-Internet days. In fact, 91 percent of recruiters acknowledge running searches of job candidates on the web as a way to screen potential employees.[4] Nothing is private anymore, and nothing is ever really erased from the Internet. Monitoring your own social networking sites and those of others where information about you might be posted is essential if you want to manage the communication available to others about who you are.

To summarize, the goal of asserting individuality is centered on the act of self-expression. In presentations designed to assert individuality, you attempt to reveal aspects of your identity and to express your uniqueness as a person. The cultural context in which you are speaking and a concern for the interests and contributions of others in the interaction affect the choices you make in constructing these kinds of presentations.

To Articulate a Perspective

A second interactional goal for presentations is articulating a perspective. When this is your goal, you share information or present your viewpoint on a subject so that all participants in the interaction have a better understanding of that subject. Articulating a perspective requires that you share information or express a perspective as fully and carefully as you can.

Articulating a perspective is different from advocating for a position. When you articulate a perspective, you may believe strongly in your perspective and may hope that your audience members find it attractive enough to consider adopting a similar point of view. But your goal is not to persuade them to adopt it. Instead, you are interested in explaining the perspective, developing it in all of its richness and complexity, and giving it the best opportunity to be understood. Presentations focused on articulating a perspective are designed to offer—not to advocate for—a perspective.

Presentations in which your goal is to articulate a perspective involve providing information of some kind. When a professor explains an assignment to a class, a supervisor tells a new employee the correct way to fill out a time sheet, or a clerk explains where to find the shoe section in a department store, information is being shared. What you think about the information is not the issue. In a professional situation, you might be asked to present a report on your findings about the advantages and disadvantages of moving the organization to a new location. You do not advocate for or against such a move but lay out the relevant information for making the decision.

At other times, you hold a particular perspective and offer it to others. In this kind of presentation, your focus shifts from the information itself to your view about that information. In a discussion with friends about the movie you just saw, for example, you might offer your opinion about how good you thought the movie was. Even when you have a particular perspective you are offering, keep in mind the basic point of this goal—you are explaining why you feel as you do rather than trying to convince others to share your view.

Clearly, however, presenting information and presenting your perspective are not separate processes. When you are presenting information, you are also offering your perspective. This is because language is always a "carrier of tendency."[5] Rhetorical theorist Richard Weaver describes this characteristic of language by suggesting that "we have no sooner uttered words than we have given impulse to other people to look at the world, or some small part of it, in our way."[6] Because you can never communicate everything about a subject, you are making selections about content and language, which means you cannot help but communicate your way of seeing that subject matter.

Articulating a perspective is used more than any other interactional goal because it is the foundation of any presentation. For example, when you give a presentation in which you assert individuality, the nature of your unique perspective is the starting point for asserting your individuality. You cannot help but articulate a perspective as you talk about those areas of your life that you see as original, interesting, or noteworthy. Virtually every presentation, then, has some element devoted to articulating a perspective. You need to make choices about how much of your presentation to devote to this goal, what information to include, and how you want to present it to an audience so that it serves as the foundation for your other interactional goal(s).

To Build Community

At times, the interactional goal you choose is to build community. A community is a group of individuals who share core values, ideas, interests, beliefs, and/or practices and feel connected to one another as a result of what they have in common. When community is a value, qualities such as connection and shared interests are privileged over individual interests. When you privilege the interactional goal of creating community, you are concerned about and committed to the stability and preservation of the knowledge, themes, beliefs, values, and practices that form the core allegiances of the community you are addressing. Presentations to build community are of three main types: (1) creating community when it does not exist; (2) reinforcing a sense of community when it already exists; and (3) restoring community when it has been disrupted.

Creating Community

When a sense of community does not exist and you want to create it, your efforts are focused on encouraging people to get to know and trust one another. Burke discusses the way identification works as a rhetorical strategy to bring people together. For Burke, identification with another—whether through "speech, gesture, tonality, order, image, attitude, idea"[7]—is a way of making connections and forming relationships. In a presentation oriented toward building community, you help people see what they have in common. You might want to try to create community, for example, among new members of a team or among neighbors in a newly formed neighborhood association.

Community can be created in another way as well—through identifying a common enemy. Individuals who ordinarily might be on different sides of an issue or belief often come together against a shared opponent.

Those who support different soccer teams, for example, might join together in support of a single national team if their country makes it to the World Cup. Similarly, many in the United States from different political persuasions have come together against the common enemy of terrorism. In every case, a group comes together because of a perception that differences among them are less important than the differences between them and another group.

Reinforcing Community

Most of the time, you do not need to create community where none exists. Rather, your primary task is to reinforce existing feelings of community. You want to reiterate and reemphasize the core commitments and values that are central to group members—to remind them of what they already share with one another.

Reminders can be communicated in a number of ways. Asking the group to engage in a shared ritual—reciting the Pledge of Allegiance, singing "Amazing Grace," or marching together in the annual Gay Pride parade, for example—reinforces solidarity and reinvigorates commitment to the community. Organizations often institutionalize rituals to reinforce community. One such example is the company picnic at which the founder speaks.

Telling stories about events and experiences important to the group is another way to remind group members of their shared sense of community. Perhaps a particularly inspirational moment was the catalyst for the group's formation. Sharing the story of that moment highlights the values on which the community was built. Or maybe the group bonded during a river-rafting trip, and your references to that weekend are enough to reaffirm the group's commitments to one another. In a presentation in which your goal is building community, your focus is on strengthening the shared bonds and common worldview that created the initial in-group feeling that is the basis of community for members.

Restoring Community

Disruption of an existing community can stem from a conflict in a group or an unexpected event or tragedy. Perhaps a faction of a church has split from the main congregation, a strike has divided a community, or a conflict between two coworkers is harming the collegial atmosphere at work. Other examples are when a new manager has been brought into a work group or a divorce has disrupted a group of friends. Abraham Lincoln's Gettysburg Address, in which he sought to unify the North and the South, is an example of a presentation designed to restore community.

When a community has been disrupted, you attempt to reestablish the shared worldview that once bound the community together. This can involve efforts to reenergize the group by talking about perspectives group members once shared and/or about the experiences and commitments important to them. Sometimes, your task will be to focus on helping the group come to terms with the disruption. The killing of 17 students and staff and the wounding of 17 others at a high school in Parkland, Florida, is an instance of a major disruption of a community. If you were speaking to members of this community, you would want to address topics such as the values of the high school, the ways in which the victims will be remembered, and how the community will care for the survivors.

When the disruption is less severe than what occurs with a death or some kind of disaster, you might simply need to direct a community's attention beyond the situation or events that led to the disruption. This might mean minimizing the importance of an event or experience—showing the group's members why they need not be concerned with certain issues or allegations. Or it might mean suggesting that certain problems that are disrupting the group can be handled fairly easily. If a central group member has resigned, for example, and group members are wondering how to address it, you can show the group how the resignation can be dealt with efficiently and effectively by following procedures laid out in the organization's bylaws. You also can assure them that all of the group members are talented and can learn to fill the shoes of the member who resigned.

Another approach to restoring community is to find common ground among parties by transcending the differences dividing them. To redirect the energies of two coworkers whose behavior is disrupting the workplace, you can help them see that they both care about the success of the company. A divorcing couple might find common ground in what is best for their children, reaching a new sense of togetherness based not on their own relationship but on their mutual desire to have their children thrive. Winning the state championship may become the common ground that unites a sports team that has been fractured by infighting among players.

The interactional goal of building community is used when collective interests are valued over individual ones, and your task is to create, reinforce, or restore the feelings of community present within a group. To accomplish this goal, your focus is on highlighting the elements the group shares by discussing what group members have in common, reminding them of experiences important to them, and anticipating a future in which the community continues to thrive.

To Seek Adherence

In some presentations, you advocate for certain beliefs or behaviors that you want your audience to adopt. You hope to persuade your audience to change in some way—to take your perspective or to agree with you about something by changing an attitude and/or a behavior. In these cases, you are seeking adherence. *Adherence* literally means to bind—to stick to or to hold fast. Seeking adherence, then, involves an effort to convince others to accept, adopt, support, or align with your point of view.

The Black Lives Matter movement calls attention to the fact that black citizens are more likely than whites to die at the hands of police—and attempts to change racist attitudes that persist against people of color.

You may choose to seek adherence as your interactional goal in a variety of situations. Sales and marketing are primary contexts for this goal. Efforts to sell or advertise a product, proposal, or idea involve presentations in which you seek adherence. In these contexts, you believe strongly in a product or plan and its benefits and would like your audience members to choose it over others so that they can realize the same benefits.

Another common situation in which your interactional goal is to seek adherence is when you are in a supervisory role. You may be responsible for producing particular results within an organization, and you want to persuade your employees to work together to achieve the desired results. You have a particular outcome in mind, and your presentations to your staff would be designed to help them realize that desired outcome.

Seeking adherence is also your goal when you offer advice in personal relationships. As a parent, you seek adherence when you talk with your child about choices you believe would help create a positive and productive future. A mother might ask her son to consider the consequences of dropping a particular class or to consider certain factors when choosing a college. In a romantic relationship, you might use the goal of seeking adherence when you encourage your partner to do any number of things you think would be good—to dress up for a holiday party, go back to school, or give up smoking, for example.

The goal of seeking adherence may seem antithetical to invitational rhetoric. After all, many of the assumptions of invitational rhetoric—for example, that understanding is the purpose of communication or that the speaker and the audience are equals—seem to contradict the effort to seek adherence. There are ways to engage in seeking adherence, however, that do not violate the principles of invitational rhetoric.

Seeking adherence can be invitational if you express your position with care. Offer your audience members as complete a picture as you can of your viewpoint—articulating your beliefs clearly, comprehensively, and respectfully. If audience members have the opportunity to consider a well-expressed perspective that avoids manipulation or deception, they may choose to change. Burke suggests the importance of offering a complete perspective when he asks communicators to "advocate their choice by *filling it out!* That is: let each say all he can by way of giving body to the perspective inherent in his choice. Let each show the scope, range, relevancy, accuracy, applicability of the perspective. . . . And only after each has been so filled out, can we evaluate among them."[8] Offering your perspective as carefully, thoughtfully, and completely as possible is one way in which seeking adherence can be accomplished invitationally. A presentation to seek adherence would look very much like a presentation to articulate a perspective when this particular strategy is used.

A second way in which you can invitationally seek adherence is by including in your presentation opportunities for you to learn about and understand the audience's perspective. One common way to do this is to ask for questions at the end of your presentation. Instead of assuming that you have the best, most efficient, or productive perspective on an issue, you enter the interaction interested in what your audience members believe about it, and you are willing to alter your perspective once you hear from them. The perspectives audience members share may allow you to come up with an idea that is even better than your original one. Furthermore, because you are taking into account your audience members' views, they are more likely to continue sharing ideas, which leads to the generation of even more ideas. What is most important here is your willingness to be open to perspectives other than the one you initially held. You may not be able to incorporate such shifts in the course of your actual presentation, but as you think further about the issue, you can take these other perspectives into account.

You also seek adherence invitationally when you unequivocally communicate to your audience members that they are free to decide whether they want to do what you are asking. A speaker who makes clear to audience members that they have choices and can exercise them creates a very different atmosphere for an audience than a speaker who argues for a point of view as if it were the only reasonable view to hold. When you speak to your audience members in a way that acknowledges and values their perspectives, they will be more willing to listen, knowing they can choose whether or not to change.

The interactional goal of seeking adherence can be enacted in ways that honor the integrity of others and their viewpoints. Such an approach to persuasion is more respectful of the range of perspectives on any given issue. Individuals are more willing to change when they do not feel coerced, and the changes that do occur typically are more thoughtful, better integrated, and longer lasting than ones produced in more manipulative ways.

To Discover Knowledge and Belief

In some interactions, the speaker and audience are unsure of their views on a situation or uncertain about how to handle something. They come together to figure out what they know and to discuss the options available to them. The interactional goal in this situation is discovering knowledge and belief. Together, the speaker and audience members explore a subject to discover what they know and believe about it and how best to respond on the basis of that information. When you choose this interactional goal, you assume the role of facilitator, but you do not have any more answers than other group members about how to address the issue. You are not there to control or dictate what others say but to ensure that participants feel comfortable sharing their opinions about an issue and to keep the group on task.

To discover knowledge and belief is substantially different from the other four interactional goals. You do not enter the interaction with a clear idea of what you think or believe or with a proposal already prepared. Instead, you genuinely do not know to handle a situation. You hold no perspective yet or, at best, have a sketchy, tentative one, and you allow the discussion to direct the development of your perspective. Discovering knowledge and belief, then, is selected most often in two situations—when you want to generate new ideas or find solutions to a problem that will take advantage of all of the expertise in a group or when you are unsure or unclear about what you know or believe and use talk with others to figure things out. In both cases, you are relying on others to help you come to a decision about something.

The most common situation in which discovering knowledge and belief is your interactional goal is when you want the group to help you solve a problem or figure out how to do something. Involving the input of others usually means that you will come up with a more comprehensive set of options than if you tackled the problem alone. The assumption is that more options will allow you to make a more informed, effective, and productive decision.

Let's assume, for example, that you are a manager at a department store, and your boss has asked you to develop a plan for distributing holiday bonuses. You want the input of the other workers in order to devise a plan that is fair and equitable. You call a meeting and facilitate a discussion that allows multiple proposals to be voiced and discussed. After hearing all of the ideas, you can choose to adopt one of the proposals in its entirety or to develop your own plan by incorporating various elements from the proposals. Or perhaps you are the advisor to a school newspaper and are trying to decide what kinds of changes in format would be beneficial. You realize that you do not know what students think of the newspaper, and you call a meeting at which students can express their views about it.

Although the goal of discovering knowledge and belief is common in workplace and educational settings, these are not the only contexts in which such presentations occur. Perhaps a friend talks to you about the difficulties he is having in an intimate relationship, and you help him figure out what to do. When your daughter comes home from junior high, discouraged by always being picked last for teams in her PE class, you help her see what her options are. Maybe your partner is trying to decide whether to change careers, and together you brainstorm other career possibilities.

Presentations to discover knowledge and belief also offer opportunities to enhance understanding because they allow participants to gain clarity about something not previously articulated. A group that gathers to develop its mission statement, for example, may have a vague idea that there are some principles and commitments that unite all of the group members. As they think together about their mission, they voice various principles and select language to communicate the group's commitment. Theologian Nelle Morton labels this phenomenon *hearing into speech*.[9] Hearing others' views in the course of a discussion enables the group to more clearly understand and articulate what they would have been unable to do previously.

Through the discovery process, you and the group arrive at an opinion or decision and also learn how productive different opinions and ideas can be in helping frame an issue more fully. You often have a more creative and comprehensive understanding than if you had tackled an issue on your own. Furthermore, the process of discovering knowledge and belief may strengthen group solidarity and foster a greater commitment to the ideas or solutions generated by the group. People support what they create, and when they are part of the process that brings new ideas into being, they are more likely to commit to and advocate for those ideas.

For the interactional goal of discovering knowledge and belief to be successful, it must take place in a context in which talk is valued as a means of coming to know and making decisions. Everyone involved must share a belief in the possibility of arriving at an acceptable solution or decision by talking things through. This kind of talk is valued in the US educational system, where many classes incorporate some kind of sharing of opinions, beginning with show and tell in kindergarten and progressing to more formal kinds of discussions in high school and college.

In contrast, there are cultures in which joint talk to discover or create ideas is not seen as appropriate or useful. In a situation with a highly authoritarian parent, for example, the goal of discovering knowledge and belief between parent and child is very unlikely. A father who "knows best" and does not tolerate challenges to his authority probably will not be willing to hear his daughter's opinion about when she is old enough to date. In countries such as China, discussions often are not seen as a legitimate way to develop ideas; ideas are supposed to come from experts and authorities and not through discussions among groups of nonexperts. In such cultures, classrooms reinforce this view by privileging reading, lecturing, and memorizing as primary modes of instruction. Those who grow up with these kinds of cultural rules often have difficulty participating in presentations where discovering knowledge and belief is the goal.

Facilitating the Discovery of Knowledge and Belief

As a facilitator, you have some initial responsibilities before you even engage the group. Your first responsibility is to arrange for the time and place in which the group can interact. This might happen at a regular staff meeting if the issue affects employees at your workplace. If you're talking with your teenaged daughter, the discussion might happen in her bedroom when homework is done. What's important is that there is ample time and an appropriate place to cover an issue thoroughly.

When you serve as a facilitator, you are responsible for framing the subject for discussion, guiding those present through an investigation and analysis of the subject, and summarizing the insights produced by the discussion. Even in informal situations—talking with your daughter or with a roommate, for instance—these responsibilities are still present, although the steps in the process are not as obvious as in a formal meeting. The essence of your role as facilitator, regardless of the degree of formality, is like that of a coach—assisting others to share, think through, and talk over various perspectives.

When discovering knowledge and belief is a goal in a presentation, the desired outcome is to better understand an issue, to generate new ideas for dealing with the issue, and perhaps to reach a decision that serves as the basis for action. Presentations of this type typically involve a brainstorming process that includes three possible steps: (1) definition of the problem; (2) joint search for ideas; and (3) evaluation or decision.

Definition of the Problem. In the first step of the brainstorming process, you state the problem or issue for the group as clearly, concisely, and comprehensively as you can. You want to make sure all of the participants in the interaction have a clear understanding of the subject or issue they will be discussing.

Defining terms is one way to provide an overview of the problem. For example, if you are a member of the boosters' club at your child's school and have been asked to facilitate a discussion on the best way to increase community support for the soccer team, you need to be sure those present agree on what they mean by *community support*. Otherwise, there will be ongoing confusion about what exactly is under discussion. Is the issue community apathy, a need for money for equipment and uniforms, or something else? If the group is not aware of the problem, you need to spend more time on this step. In such a case, you might want to prepare a presentational aid that provides background and summarizes the basic facts involved.

Search for Ideas. The second step in the facilitation process is a joint search for ideas. You and your audience members talk together to discover what you know or believe about a subject or to generate ideas that might solve a problem. As the facilitator, this step consists of asking questions to stimulate discussion such as: "What can you tell us about yourself and your life that would help us understand your views on this issue?" "What do we stand for as a group?" "What could we do to improve our effectiveness as an organization?" and "What are different ways that we might solve this problem?"

You might want to use formal brainstorming techniques at this stage of the facilitation. In brainstorming, you ask participants to generate as many solutions as they can to a problem while someone records all of the ideas for the group. What is important in the brainstorming process is that there is no judgment or even commentary on the ideas generated. Any idea, no matter how silly or unworkable it seems, is recorded because even those ideas that appear to be unusable may stimulate further thinking.

You may discover, in your search for alternatives, that the group needs more information. Perhaps some creative solutions have been offered to a problem, for example, but you do not know if they violate company policy or whether they can be implemented in the time available. When this is the case, you can give individuals particular assignments such as making calls to appropriate people or looking up relevant policies to get the information you need. You set another time for participants to meet and report back on what they have found, and the idea-generation process begins again, taking into account the new information.

When you are facilitating a discussion, your primary responsibility is to ask questions. You need to ask good questions to achieve the kind of interaction and input you want from the group. In advance of the interaction, generate questions you can use as needed to ensure that all perspectives are heard, to prevent any individual from monopolizing the discussion, and to keep the discussion on track. Listed below are some sample questions for handling specific situations that may arise when you are facilitating a discussion.

- To draw out a silent member.

  "Does anyone who hasn't spoken care to comment?"

  "Hui, what is your opinion of . . . ?"

  "Cecilia, from your experiences in local government, would you care to comment on that?"

- To suggest the need for sharing personal experiences.

  "Does anyone know of instances where this has worked?"

  "How has this affected each of you personally?"

  "Will each of you be thinking about your own experiences in this matter so that I can ask you for your reactions later?"

  "Have any of you had experiences with this in another company that you would be willing to share with us?"

  "What is at the heart of the matter for you?"

  "How did you get involved with this issue? What is your personal relationship to it? Do you have a personal history with it?"

- To call attention to points that have not been considered.

  "Does anyone have any information on . . . ?"

  "What has been your thinking on . . . ?"

  "Before we continue, would it be profitable to explore another angle?"

  "Whose lives are affected by the issue? How are they affected?"

  "Whose perspectives are not represented in our discussion?"

- To suggest the need for additional information.

  "Do we have enough information to decide now?"

  "Should we form a subcommittee to research this issue?"

- To prevent a few from monopolizing the discussion.

  "Excuse me, Shahid. Before you continue, may I ask if anyone has a comment on the point you've just made?"

  "Thank you, Anthony. May we hear from someone else who hasn't expressed an opinion?"

- To keep the group on track and on task.

  "That's interesting, Madison. How does this point fit in with the issue being considered?"

  "I might have missed something you said. Will you please explain the connection between your suggestion and the main issue?"

  "Does the group feel that this point bears directly on the issue at hand?"

  "Would we make more progress if we confined our discussion to the facts of the case rather than to the people involved?"

  "Since we don't seem to be able to resolve this difference now, could we move on to the next point? Perhaps further discussion will reveal additional information that will help us resolve this issue."

  "What are we hoping to accomplish in this conversation? What do we want to see happen here?"

  "Shall we go back and revisit our purpose to see if we're still working toward that end?"

Evaluation/Decision.   After a group has generated ideas, those ideas need to be evaluated. The first step in this process is to determine the criteria group members will use for the evaluation process. Criteria might include workability of the solution, simplicity of the solution, lowest cost, or whether the solution meets everyone's needs. As the facilitator, you lead the participants through the brainstormed ideas one by one, helping them apply the criteria they have developed.

As you apply the criteria to the suggested options, frame the evaluation process positively so that those whose ideas are being evaluated do not feel hurt or dismissed. Instead of asking which ideas are unacceptable or bad, ask which appear to be the most promising and should be given the most serious consideration. The discussion at this stage is a process of clarification. As each idea or proposal is discussed, group members become increasingly clear about what they want, and often the best solution becomes obvious to everyone.

The evaluation/decision step ends in one of two ways. You may evaluate the ideas and decide which one or ones are the best, and the process ends there because you are not ready to implement your decision yet. Or perhaps a single decision is not necessary—participants might implement the options individually as they choose. At other times, the group comes to a formal decision at the end of evaluating the options. They take a vote or reach consensus on which option is the best and how the group will implement it.

You might use the interactional goal of discovering knowledge and belief to brainstorm with your roommates how you can save money on the costs of living in the house you rent together. In the first stage, definition of the problem, you would let your roommates know that the landlord is raising the rent and that you all need to figure out ways to cut back on expenses. In the second step of the process, the joint search for ideas, you would ask your roommates to brainstorm ways in which you can reduce costs. The group might generate ideas such as getting an additional roommate, being more conscious about turning off lights and electrical appliances when not in use, eating more meals at home instead of going out, taking showers instead of baths, taking shorter showers, and buying a coffee maker to use at the house instead of going to Starbucks every morning. In this case, the consensus or evaluation step probably would not be necessary because, with the exception of the option of adding a roommate, there is no need to come to consensus on which option the roommates will use. All ideas can be used to reduce their living costs. The session would end with you encouraging your roommates to use all available options and to think carefully about how their daily decisions about food, water, and electricity contribute to monthly house expenses.

Because the interactional goal of discovering knowledge and belief involves a group in the decision-making process, you cannot accomplish this goal in a short classroom presentation. If you want to try out this goal in a presentational speaking course, you probably will need to shorten the process in some way. Devote your presentation to just one step of the process—generating ideas, for example—rather than taking the group through the entire process from idea generation to evaluation. You also could make use of this goal for the introduction of your presentation only. Perhaps you ask your audience to generate definitions of something—the word *truth*, for example—that you then use in the body of your presentation. You may ask audience members to offer a few examples of their expectations about something, which you later incorporate into your presentation. Of course, if you have the option of speaking for 15 or 20 minutes, you can try out this goal in a presentation that incorporates the full decision-making process.

MULTIPLE INTERACTIONAL GOALS

We have been talking about interactional goals as if you will select only one for any given presentation. Although you are likely to have a primary goal, most presentations have multiple goals. If you want the approval of your manager to change the accounting process for a project, your primary goal will be to seek adherence. As part of that presentation, you need to explain why the proposed change makes sense in light of the overall project, which requires you to put together information about the nature and status of the project—to articulate a perspective. At the same time, you are seeking to present yourself in a positive light to your manager—to have her see you as a competent individual—so the goal of asserting individuality also is at work.

Interactional goals are the core of a presentation. The goal you select—to assert individuality, articulate a perspective, build community, seek adherence, or discover knowledge and belief—names a situation in some way and encompasses your response to it. It addresses the need you have identified as most important to your presentation. The goal you choose serves as your guide for the other decisions you will make about your presentation.

3

Creating Environment

Now that you have identified the interactional goal or goals of your presentation, you are ready to begin thinking about your specific speaking context. You want to create an environment that will facilitate an invitational approach. Your aim is to encourage your audience members to consider your perspective carefully as well as to share their perspectives with you.

CREATING EXTERNAL CONDITIONS FOR TRANSFORMATION

To create an environment that allows audience members to be receptive to transformation, you want to create particular external conditions in a speaking situation. When these conditions are present, the possibilities for transformation on the part of the speaker and the audience increase, and audience members feel free to contribute to the interaction. When both you and the audience consider new perspectives, the opportunity to understand one another is enhanced. As you prepare and deliver your presentation, the communication options you select either will facilitate or impede the development of these conditions in your particular speaking situation. The four external conditions you want to create in the speaking environment are: (1) safety; (2) openness; (3) freedom; and (4) value.[1]

Safety

Safety is the condition of feeling free from danger or risk. When you create safety in a speaking situation, audience members trust you, are not afraid of interacting with you, and feel as if you are working with and not against them. If participants in an interaction do not feel safe, they are reluctant to share ideas, making the emergence of new perspectives difficult. In a speaking situation, safety means feeling secure physically and intellectually.

The foundation of safety is the experience of well-being at a physical level, which includes the physical environment in which the interaction occurs. Physical safety may be an issue if you are communicating in a difficult physical situation—the site of a recent natural disaster such as an earthquake or a hurricane, for instance. If you are using dangerous equipment or tools as part of your presentation—weapons or power tools, for example—you and your audience undoubtedly will be aware of issues of physical safety.

Issues of physical safety, however, are rare in most presentational speaking situations. Most meeting rooms, classrooms, and auditoriums are safe physical spaces. What you have to contend with more often is a general context of fear about safety in contemporary culture. Several explanations can be offered for such feelings. The mean-world hypothesis suggests that the media—and television in particular—have projected a distorted view of how dangerous life is. As a result, people believe the world is a violent place.[2] Shootings such as the one at the Route 91 music festival in Las Vegas or at the Pulse nightclub in Orlando have intensified such fears. And, of course, the terrorist attacks of September 11, 2001, led many US citizens to feel fearful in ways they had not before—afraid to fly, afraid of anyone of Middle-Eastern descent, and afraid for the sanctity of US boundaries.

As a result of such fear, people with whom you are interacting might be afraid for their own safety and the safety of their families; they might be afraid to take risks or to go beyond what is comfortable and familiar. What this means for a speaking context is that some individuals may be generally less adventurous, less willing to try new things, and less willing to take risks. When individuals are affected by vague concerns about physical safety, your efforts at achieving understanding and transformation may be less effective than they might be in a different climate.

In most speaking situations in which safety is a concern, intellectual safety rather than physical safety is the issue. Intellectual safety concerns the degree to which participants feel they can safely explore, question, and share ideas and whether those ideas will be treated with respect and care. Certain audiences do not feel safe, for example, expressing perspectives that differ from those of their supervisors, church or government officials, or even the majority view in a group.[3] Intellectual safety also means that both speaker and audience members allow for and value the expression of ideas with which they do not agree. Rather than immediately judging someone as silly, stupid, or ignorant for believing something, both the speaker and audience must be willing to listen to ideas that are different from their own in order to gain the fullest possible perspective on an issue. Also important to intellectual safety is a willingness, on the part of both the speaker and audience, to admit they do not know something. Admitting ignorance can be as difficult for some people as listening to differing perspectives.

In a speaking situation, you can facilitate a feeling of safety in several ways. One is to make careful decisions about your format for interaction depending on your audience. Some participants may feel safest in a setting in which the chairs are arranged in an intimate circle. Others feel safest sitting in rows of chairs in a large lecture hall, where there is no expectation for them to reveal their perspectives. Safety for some might mean energetic participation in heated debate; for others, such participation feels very unsafe.

You also can generate a feeling of safety by asking a group to construct its own guidelines for interaction. Typically, these guidelines include some topics explicitly designed to help participants feel safe. A group might develop ground rules such as "speak only for yourself, not others"; "be respectful when commenting on the opinions of others"; "try to understand where others are coming from when they express an opinion"; and "give everyone who wants to speak the opportunity to do so." With these kinds of guidelines in place, participants might feel safe to share their perspectives with other group members.

Keep in mind that there will be some in your audience, no matter the size or the number of guidelines the group has developed to encourage participation, who do not feel comfortable speaking up. With a bit of planning, you can ensure that the perspectives of these audience members are "heard" without violating their sense of safety. At the beginning of your presentation, for example, you might ask audience members to write down questions or comments, which you then collect and incorporate into your presentation or address in the question-and-answer session at the end. You also can ask for a written straw vote to see how audience members feel about an issue.

Another way in which you can help create the condition of safety for your audience members is by modeling how to respond to others in ways that facilitate a feeling of safety. If you listen to the ideas and feelings of others with respect and care and do not degrade or belittle them or their beliefs, you will show that you truly value all opinions and perspectives. If an audience member challenges you, make a real effort to understand the perspective of the challenger.

You also want to model that you feel safe yourself, perhaps by taking some risks. If self-disclosure is a feature that means safety for your audience, you might want to talk about your children or tell a story about a time you made a mistake. Such disclosures can communicate to audience members that they also can feel free to take risks. As consultant Annette Simmons suggests, "Use yourself as 'exhibit A' to prove this is a safe place."[4] She adds, "If you feel safe, you communicate that to everyone. If you don't, you can't."[5]

Openness

The second characteristic required for a transformative environment is openness, a genuine curiosity about perspectives different from yours. Openness is the operationalization of the key idea behind invitational rhetoric—diverse perspectives are resources. Both you and your audience members acknowledge that the greater the diversity of perspectives available, the greater the understanding you will have of a subject. The availability of diverse perspectives, then, increases opportunities for transformation. If both speaker and audience approach such diversity thoughtfully and respectfully and with an attitude of appreciation and delight, openness will function as a resource.

One way to communicate openness to your audience in your presentation is to acknowledge other perspectives on an issue. Showing awareness of alternative viewpoints reveals that you have considered perspectives other than your own, which will go a long way toward creating an environment in which transformation is possible.

Another way to demonstrate openness is to allow your audience members an opportunity to articulate their perspectives on an issue—in small breakout groups, by sharing their opinions on flip charts, or by voting on ideas or formal propositions, for example. A question-and-answer session after the presentation also allows audience members to hear the perspectives of others and further facilitates an environment of openness.

Freedom

Freedom is the power to choose or decide from among available options. It allows each participant in the interaction to make decisions about what to believe and how to act. When freedom is present in a speaking situation, there is no pressure on audience members to make the same choices as the speaker.

You can develop freedom in a speaking situation in a number of ways. Freedom is created when you do not place restrictions on the nature of the exchange. Participants feel free to bring up any topic; they are not limited to discussing only the topics you raise. In other words, if audience members challenge beliefs important to you or bring up topics you would rather not talk about, you do not exclude those topics from the discussion. In addition, all assumptions are open to questioning and rethinking. Probably the most important way you can create the external condition of freedom is to communicate to listeners that they do not have to adopt your perspective. If your audience members are truly free, they can choose not to accept your viewpoint without fear of ridicule, punishment, or humiliation. You communicate to them that your relationship with them is not contingent on their agreeing with your point of view.

The condition of freedom is at the heart of an invitation to transformation because whether to change or not is a choice. If your interactional goal is seeking adherence, for example, you help create the condition of freedom by conveying to your audience that changing minds or behaviors is not the most important aspect of your interaction with them. You are more interested in maintaining your connection with them, understanding them, learning from them, and enjoying the process of interaction than you are in convincing them to change in a direction you advocate. One of Sonja's students, who was working on a PhD in communication, has decided she does not want to become a professor; she wants to own and manage a food truck instead. Some of her professors are telling her that she is good at research and has what it takes to make it in the academy, so she should continue on that path. In their interactions with her, they are not supportive of her decision. Other professors demonstrate what we mean by *freedom*—assuring her that her friendships with them will not be damaged because she has left the academy, that her happiness is their most important concern, and that they will continue to support her occupational choices.

A commitment to the condition of freedom means, then, that you cannot control the end result of the process of presentational speaking. You enter the situation inviting others to explore a subject with you, and you trust that what you create together will be beneficial for everyone involved. You are willing to live with and even to appreciate the "creative, messy, unfolding"[6] of perspectives that occurs because you are committed to letting others make their own choices for their lives.

Value

The external condition of value honors the intrinsic or inherent worth of each individual. It communicates that each participant is a significant and critical part of the interaction because each individual's perspective is unique. To gain a full understanding of an issue, everyone's perspective must be heard and appreciated. If some perspectives are privileged and others are ignored or devalued, only partial understandings are possible. When value is created in a speaking situation, audience members feel that they have something important to contribute and that the speaker cares about and appreciates their contributions.

One way in which you can convey that you value your listeners is by inviting and encouraging all participants in the interaction to be heard. By structuring opportunities for discussion into your presentation and using a question-and-answer session, for example, you demonstrate that you value the views of all audience members and want those views to be included in the conversation.

At times, the task you face in terms of value is not figuring out how to get shy or reticent audience members to share their perspectives but how to prevent one person from doing all the talking. You undoubtedly have been in situations where one person dominates the interaction, apparently believing that his perspective is more valuable than those of the others in the room. In such a case, your task is to limit this person's input without devaluing him. You can say things like, "We have a pretty good understanding of your perspective, Jason. Let's see if anyone would like to share some ideas we haven't heard about yet." Or you might say, "I appreciate your willingness to help us understand and develop that particular perspective, Anna. I wonder if others have suggestions that we may not have considered yet?" (Chapter 2 also offers suggestions for ensuring that all parties are heard.)

ANALYZING THE SPEAKING ENVIRONMENT

In the ideal speaking situation, you want the conditions of safety, openness, freedom, and value to be present. To create such conditions, you must assess your speaking environment to discover the elements that are available to you. If your analysis reveals that certain factors are likely to facilitate a transformative environment, you will organize your presentation to emphasize these factors. If other factors in the situation appear likely to be obstacles to transformation, you want to adjust them or neutralize their impact so that they do not hinder the creation of safety, openness, freedom, and value.

The four primary components of the speaking environment to consider when creating the external conditions for transformation are: (1) setting; (2) audience; (3) speaker; and (4) subject. Below are lists of questions to stimulate your thinking about each of these components. Your goal is to discover the factors that are likely to facilitate or hinder your creation of safety, openness, freedom, and value. These questions are only starting points. The details of your particular speaking situation undoubtedly will suggest other factors that you will want to consider.

Setting

Date
What is the date on which you are speaking? Is there anything unusual or significant about it for either you or your audience? If you are speaking on September 11 in the United States, audiences are likely to expect some kind of reference to the events of 2001.

Hour
At what time of day are you speaking? Is it early in the morning or late in the evening, after the audience has had a full day of other speakers or activities? Are you a morning or an evening person? If the hour is not the best for either you or your audience, you will need to pay extra attention to how you can encourage audience members to listen, to engage various perspectives, and to contribute.

Meeting place
What are the characteristics of the place in which you are speaking? Is it indoors or outdoors? What is the shape and size of the space? Are

there acoustical problems? Is the room a comfortable temperature, or is it too hot or too cold? What kind of lighting is available in the room? What is the noise level? Are there features of the room that might function as distractions for the audience? Will the audience be standing or sitting in rows of chairs, at tables, or on the floor?

Size of audience

How large is your audience? Are you speaking to one person? To a small group? To a large group? Can the space accommodate your audience comfortably?

Purpose for gathering

What is the purpose of the event, meeting, or gathering at which your presentation will be given? Is it to conduct business? To socialize? To solve a problem? To reinforce community ties?

Order of events

What or who precedes and follows your presentation? Are other presentations planned? On what subjects? How long has your audience been listening to presentations before yours? Are food and refreshments to be served and, if so, when?

Time constraints

How much time do you have for your presentation? Is there enough time for you to accomplish your interactional goal(s)?

Presence of an interpreter

Will someone be translating your presentation into another language? Will that translation be simultaneous or sequential? If it is not simultaneous, your presentation will take twice as long as usual, so you will need to plan carefully so you have time to develop your perspective fully. Will someone be signing your presentation for deaf members of your audience? Do you need to make adjustments so that the presence of the interpreter does not distract other audience members?

If an analysis of your **setting** tells you, for example, that you will be speaking following dinner at a conference that has been going on all day, you can assume that your audience members probably will be tired of thinking, tired of sitting, and tired of listening to speakers. Consequently, they are not likely to be able to engage in the sustained listening necessary to fully attend to your presentation. Instead, they are likely to stick with their current ways of thinking because they are interested in other things—perhaps joining friends for after-conference partying or going home to bed. To convert this obstacle into a dimension that facilitates transformation, keep your presentation short, and develop your topic in ways that will connect particularly strongly with your audience. Think about ways to involve your listeners in a discussion of the subject rather than simply presenting your ideas to them. When taking setting into account, select communication options that enable the setting to enhance rather than distract from the presentation of your perspective.

Audience

Knowledge of and interest in subject

How much do your audience members know about the subject of your presentation? Do they care about your subject? To what degree? Those who care a great deal may have developed strong views about it, while those who are unfamiliar with it or do not think it is very important will be more neutral. Will audience members be distracted by their cell phones and laptops and be more interested in their devices than in the subject of your presentation?

Perspective on subject

What perspectives do audience members have about your subject? If the subject is controversial, what positions do they hold? What experiences are influencing the perspectives audience members hold? What demographic variables of the audience—age, gender, economic status, religious affiliation, political affiliation, or cultural identity, for example—are likely to influence their perspectives?

Receptivity to change

How committed are your audience members to their perspectives? To what degree are they willing to change those perspectives?

Homogeneity

To what degree are your audience members homogeneous? Are they the same age, for example? The same race? Members of the same political party?

Cultural/personal identities

What cultural identities are important to audience members? Gender? Race? Ethnicity? Occupation? Hobby or interest? What are their cultural expectations about speaking situations?

To give you an idea of how your analysis based on **audience** factors might proceed, suppose you have been asked, as the best man, to give a toast at a wedding. Both you and the groom are electrical engineers, and you were students together in college. But you know that most of the others who will be attending did not go to college and are certainly not familiar with the engineering field. In your toast, you probably would not want to make a joke using the specialized jargon from your field because, no matter how funny it might be to the two of you, the others in the audience will be left out. Using jargon also might keep others from giving their toasts if they feel intimidated by your level of education. The choices you make in terms of topic, language, and style of delivery for your toast should make your audience members feel safe and free to share their own experiences about the couple in their own toasts.

Speaker

Position
What is your position, title, or rank? How is it likely to be perceived in this situation?

Attitude toward self
How do you feel about yourself in this speaking situation? Confident? Excited? Tentative? Intimidated? Scared?

Cultural/personal identities
Which of your cultural identities are evident to your audience? Race? Ethnicity? Gender? Sexual orientation? Economic class? Will you choose to reveal some aspects of your identity that are not readily apparent? How will these identities affect the audience's perceptions of you and your presentation?

Speaking competencies
What kinds of communication competencies are required in this situation? The ability to explain clearly? To lead a discussion? To generate excitement? How confident are you about using the necessary skills effectively? Do you experience communication anxiety that may interfere with your ability to communicate competently?

Vulnerabilities
Are there aspects of the speaking situation that make you feel vulnerable? Are they related to your subject? To your communication ability? To your relationship with your audience?

Attitude toward audience
How would you describe your attitude toward the audience? Is it one of affection? Respect? Compassion? Irritation? Frustration? Do you have prejudices that may affect your attitude toward your audience?

Previous experience with audience
Are your audience members acquainted with you? From what context? What experiences, if any, have you previously had with your audience that might affect this speaking situation?

Knowledge of subject
How much do you know about the subject on which you will be speaking?

Comfort with subject
How comfortable are you talking about this subject?

Perspective on subject
What is your present viewpoint on the subject?

Receptivity to change
How committed are you to your perspective? To what degree are you willing to shift your perspective? To see it from multiple vantage points?

In your analysis of the factors that you as the **speaker** bring to the speaking situation, think about your strengths, weaknesses, and degree of comfort. You may find that you are less comfortable with particular forms of communication. If you feel removed and distant from your audience when you stand behind a lectern, walk around the room as you speak and encourage your audience members to ask questions during your presentation. Conversely, if you feel you lack the skills to lead a discussion well, you probably will not be comfortable incorporating a great deal of discussion into your presentation. Your discomfort and feeling of vulnerability may prevent you from modeling a feeling of safety for your audience.

Subject

Comfort level
Is the subject a comfortable and easy one for your audience members to listen to and discuss?

Complexity
How complex is the subject?

Nature of evidence
What sources of information or evidence about the subject are allowed or privileged? Scholarly research? Personal experience? Testimonials from others?

Controversial nature
How controversial is the subject? Are there likely to be opposing perspectives on it among audience members? How likely are they to share those perspectives during your presentation?

Interactional goal
What is the interactional goal guiding your presentation? Will your effort to invite transformation assume the form of asserting individuality? Building community? Articulating a perspective? Seeking adherence? Discovering knowledge and belief? What expectations and constraints are generated by your goal?

Your analysis of **subject** dimensions suggests how to proceed as you develop and deliver your presentation. Perhaps your analysis suggests that your subject is a highly controversial one. By selecting communication options that encourage your audience to be open and receptive to your message, you can create conditions of safety, openness, freedom, and value despite the difficult topic. For example, you could select as your interactional goal articulating a perspective rather than seeking adherence. This goal will allow full presentation of multiple views and convey to participants that they are being heard. Incorporate into your presentation self-disclosure about your own background and the influences that led you to adopt the perspective you hold, helping other participants understand the context for your perspective. As you lead the discussion or answer questions, be careful not to belittle or devalue the opinions of others.

Each of the questions above concerning setting, audience, speaker, and subject can help you identify elements that will contribute to or detract from your ability to create the conditions of safety, openness, freedom, and value in your presentation. As always, these elements are created in conjunction with your audience. No matter how carefully you have considered your options, your audience members may have different ideas about the subject and how you are choosing to approach it.

MANAGING DIFFICULT ENVIRONMENTS

There are two environments that frequently give speakers difficulty. One is when you find yourself being confronted with conquest or conversion rhetoric, and you want to try to communicate invitationally. The second is when your audience members are on their mobile devices and do not seem inclined to pay any attention to you. Let's take a look at what your options might be in these situations.

Dealing Invitationally with Conquest and Conversion Rhetoric

Even if you are inclined to communicate invitationally, the creation of the conditions of safety, openness, freedom, and value is not always easy. The process is much more difficult in interactions framed in the conquest or conversion modes of rhetoric. You might find yourself, for example, in an environment in which someone is trying to convert you to her point of view. Perhaps your roommate is upset over a Supreme Court ruling that was just issued about immigration and is trying to persuade you that her position, which is different from yours, is the correct one. You do not want your communication to contribute to an environment of conversion; instead, you want to see if you can communicate invitationally. In such instances, you might want to engage in re-sourcement.

Re-sourcement is a term coined by rhetorical theorist Sally Miller Gearhart that means "going to a new place" for energy and inspiration: "To re-source is to find another source, an entirely different . . . one."[7] Re-sourcement involves choosing not to respond within the original frame of the interaction. Instead, for your response, you pivot and choose a different frame in order to turn the interaction in a different direction. Re-sourcement involves two processes: (1) disengaging from the conquest or conversion frame of the precipitating message; and (2) formulating a response within a new frame.

Disengagement

If the message to which you are responding is framed as conquest rhetoric—for example, the speaker is trying to dominate or bully you into agreement—the first step in the process of re-sourcement involves stepping away from that frame. When you decide to disengage, you do so because you recognize that you have options for how to respond, and you choose not to respond within the original frame of the interaction. You understand that nothing will be gained through communicating in that frame. In fact, the relationship and future interactions may be jeopardized. So the first step in this form of disengagement is an awareness that you want to respond differently.

Sometimes, disengagement itself constitutes the entire process of re-sourcement. You literally might choose to walk away from an encounter rather than continue a negative interaction. Karen's grandson talked to her about having to fight the school bully. He acted very surprised when she suggested he just walk away without fighting. Such responses tend not be valued in our culture because they are interpreted to mean that the person is a spineless wimp or a coward. The tendency not even to see disengagement as an option is illustrated in an episode of the comic strip *FoxTrot*, in which Jason Fox, a video-game fanatic, spent a month trying to kill off a particular enemy to get to the next level of the game. When his sister quickly made it to the next level simply by walking past the enemy, Jason responded: "I spent an entire month trying to kill this one video game foe, and it turns out all I had to do was walk past him! Who knew you weren't supposed to club him or kick him or lob fireballs at his head, just because he's huge and fierce and can squash you at will!"[8]

Disengagement can occur in the daily interactions that mark our professional and personal lives. Sonja once received an email message from a colleague who viciously attacked her for a position she had expressed on a departmental issue. After working very hard to formulate a productive response to the message, Sonja realized that she had another option as well—simply deleting the email and not responding at all—which is what she did. She heard no more from her colleague on the issue. When you do not participate in conquest or conversion rhetoric, it cannot continue. Not taking the bait can change the dynamics of the interaction and open up a space in which safety, openness, freedom, and value can begin to develop.

Formulating a response within a new frame

A second step you may want to use in re-sourcement is to devise a creative invitational response to the conquest or conversion message by engaging in communication that does not directly argue against or even address the message being offered. It presents a response addressed to a different exigence from the one implicit in the conquest and conversion rhetoric. In other words, by offering a message that comes from a different source or different frame from that of the initial message, you shift the interaction out of the conquest or conversion mode. In doing so, you increase the possibility that an invitational interaction is possible, and you enable the conditions of safety, openness, freedom, and value to begin to develop. This kind of response is designed to foster understanding, communicate that the speaker and audience are equal, and signal an interest in continuing to interact without denigrating the other's perspective. At the very least, this kind of message makes future interactions possible by preserving enough of the relationship so that the parties are willing to interact again.

An example of the use of re-sourcement as a response to conquest or conversion rhetoric occurs in the movie *The Long Walk Home*. The movie recreates the bus boycott by African Americans in Montgomery, Alabama, in 1955–1956 that was designed to end racial segregation on buses. As the boycott continued, white women began to drive their black maids to and from their homes, often in defiance of their husbands. In one scene, white men surround a group of white women and their black maids heading for their cars, jeering and taunting them, clearly ready to attack. The women respond by joining hands and singing a gospel song, and the men back away without harming them. The men's message was one of anger and conquest, and the women's message in response communicated compassion, respect, and solidarity. They acknowledged the perspective of the men but did not try to change it. Instead, they enacted solidarity, safety, friendship, and respect among themselves.

Linguist Suzette Haden Elgin provides an example of re-sourcement as a response to sexual harassment. If a colleague, customer, or supervisor makes a sexual proposal or sexually suggestive remark, Elgin suggests using the Boring Baroque Response. This response involves ignoring the content of the message and responding by telling a long story with many tedious details that doesn't address the unwanted message.[9] Such a response to an unwanted sexual comment might go something like this:

> That reminds me of the first time I heard jazz. My parents and I were visiting friends, and an album by Dizzy Gillespie was playing on a stereo. I was probably 10 or 11 years old. I don't think I'd seen a turntable before then because my parents had given their record player and albums away a long time ago, and I certainly hadn't heard anyone play the trumpet like he did. I remember being just mesmerized. I wanted them to play that record over and over, all evening long. And as soon as I got home, I asked my mom if she would buy me that CD. From that point on, I started paying attention to all kinds of jazz musicians, but trumpeters have always been my favorite—Miles Davis, Chet Baker, Louis Armstrong, Al Hirt. I just can't get enough of them.

This is an example of re-sourcement in action because the speaker refuses to participate in the frame established by the harasser—a frame of conquest—and creatively devises a response that is outside of that frame. The Boring Baroque response can be as eloquent as the example above, but creating a story with tedious detail does not require special training, talent, skill, or access to legal and financial resources.

Re-sourcement is useful in a variety of other situations in which a communicator tries to goad you into participating in conquest rhetoric. Kathy, a friend of Karen's who is a facilitator and trainer, is the daughter-in-law of a prominent politician. In the middle of a training session, one of the participants asked her about her name and whether she was related to the politician. When she learned that they were indeed related, the participant said, "That's interesting because your work and your perspectives seem so at odds with his views." Rather than denigrate or defend her father-in-law, which would have maintained the conquest rhetoric frame, Kathy engaged in re-sourcement by using the participant's own term—*interesting*—differently from how it was intended: "Yes, the work I do is very interesting; it allows me to work with diverse issues and to meet lots of people. I like it very much."

Another form re-sourcement can take is appreciation. When others attack or criticize, your typical response might be to attack back. In response, the attackers defend themselves and often launch new attacks, creating an exchange that tends to destroy any feelings of safety, openness, freedom, and value. Appreciating instead of criticizing sometimes can change the entire nature of the interaction because it deliberately reintroduces and focuses on the conditions desired. At Sonja's university, there was a period when the mail room was not operating well because of high turnover among staff and lack of training for new staff members. As a result, her department consistently received the mail intended for other departments, and the mail the department sent out was very late in reaching its destination. Sonja's program assistant repeatedly complained to the mail room supervisors about the problems, with no noticeable impact. Sonja and her program assistant then decided to try appreciation. They brought boxes of chocolates to the mail room employees with a note acknowledging how hard the employees worked, how difficult their jobs were, and how much their department appreciated what they did. Mail service to the department improved dramatically. The environment in which the initial interaction was framed was one of opposition and defensiveness, but Sonja and her assistant chose to communicate instead within a frame of appreciation.

Poet Adrienne Rich demonstrated re-sourcement when she was awarded the National Book Award's prize for poetry. When she accepted the award, she read a statement she had coauthored with Audre Lorde and Alice Walker, both of whom also had been nominated for the prize. In the statement, the three women announced that they were accepting the award together and would share the prize: "We believe that we can enrich ourselves more in supporting and giving to each other than by competing against each other; and that poetry—if it *is* poetry—exists in a realm beyond ranking and comparison."[10] Rich, Lorde, and Walker chose not to respond with a message congruent to the conquest rhetoric of the award, which would have supported the competitive, hierarchical system in which one person wins and others lose. They responded instead with a message of cooperation, creating a collaborative rather than a competitive frame for the poetry competition. (Their complete statement is one of the sample presentations included at the end of this book.)

President Barack Obama used re-sourcement in his eulogy following the killing of the Reverend Clementa Pinckney and eight other members of the African Methodist Episcopal Church in Charleston, South Carolina. In his presentation, Obama described the usual way gun violence is framed: "The killer . . . surely sensed the meaning of his violent act. It was an act . . . that he imagined would incite fear and recrimination; violence and suspicion. An act that he presumed would deepen divisions that trace back to our nation's original sin." Obama shifted out of the conquest frame with his transition: "Oh, but God works in mysterious ways. God has different ideas." Obama then placed the killer within an invitational scenario:

> Blinded by hatred, the alleged killer could not see the grace surrounding Rev. Pinckney and that Bible study group—the light of love that shone as they opened the church doors and invited a stranger to join in their prayer circle. The alleged killer could have never anticipated the way the families of the fallen would respond when they saw him in court—in the midst of unspeakable grief, with words of forgiveness. He couldn't imagine that. . . . Blinded by hatred, he failed to comprehend what Rev. Pinckney so well understood—the power of God's grace.[11]

Obama chose to alter the expected framing following a shooting—a frame in which the shooter is typically demonized—and instead to highlight a frame of grace and forgiveness.

Re-sourcement, then, is a response you can use to communicate invitationally and to create safety, openness, freedom, and value when those around you are communicating noninvitationally. It consists of disengaging from the frame of conquest or conversion in which a message is crafted and instead constructing a response from within a different frame. Re-sourcement enables you to continue to value others because you do not engage them in negative confrontation, and you are able to respond in a way that keeps the interaction invitational. Re-sourcement also opens up possibilities for a greater array of options for communication in the future. Because you have not cut off other communication options for interacting with someone, you may go on to offer your perspective in more traditional ways, using any of the five interactional goals.

Dealing Invitationally with Mobile Communication Technologies

When you want to speak with an individual or a group of people, you may find yourself competing with the smartphones, tablets, or laptops of potential audience members. They may be conversing with others via text, reading and responding to emails, doing some online shopping, watching videos, or playing games. You are likely to find, as a result, that your audience members "are actually only half-present. They are present in body, but their attention, mind and senses can at any moment . . . be drawn elsewhere."[12] Even securing the attention of your audience in an environment of mobile communication technologies, then, can be difficult.

Another obstacle to securing the attention of others is that your potential audience members are often not motivated to communicate with individuals outside of their social networks and thus are not receptive to your efforts to communicate with them. In all likelihood, your potential audience members are engaging in "chosen socialness"—preferring to communicate with those who are familiar to them—rather than engaging in "chance socialness"—taking an opportunity to communicate with a less familiar or unknown person.[13]

You have to make yourself present to audience members who may not be interested in paying attention to you and your presentation. You must insert yourself into their life worlds—somehow you must shift the attention of potential audience members from whatever they are attending to at the moment to you.

Let's take a look at some of the options for getting audience members to pay attention to you and to your presentation. One option—and the one that speakers use most often—is to limit the number of messages that are available to audience members in the environment. You essentially try to secure attention by limiting audience access to other messages so they are more likely to attend to yours. You can do this, for example, by collecting audience members' cell phones, tablets, or laptops at the door or asking everyone to put their mobile devices away. When you employ this strategy, you essentially are saying that you believe your message is important and will benefit the audience, so you assume that it should be privileged over other messages that audience members are sending or receiving. This strategy doesn't ensure that your audience members will pay attention to you (they can be thinking of all sorts of things other than your presentation even without their mobile devices), but it increases the likelihood that they will.

Another option for dealing with the potential lack of attention by audience members is to try to make your message so compelling that your audience members will want to attend to it instead of the messages on their mobile devices. You recognize that your message potentially has competition from many different messages or conversations that are likely to be relevant to the members of your audience, and you want your message to win the competition. Your strategy here is to develop an engaging message, whether through the kind of content you present or the strategies you choose for delivering the message. When you use this approach, you are giving your audience members a high degree of control over the interaction because they have a choice about whether to attend to your message. Although both of these first two options are commonly used, they are not invitational because they involve efforts to control your audience.

Given the pervasiveness of and difficulties inherent in today's mediated environment, is it even possible to communicate invitationally with audience members about digital devices? One approach to dealing with the potential lack of attention to and interest in your message is to issue an invitation to your audience members to enter into an interaction with only you. You might explain why you are interested in sharing your perspective with them and why you want to get to know them and their perspectives. Your audience members, of course, may refuse your invitation. They may choose to continue to interact with others on their digital devices and ignore you, but that is their right. You offer the invitation as eloquently as you know how and hope they accept it.

A second invitational approach is to model the behavior you would like your audience to enact. If your cell phone is lying next to you on a table or the podium, you are implicitly communicating, "I am so ready to drop my focus on you and pick up my phone." So put your own laptop or cell phone away so it is not even visible during your presentation. Signal to audience members that you are committed to the interaction at hand and are willing to focus on them. Another method is to explicitly discuss mobile technologies at the beginning of your presentation. You do so not to insist that the audience members put their mobile devices away but to invite everyone to join in the interaction and to share their perspectives because their input is important for the interaction. This might take the form of something like, "We're going to have a really sensitive conversation that will probably be rather difficult, so let's be present for each other and begin by putting our phones away." Another approach that involves explicitly addressing technology in an invitational way is to establish, as a group, some ground rules for the use of mobile technologies during your presentation or during all of the presentations on that particular occasion. This involves spending some time at the beginning of your presentation asking the group to decide how to handle mobile technologies. Of course, you then have to be willing to go along with whatever the group decides.

Whichever option you choose for approaching mobile technologies in the speaking environment, you are still likely to encounter people who are talking or texting on their cell phones or who are surfing the web. Your responses in such a situation can range from the confrontational to the more respectful. If someone's cell phone rings, for example, you can walk over to that person and answer it. This is clearly an approach that is likely to embarrass the individual and is not likely to contribute to feelings of safety, openness, value, and freedom. If you feel you need to address this situation with your audience, you have the option of doing so in a way that is more respectful and saves the face of that person. This might take the form of a question such as, "Hey, is everything okay? Do you need to take a minute?"

A key tenet of invitational rhetoric is that the purpose of an invitational interaction is not to persuade but to understand. Another is to allow individuals self-determination in their actions. Because some of the options suggested privilege the perspective of the speaker over the audience and are sometimes very directive in terms of audience behavior, the options are not always invitational. But dealing with mobile devices is difficult because the problem is so ubiquitous, and there are not many models for how to handle it in an invitational manner. The approaches suggested here are starting places to try to respond invitationally to what has become a very common and challenging kind of environment. We encourage you to come up with ways of approaching the problem that are consistent with the principles and assumptions of invitational rhetoric and that encourage you and others to engage in the kind of focused, sustained interaction you want to have.[14]

In the ideal environment for invitational rhetoric, the conditions of safety, openness, freedom, and value are present and increase the possibilities of mutual understanding, growth, and transformation. An analysis of the dimensions of the speaking environment—setting, audience, speaker, and subject—reveals which factors are likely to facilitate the creation of a transformative environment and which are likely to obstruct it. If you determine that the creation of these conditions will be very difficult because the interaction is framed as conquest or conversion rhetoric, re-sourcement may create a space in which a wider variety of communication options remains possible. Using re-sourcement, opportunities for transformation might emerge that may have seemed virtually impossible at the start of an interaction. If you find that mobile communication technologies are posing a threat to the possibility of having the kind of invitational exchange you intend, you must secure the attention of your audience members and insert yourself into their life worlds before you can even begin your presentation. To do so in a way that is consistent with invitational principles is the challenge.

4

Focusing

After you have decided on your interactional goal; analyzed environmental factors relevant to your speaking situation; and planned how to use them to create safety, openness, freedom, and value, you are ready to begin preparing your presentation. Although the various processes involved in developing your presentation—focusing, framing, elaborating, beginning and ending, connecting ideas, and delivering—are treated here as a series of discrete steps, they overlap considerably. For example, when working on elaborating your ideas, you simultaneously will be working on how you are going to connect those ideas and how you are going to express them when delivering your presentation.

Three preliminary processes will help you focus your presentation: (1) developing a thesis statement; (2) generating the main ideas for your presentation; and (3) making use of speaking resources. The processes involved in focusing are those that get you started on a presentation—clarifying your thesis statement, generating and selecting your main ideas, and seeking out resources that will help you throughout the process of preparation. By the time you have completed these steps, you will have a good sense of the basic elements of your presentation and will be ready to shape and refine it.

DEVELOPING A THESIS STATEMENT

The first task in terms of focusing your presentation is to craft a thesis statement. This is a statement that summarizes the subject matter or gist of your presentation, offers your initial commitment to a position, and suggests your interactional goal. A thesis statement guides you in developing your major ideas and sifting through and organizing the ideas you generate.

A thesis statement is not the same as a subject or topic. A subject simply names a field, a body of knowledge, or a situation. A thesis statement, in contrast, incorporates your perspective on the subject you intend to explore, explain, or support in the course of your presentation. For example, if the subject is accounting, a thesis statement on the subject could be, "I believe accounting currently offers excellent employment opportunities." This thesis statement signals that you have a perspective regarding the accounting field and that you will be articulating that perspective for your audience. In your thesis statement, you should be able to locate the subject of your presentation, your particular perspective on it, and your interactional goal.

The thesis statement represents only a preliminary or initial commitment to a perspective. If you think of your thesis statement as tentative, it serves as a reminder that your position is evolving and that you are willing to be changed as a result of the interaction, just as you hope your audience will be. Implicit in the thesis statement, then, is the recognition that the interaction is not complete without the incorporation of the audience's perspective. The audience has a central role to play in the further development of your thinking on the subject.

The function of a thesis statement is not unlike the planning you do when you host a Super Bowl party. The thesis statement is equivalent to initial preparation for the gathering—cleaning your house or apartment, buying some drinks, and perhaps ordering some pizzas. Your thesis statement communicates to the audience that you have thought about the subject and how to communicate the results of that initial thinking in a presentation. Important to remember is that you do not know how the party or the presentation will go, and the outcome may be different from what you expect.

How you word your thesis statement will vary depending on your interactional goal. Thesis statements usually can be identified by certain words or phrases that indicate to your audience which goal is guiding your presentation. Thesis statements for the interactional goal of **articulating a perspective** often begin with or imply phrases such as *I'd like to share information about, I believe, my view is, I think,* or *my current understanding is.* Below are some sample thesis statements for the goal of articulating a perspective.

- I would like to share some information about how various school systems have implemented a foreign-language requirement.

- I believe that moving to a voucher system in our schools would improve educational opportunities for our children.

- I have a particular perspective on ethics concerning artificial intelligence that I would like to share with you.

When your interactional goal is **asserting individuality,** phrases such as *I am, I have certain skills and abilities,* and *I want to* are included or implied. With this goal, your focus is on certain aspects of yourself that you want to highlight for your audience. Below are sample thesis statements for presentations to assert individuality.

- I am a bilingual speaker and personally understand how valuable knowing more than one language is.
- Because of my extensive experience implementing voucher systems in schools, I am an excellent choice for the position you have open.
- I am delighted to be joining this company and would like to share some of my background in the area of artificial intelligence with you.

When your interactional goal is **building community**, your thesis statement is likely to begin with phrases such as *we can, we share, we appreciate,* and *we value.* Your focus is directed collectively rather than individually, and your language is similarly inclusive. Thesis statements that have building community as an interactional goal typically follow the forms in the samples below.

- As bilingual speakers ourselves, I know we all share the value of speaking more than one language.
- We all want the best possible education for our children, and a voucher system is the best route to take to improve education in this community.
- All of us here appreciate the critical importance of artificial intelligence to this line of work, and I hope that after we've talked, the ways each of us can contribute will be clear.

Thesis statements for the interactional goal of **seeking adherence** often use phrases such as *should, would, could, benefit, best,* and *desirable.* With such thesis statements, you are seeking the assent of audience members to something or asking them to adopt a particular idea or plan. The following thesis statements are examples of statements appropriate for presentations centered around seeking adherence as a goal.

- We should adopt a foreign-language requirement for students in our school.
- Our educational system would benefit from the introduction of vouchers, and I urge us to vote to implement the proposed voucher system at this meeting.
- Our organization should develop our resources in artificial intelligence so that we can distinguish ourselves from others in the field.

Discovering knowledge and belief is the fifth interactional goal, and thesis statements associated with it often incorporate words such as *explore, determine,* and *decide* and phrases such as *I'd like you to help me with . . . , how can we solve . . . ?,* and *what ideas do we have for . . . ?* The exploration process central to this interactional goal is the focus of these thesis statements. Thesis statements for discovering knowledge and belief take the form of the examples below.

- I need your help to figure out when a student is exempt from our foreign-language requirement.
- I would like to explore how a system of educational vouchers might benefit our school district.
- How can we use artificial intelligence to benefit the company?

The thesis statement is central to your presentation. It communicates your general subject matter and reveals your commitments around that subject. Although you may find that you often are asked to speak on the same subject matter—the area of your expertise—your choice of interactional goal affects how you word your thesis statement.

GENERATING THE MAIN IDEAS

Once you have developed your interactional goal and your thesis statement, you are ready to move to thinking about the main ideas of your presentation. They should relate to and develop your thesis statement, and they should be consistent with your interactional goal. Often, the main ideas emerge naturally from the thesis statement. Some sample interactional goals, thesis statements, and main ideas are listed below to show the connections among these components.

Scenario 1

Audience: Manager
Setting: Job interview
Interactional goal: To assert individuality
Thesis statement: I am well prepared for this position.
Main ideas:
- My educational background prepared me for this position.
- My previous positions provided experience for this job.
- I am dependable and also have the creativity necessary for this position.

Scenario 2

Audience: City council members
Setting: City council meeting
Interactional goals: To articulate a perspective; to seek adherence
Thesis statement: The noise problem downtown needs to be taken seriously, and I urge the city council to pass a noise ordinance.
Main ideas:
- Noise from downtown bars is excessive and disruptive.
- Passage of a noise ordinance will manage this problem.

Scenario 3

Audience: Web designer
Setting: Meeting to revamp company's website

Interactional goal: To discover knowledge and belief
Thesis statement: I want to explore ways to improve our website.
Main ideas:
- What is effective about the current website?
- How can the website be improved?
- Which of the proposed changes are most cost effective for the company?

Scenario 4

Audience: State legislators
Setting: Legislative hearing
Interactional goal: To seek adherence
Thesis statement: Our state should legalize marijuana.
Main ideas:
- A majority of the public favors legalization of marijuana.
- Marijuana can improve the quality of life for individuals suffering from a variety of illnesses, including PTSD and various forms of epilepsy.
- Legalized marijuana would be a new source of revenue and jobs for our state.

In all of these scenarios, notice how the main ideas are a natural extension of the thesis statement. Once you have your thesis statement, you are likely to have a good idea of some of the major ideas to develop in your presentation. Locating some sources to help you develop those ideas is very useful at this stage in the process of creating your presentation.

DOING RESEARCH TO DEVELOP IDEAS

Developing the ideas in your presentation often requires that you do some kind of research. When you are asked to speak because you have developed a particular perspective on a subject, you probably will rely on resources already at your command such as your current knowledge of the topic and your personal experience with it. If you are developing a new presentation on a topic you haven't spoken about before or a presentation where you develop a new perspective on a subject, you probably will want to turn to external, secondary resources of various kinds to assist you. Researching the topic will allow you to present the most current information, to take into account how your perspective is evolving, and to analyze alternative viewpoints.

In suggesting possible speaking resources, our intention is not to instruct you in how to do research. If you are a college student, you undoubtedly are familiar with how to search the Internet, how your library works, and how to access other useful sources on your campus. If you are a first-term freshman, you may be less knowledgeable about these resources, but your campus, if it is typical, offers workshops, tours, and programs for new students to learn how to do research. For those of you who have been out of school for a while, you undoubtedly are familiar with how to access resources for research in your organization or community. Our intent here, then, is simply to remind you of some of the major speaking resources available to you when preparing a presentation. There are two main types of research: primary sources and secondary sources. You use secondary sources when you make use of the research or information compiled by others. Primary sources are those you develop by doing your own research or relying on your personal experience.

Secondary Research

Traditional sources for finding the materials you need for your presentation are those available in print—books, newspapers, journals, and magazines. Each of these sources is valuable for different reasons. Although books are the least current source of information due to the extensive time required to write and publish them, they provide historical information and more in-depth analyses than what is offered by publications devoted to current events. Newspapers and magazines provide up-to-date information, with magazines usually providing more in-depth coverage than newspapers simply because their deadlines are not as immediate. A newspaper story reports daily information about an incident, while a weekly news magazine can provide an overview of a story from start to finish.

Journals or scholarly periodicals provide another useful source for developing your presentation. The journals published by academic disciplines include current research findings on various topics. In the discipline of communication, for example, there are many journals that publish articles about all aspects of communication as well as journals that specialize in areas such as media studies, communication theory, applied communication, health communication, gender communication, and intercultural communication. You can find research in these journals on such diverse topics as the process of compliance gaining in interpersonal communication, religious communication, public relations campaigns, organizational communication, and analyses of television programs and films.

The Internet has changed how research is conducted, and you are now able to find books, newspapers, journals, and magazines online. Websites, videos, electronic mailing lists, newsgroups, discussion forums, blogs, wikis, and social networking sites can provide you with additional sources of information on your topic. When you use the Internet as a source for your presentations, you must deal with two primary problems—how to find relevant information and how to find reliable information.

You may find that a search on a particular subject produces many screens and includes hundreds or even thousands of items. Deciding which Internet sources are most valuable for your project requires patience and practice. Although you may be able to find much of what you need by searching various websites on your own, numerous databases exist that can assist you with specialized information relevant to your topic. The LexisNexis database (lexisnexis.com), for instance, catalogs legal material, newspapers, and public records and may provide you with more detailed information than you could find in a more random search. Other examples of specialized data bases are WorldCat (worldcat.org), Academic Search Complete (academicsearchcomplete.com), and Google Scholar (scholar.google.com). USA.gov allows you to search for publications authored by federal agencies and institutions.

In addition to searching for relevant information, a second problem you face when using Internet sources is how to evaluate the quality and legitimacy of the information you find. Because of the democratic nature of the web, there is no oversight body or organization that evaluates the credibility, trustworthiness, and reliability of Internet publications. Anyone can put anything on the Internet, whether it is true or false, accurate or inaccurate, so much of the information available online is sensationalist, heavily biased, and deceptive. Among these are hyperpartisan websites and social media pages that foster a particular political view through a highly biased lens as well as fake news—information that is fabricated, packaged, and distributed to appear as legitimate news.

The challenge of evaluating what you find on the Internet is compounded by the fact that individuals now can control the information they receive via the Internet, and you are able to live in an online world that only lets in information that aligns with your preferences and tastes. Personalization algorithms used by online services prioritize, filter, and hide information, depending on your previous interaction with the system, so you are fed news, advertisements, and other messages consistent with your browsing history.

Even when algorithms are not dictating the content to which you are exposed, you have the option of personalizing that content, limiting your exposure to a variety of sources. You are able, for example, to filter content on Twitter, only following those individuals in whom you are interested and whose perspectives align with yours. On Facebook, you are able to be friends with those with whom you agree and to unfriend or untag those with whom you do not. As a result of these filters, you, like many others, are likely to be living in a "filter bubble" [1] or an "information cocoon," [2] in which you are exposed only to what you select and to what pleases you. Consequently, you create a unique universe of information that fundamentally discourages you from encountering a variety of ideas and information and makes gaining access to a wide variety of sources on a topic more difficult.

Five criteria can help you evaluate information you find on the Internet: (1) authorship; (2) publishing body; (3) referral to and/or knowledge of other sources; (4) accuracy or verifiability; and (5) currency. If you are conscientious about your Internet research, you can be confident that the information you use in your presentations is accurate and trustworthy.

Authorship

You want to establish the author's qualifications for making the claims you want to incorporate into your presentation. Look to see if a website gives credit to an author. If it does, that is one indication of a credible site—the author is willing to stand behind the information presented. See if there is a link to a website or a background page that tells you more about the author. Such links may provide information about the author's credentials—perhaps the author's occupation, education, and position—that will help you determine whether the author is an expert in a field and qualified to write about the subject. This background information also may tell you whether the author is presenting a neutral perspective on a topic or is advocating a specific view. In addition, seek out comments from others about the author's work to establish context for that individual's credentials and perspective.

Publishing Body

This criterion deals with the credibility of the publishing source. If possible, determine what institution—company, university, or government body—is presenting the content on the website and is standing behind a document on the Internet. The easiest way to find out about the publishing body is to look for an "About Us" section on the website. Is the website part of a commercial organization or an organization with a specific agenda, such as a political party, for example? Knowing who is behind the website's creation can suggest motives for the content—to provide information, to demonstrate or explain, to sell a product, or to provide news specific to a trade or profession, for example. Two indicators that a website is not going to provide you with legitimate information is if it urges you to dox an individual or organization—to publish private information about a person or organization online—or if it includes clickbait—sensationalist headlines and odd photos designed to encourage you to click on the website and thus increase traffic to it.

If the owner or publisher of the website is not identified, you can tell something about the origin of the site from the domain name or URL (Uniform Resource Locator). A *.com* ending to the domain name, for example, tells you the website is a commercial one; an *.edu* extension denotes a website for an educational institution; *.mil* is a military organization; *.gov* designates a governmental organization; and *.org* generally means a nonprofit organization. However, any organization can register a *.org* address, and websites that contain the suffix *lo* (as in *Newslo*) or that end in *.com.co* often present false information for satirical purposes. The URL also indicates the country where a website originated. A website from the United Kingdom, for example, will have *.uk* at the end of its

URL, and one from Brazil will have *.br*. If no country is indicated in an address, that means it is a US website.

Referral to and/or Knowledge of Other Sources

This criterion has to do with how a website treats other sources. You can use two approaches to help you make this assessment. The first and easiest way is to examine the content of the document itself. Does it reference or recognize other sources? Does it represent other sources fairly? The second is to seek out other sources on the topic to see if the author of the information you are trying to evaluate has considered a sufficient number of alternative views.

Accuracy or Verifiability

Accuracy or verifiability has to do with establishing the accuracy of data you find on the Internet. To see if information meets this criterion, check to see if sources are clearly listed so that the information can be verified. You want to be able to verify the information you use in your presentation from independent sources or from your own knowledge. The publisher of a website that values accuracy will often provide direct links from the website to the sources cited on it. You then can go to those sources to see if the author of the document you are reviewing has summarized the perspective appropriately and cited from it accurately.

If the information in an Internet source is free of spelling, grammatical, or typographical errors, that also suggests that the publisher of the website takes care both with what it presents and the form of presentation. Beware of websites that have amateurish design elements and/or use all capital letters. These are often signs that information is not trustworthy and that you should research your topic via other sources. Also be careful about memes making the rounds on Facebook or other social media sites. Try googling the topic of a meme or other doubtful story or piece of information. If it is a legitimate story, you will probably find it covered by an established source like a major newspaper or television news channel.

Currency

Currency deals with when information was published. You want to know how timely the information is that you are using in your presentation if your topic deals with a contemporary issue. A well-maintained website generally will state when it was last updated and perhaps when it was originally created. Another way to tell if a website is updated regularly and is being maintained is if the links are up to date and working. If there are many broken or dead links on the website, the article you are assessing is likely to be old.

Primary Research

Research that relies on primary sources is research you have conducted yourself by doing experiments, coding qualitative data, conducting surveys, interviewing others, or using your own personal experience. If you are an undergraduate student, you probably have not had much chance to do original research or to conduct surveys that could serve as sources for your presentations, but you can do interviews and make use of your personal experience. Interviewing does not have to be a formal process like a job interview or the interviewing a reporter does with a source for a news story. It can be an informal process of discussing a topic with another person. If you want technical or specialized information about a subject, interview someone who is an expert in the field. If you are working in or hope to be working in a particular field, you undoubtedly have or can gain access to a variety of individuals with expertise in that field. If you want to learn what people in general think about something, talk to several people who have been affected by an issue—perhaps employees of the organization for which you work who have been harmed by a policy you will be discussing in your presentation. In addition, interviewing individuals gives you an opportunity to obtain brochures, reports, and other documents from the organizations with which the individuals are associated, which may be useful sources for your presentation as well.

Don't forget your own experience as a resource for your presentation. Thinking through how you came to hold a belief about something can help you articulate the various facets of your perspective and can help you make decisions about how to present that perspective to your audience. Realizing how your own perspective developed also can make you more sensitive to and appreciative of the variety of perspectives your audience members hold. Finally, thinking about the experiences responsible for your perspective can be a source of stories and other forms of elaboration that you can incorporate into your presentation.

You will make use of secondary and primary sources for your research at a number of places in the process of creating your presentation. Such sources are critical in the early stages of your thinking about your presentation as you select your topic, develop your thesis statement, and select the main ideas of your presentation. You will continue to make use of these sources in other parts of the process as well. When you develop your introduction and conclusion, for example, you may find that some of these sources are useful for providing a beginning or ending to your presentation. When you refine the specific ideas of your presentation, you also will draw on these sources for the forms of elaboration that will support and enhance the main ideas in your presentation.

The process of focusing gives you the materials that form the essence of your presentation. Crafting a thesis statement, developing your main ideas, and doing the research for those ideas lead to a consideration of the frame or structure you will create for your presentation. Framing provides the container into which to put your emerging presentation, and it is the subject of the next chapter.

5

Framing

Framing is the process of choosing an organizational pattern for the main ideas of your presentation. There is no one right way to frame or organize a presentation. To decide which frame works best to show the relationships among your ideas, take into account the preferences and expectations of your audience, the cultural context in which you are speaking, your subject, your interactional goal, and your own personal style. Because a frame increases the ease with which your audience members can understand your ideas and allows them to retain information more easily, it communicates to your audience members that you value them.

You do not have to begin from scratch to structure your presentation. Ideas for any presentation tend to sort out into some basic or conventional organizational patterns frequently used by speakers and writers. You probably will discover that many of these patterns are familiar and that you automatically use some of them to organize your ideas, even though you may not have known their formal labels.

OPTIONS FOR FRAMING

This section discusses examples and descriptions of some conventional organizational patterns. The patterns are arranged in alphabetical order because we do not want to privilege some over others. We want to encourage you to consider all possible organizational formats for a presentation rather than selecting one that is familiar or formulaic. In the few cases where a specific pattern is appropriate for only one interactional goal, that goal is noted in the description of the pattern.

Alphabet

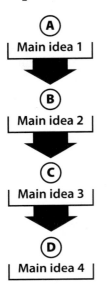

The alphabet pattern involves arranging ideas in alphabetical order. You can organize a presentation on the importance of the arts, for example, around three values that you link to letters of the alphabet: A is for awareness, B is for balance, and C is for creativity. A variation of this pattern is the structuring of a presentation around an acronym that uses letters of the alphabet such as *SAFE* to discuss earthquake preparedness. *S* might stand for securing the environment, *A* for advance planning, *F* for family meeting place, and *E* for emergency supplies. In her TED Talk with Ari Seth Cohen about *Advanced Style*, a project in which Cohen photographs older women and men and their stunning outfits on the streets of New York City, Debra Rapoport discussed "the ABCs"—assembling, building, constructing—she uses to put together her eclectic outfits.[1]

Category

You can organize ideas around the categories that naturally arise from your subject matter. The major components, types, questions, functions, or qualities of a subject can be used as the categories in this organizational frame. Because almost any subject can be divided into categories, this is a very common organizational pattern. President Donald Trump used a category pattern when he addressed the nation on the subject of US involvement in Afghanistan. He discussed four pillars that represented his new approach to the issue: (1) using conditions on the ground and not arbitrary timetables to guide the strategy; (2) integrating all instruments of American power, including diplomatic, economic, and military, to produce a successful outcome; (3) adopting a new approach to Pakistan, which receives billions of dollars of aid while harboring terrorists; and (4) asking India to provide the United States with more help with Afghanistan, especially in the area of economic assistance and development.[2]

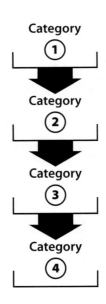

Causal

A causal (not *casual*) organizational pattern is structured around
a cause or series of causes that
account for an effect or effects. In
a causal pattern, you can organize
ideas by beginning either with the
cause or with the effect. You can
analyze the conditions that produce a particular effect, or you can
discuss the end result first and
then go back and discuss the factors responsible for that effect. If
your presentation is about an eco-

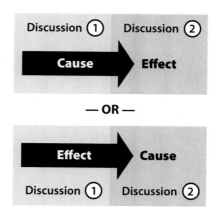

nomic crisis, for example, you could begin by discussing the major reasons (causes) for the crisis and the consequences (effects) of those
economic behaviors. In a speech to the Heritage Foundation, US ambas-
sador to the United Nations Nikki Haley explained that the United States
had withdrawn from the United Nations Human Rights Commission
(the effect). She then explained the two causes for the withdrawal: Some
members of the Commission are some of the worst human rights viola-
tors, and pro-human rights countries refuse to speak up publicly about
human rights violations.[3]

Circle

In this structure, ideas follow a circular pattern. You develop one
idea, which leads to another, which leads to another, which leads to
another, which then leads back to the original idea. You might suggest to
your coworkers, for example, that greater cooperation is needed to
accomplish your unit's
goals. To achieve this
cooperation, you pro-
pose that the members
of the unit establish a
goal of being honest
with one another. You
then discuss how hon-
esty can contribute to a
greater feeling of trust,
and trust, in turn, con-
tributes to an environ-
ment in which team
members are more like-
ly to cooperate.

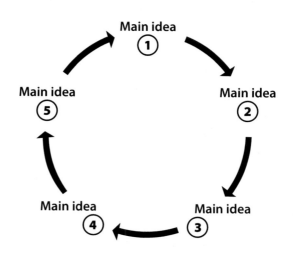

Continuum

Ideas can be organized along a continuum, spectrum, or range. All of the ideas along the continuum share some common quality or substance, but they differ in the degree or level to which they contain that quality. Using this pattern, you move from one end of the continuum to the other to discuss your ideas. You might organize a presentation using a continuum pattern by discussing ideas from small to large, familiar to unfamiliar, simple to complex, or least expensive to most expensive.

Chapter 1 of this book contains an example of a continuum organizational pattern. In the discussion of different modes of rhetoric, five kinds of rhetoric are organized and discussed along a continuum that moves from conquest rhetoric to conversion rhetoric to benevolent rhetoric to advisory rhetoric to invitational rhetoric. All of the points along the continuum—the different modes of rhetoric—share the quality or substance of being rhetorical modes, but they differ in the degree to which the speaker seeks to change the perspectives of audience members.

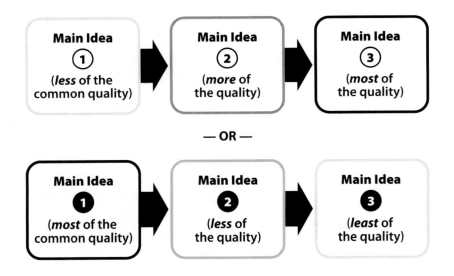

Elimination

An elimination organizational pattern begins with a discussion of a problem, followed by a discussion of several possible solutions to that problem. You examine each solution in turn and eliminate each one until the one you prefer remains. In a speech about immigration, David Cameron, Prime Minister of the UK, introduced three perspectives on the issue that he believed were dangerous: (1) recent levels of immigration are not problematic because mass migration is simply an unavoidable aspect of globalization; (2) countries can retreat from the world,

ignoring immigration entirely; and (3) a successful plan to deal with immigration is only
about immigration policy. Cameron rejected
these three solutions and then proceeded to
offer his own solution to the problem of immigration—a policy that would provide restrictions on immigration while also recognizing its
benefits to the UK.[4]

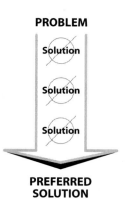

Location

In an organizational pattern of location, ideas are assembled in terms
of their spatial or geographic relationships. This pattern only works
when you have ideas that can be discussed according to places or locations. In a presentation titled "Asia's Rise: How and When," Hans
Rosling discussed major events in 1858 that transformed world cultures
and economics. He started with the United States and Great Britain and
moved east across the globe to India, China, and Japan, discussing the
events that occurred in each location.[5]

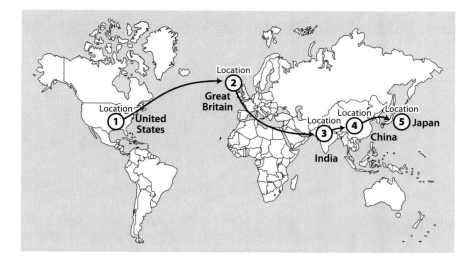

Metaphor

A metaphor is a direct comparison between two ideas, concepts, or
objects. When you use this pattern, you compare an item, idea, or experi-

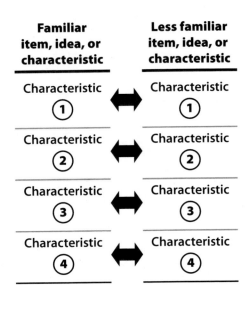

Familiar item, idea, or characteristic	Less familiar item, idea, or characteristic
Characteristic ①	Characteristic ①
Characteristic ②	Characteristic ②
Characteristic ③	Characteristic ③
Characteristic ④	Characteristic ④

that is familiar to audience members with one that is less familiar to help them understand the less familiar subject. One example of metaphor used as an organizational pattern was a presentation by China's president Xi Jinping at the opening ceremony of the Nineteenth Congress of the Communist Party of China. He compared the silk road, an ancient network of trade routes, to current digital infrastructure to suggest how Chinese telecommunications companies can access new markets by improving infrastructure in Asia and Africa.[6]

Motivated Sequence

The motivated sequence is a five-step organizational pattern designed to encourage an audience to move from consideration of a problem to adoption of a possible solution.[7] This pattern is appropriate only for the interactional goal of seeking adherence, although it is not the only pattern that can be used for that goal. The steps in the sequence are described below.

Attention

The introduction of a presentation that uses motivated sequence is designed to capture the attention of audience members. In a presentation to highschoolers on the sexual transmission of AIDS, for example, you might begin by citing statistics on the number of students who are HIV positive.

Need

In the need step, a problem is described so that the speaker and audience share an understanding of the problem. At this point, you talk about how sexual intercourse is the major means of transmission of the AIDS virus and suggest that there is a need for young people to engage in honest, explicit discussion about sexual practices with their partners.

Satisfaction

A plan is presented to satisfy the need created. You might suggest various ways in which young people can initiate talk about sex with their partners.

Visualization

In the visualization step, what will happen once the plan is implemented is described. Here, you encourage the audience to imagine and anticipate the results of the proposed plan—in this case, the reduced risk of AIDS and more open communication in relationships.

Action

The audience is asked to take action or approve the proposed plan. You ask audience members to use the techniques you have offered to discuss sex more explicitly and openly with their partners.

Multiple Perspectives

An organizational pattern created around multiple perspectives is one in which an idea or problem is analyzed from several different viewpoints. This pattern is designed to generate a full understanding of a subject. There are several forms this pattern can take. Summarizing different perspectives on an issue is the most common. Each perspective you discuss is a different lens through which the issue can be viewed or a different way of looking at the problem as a result of different areas of specialty, interest, or expertise. In a presentation on the state's budget deficit, for example, you might suggest solutions such as imposing an additional tax on cigarettes, cutting state programs, raising property taxes, and legalizing marijuana. You discuss the advantages and disadvantages of each of the proposed solutions. All of the perspectives offered are considered part of the dialogue about this issue, and in your presentation, you represent and do not dismiss any of them as legitimate points of view.

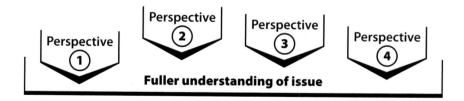

When the perspectives you are choosing to present are in opposition to each other, your analysis might take the form of comparison and contrast—pointing to the differences and similarities among the perspectives. You also might choose to highlight the common ground that exists among the perspectives instead of focusing on the differences among

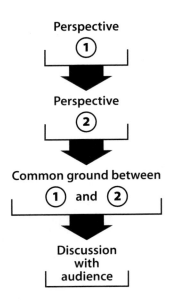

Perspective (1)

Perspective (2)

Common ground between (1) and (2)

Discussion with audience

them. In this case, you would point to potential points of unity between the two conflicting viewpoints.

If you are a supervisor who is meeting with a work group to try to resolve a conflict about how to determine salary increases, you might use an organizational pattern of multiple perspectives to begin the meeting. You could begin by summarizing the perspective of those who believe that the supervisor should determine pay increases, then summarize the perspective of those who believe that a committee should make the decision, and conclude with a discussion of what the two perspectives have in common. Both perspectives, you might suggest, are designed to make sure salaries are determined fairly, both use the same evaluation forms, and both focus on quality of work rather than length of time employed. You then would want to ask your colleagues to join you in trying to resolve the conflict.

Narrative

In a narrative organizational pattern, ideas are structured in the form of a story using characters, settings, and plots. The story may be a true story or one you invent and may consist of a single or several episodes. It is used to convey information about or illuminate a subject matter in a way that is easy for the audience to grasp. Author Ursula Le Guin, in a speech to the National Abortion Rights League, told of her own abortion by framing it as a story about a princess who fell in love with a prince. When she got pregnant, the prince ran back to his family and refused to have anything more to do with her. Her parents helped the princess get an illegal abortion, after which she finished college, went on to graduate school, got married, became a writer, and had three children. She concluded her story with the moral of her presentation: The United States cannot go back to

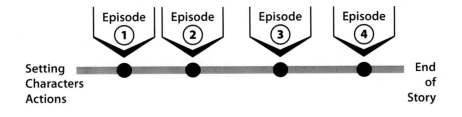

Episode (1) Episode (2) Episode (3) Episode (4)

Setting
Characters
Actions

End
of
Story

"the Dark Ages when abortion was a crime. . . . We are not going to let anybody in this country have that kind of power over any girl or woman."[8]

Narrative Progression

A variation of the narrative pattern is narrative progression, where you tell several stories, one after another. Each story leads into the next, and you conclude with the overall point you want to make based on all of the stories. In a commencement speech at Stanford University, Apple cofounder Steve Jobs offered three stories. In the first story, he told about a calligraphy class he took in college that later provided the inspiration for the fonts on Mac computers. In the second, he told about getting fired from and then rehired by Apple, which taught him what he really loved in life. The third story was about his experience with pancreatic cancer and what it taught him about living. Jobs concluded by explaining the point of all three stories: "Your time is limited, so don't waste it living someone else's life. Don't be trapped by dogma—which is living with the results of other people's thinking. Don't let the noise of others' opinions drown out your own inner voice. And most important, have the courage to follow your heart and intuition."[9]

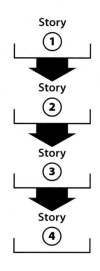

Problem/Solution

A problem/solution organizational pattern begins with a discussion of a problem and concludes with your suggestion for a solution or solutions. In a speech to the US Senate about the opioid epidemic, Senator Rob Portman of Ohio detailed a problem that contributes to the epidemic—the fact that the synthetic opioid fentanyl is shipped largely from China through the US Post Office. The legislation he discussed in his presentation—to require the Post Office to screen 100% of its packages to identify and stop opioids from entering the United States—was his proposed solution.[10]

Spiral

A spiral pattern begins by offering ideas at a broad level and moving to increasingly in-depth explanations of those ideas. You begin by talking about something at a general level and wind down into the particular, focusing in greater detail on the subject as you proceed through your presentation. You move toward greater specificity as you develop your ideas.

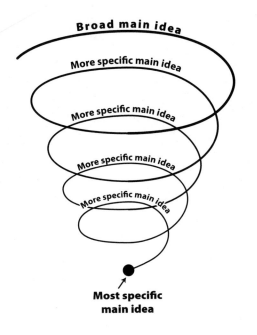

Broad main idea

More specific main idea

More specific main idea

More specific main idea

More specific main idea

Most specific main idea

In your self-presentation on a first date, for example, you tend to use a spiral pattern to offer information about yourself. You reveal something about yourself in broad, general terms—perhaps that you enjoy music. If your date is interested in this topic and asks for more information, you go into more depth. You might explain that you like many different kinds of music, that you particularly like alternative country, that you have an iTunes collection of many alternative country musicians, and that you would like to play in a band someday.

Thinking Things Through

In this pattern, you lay out the actual thought processes you followed while trying to answer a question, solve a problem, or formulate your perspective on an issue. You take your audience on the journey you took in thinking something through—helping the audience understand how you arrived at where you now stand in your thinking. Sometimes, this means that you have arrived at a particular decision, which you share with your audience. At other times, you emphasize that you have not yet finalized your thinking on the matter. This is a good organizational pattern to use for the interactional goals of discovering knowledge and belief and articulating a perspective because it helps others in the interaction understand how your thinking has evolved on the issue under discussion.

Let's assume that you are on a search committee to hire someone for a position open in your organization. At the meeting to select the person for the job, you can use the thinking-things-through pattern to explain why you are leaning toward one candidate over the others. You might tell the other committee members, for example, that you began by thinking about the skills the

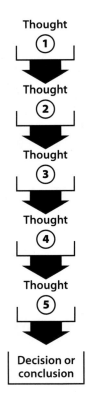

Thought
①

Thought
②

Thought
③

Thought
④

Thought
⑤

Decision or conclusion

position requires, which led you to think about the differences in skills among the candidates interviewed. You decided that the skills of candidate A are adequate for the organization's needs, although perhaps not as strong as those of candidate B. But then you thought about how each candidate would fit into the organization, and you sense that candidate A, who seems very community oriented, would work hard to fit into the organization. Continuing to reveal your train of thought, you explain that you next remembered experiences you've had with people who didn't fit into the organization and how they tend to leave the job fairly quickly after they are hired. That is why, you continue, you probably favor candidate A, who fits in, even though she doesn't have the same level of skill as candidate B. You might conclude your presentation by saying that this is where you are in your thinking right now, but you are looking forward to hearing others' thoughts on the candidates.

Time

When you present your ideas according to their temporal relationships, you are using an organizational pattern of time. Ideas presented in this form are structured chronologically from past to present or from present to past. The units also can be time periods or steps in a process. Kevin Durant, accepting an MVP award from the National Basketball Association, used this kind of pattern. He began with his childhood, thanking his mother for her sacrifices: "When you didn't eat, you made sure we ate. You went to sleep hungry. You sacrificed for us. You're the real MVP." He proceeded from there, recalling the first time he walked into a gym to play basketball. He then moved into the present, thanking his teammates for the part they played in his success.[11]

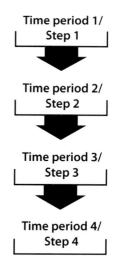

Web

A web organizational pattern revolves around a central or core idea. Other ideas branch out from the core, with each branching idea a reflection and elaboration of the core. In the web form, you begin with the central idea and then explore each idea in turn, returning to the core idea and going out from it again until all of the ideas have been covered. The web structure is especially useful when you really want to emphasize a core or primary idea in your presentation because it allows you to restate that idea frequently.

This pattern is very close to a category organizational pattern in that both patterns address different aspects or categories of a subject. In a

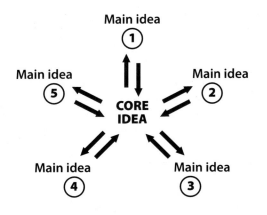

web pattern, you return to the core idea and explicitly reference it between your discussions of each of the main ideas, but in the category pattern, you explore various ideas sequentially without explicit reference to the core idea. The web pattern is also similar to the circle pattern, where each idea leads to the next. Rather than simply moving around the circle with the points you want to make, however, you move out from and then back to the main idea when using the web pattern.

A web structure could be used by a manager to explain to her new program assistant how she will be evaluated each year. The core of the job, she might emphasize, is customer service—treating the clients with respect and helping them solve their problems. She discusses the other aspects on which the program assistant will be evaluated—managing the budget, providing support to the team members, completing the paperwork when new employees are hired, processing the mail, and maintaining the organization's website. The primary function of the job, though, is customer service, and the manager would keep coming back to that point and its importance to the job between her discussions of each of the other duties.

The way you choose to frame your major ideas is an important step in helping your audience understand your perspective. Although we have provided you with a lengthy list of potential patterns, the list is incomplete. Framing is a creative act, and there are an almost infinite number of ways to organize a presentation. Now that you have a framework that effectively organizes your ideas, your next task is to elaborate on your main ideas.

6

Elaborating

Elaborating is the process of developing the ideas that emerge as you begin to construct your presentation. In the process of elaboration, you work out the specific details that will support, expand on, and give presence to the main ideas of your presentation. You make a presentation come alive for your audience through examples, figures of speech, facts, statistics, stories, or other forms of elaboration. Enlivening your presentation helps your audience arrive at a fuller understanding of your perspective.

The particular combination of forms of elaboration that you select for a presentation depends on your interactional goal; your personal and cultural preferences; and the nature of your audience, setting, and subject. As is the case with all communication options, you naturally will prefer some forms of elaboration over others. If you are uncomfortable sharing highly personal information with a particular audience, you probably will not choose to use personal narrative in a presentation. Similarly, an audience not used to discourse with a strong pattern of rhythm and rhyme might be baffled or even irritated if you incorporate it into a presentation. If you are attempting to build community, you probably do not want to use forms of elaboration that are highly individualistic. Instead, you would choose forms such as myths, participation, and proverbs that bring audience members together.

In this chapter, we discuss possible forms of elaboration you can use to develop your main ideas. These forms are designed to serve as starting points for thinking about how to discuss and extend your ideas for your specific audience. As with the organizational patterns in chapter 5, the forms of elaboration are arranged in alphabetical order because we want to encourage you to consider all possible forms of elaboration for your presentations rather than simply selecting those that are most familiar or obvious.

FORMS OF ELABORATION

Comparison and Contrast

In comparison and contrast, you develop an idea by discussing something unfamiliar through the lens of a concept or experience that is familiar to your audience.

Comparison

Comparison is the process of showing the similarities between the familiar and the unfamiliar. In a presentation about fashion, for example, you might suggest that the 1920s and the 1970s were similar in terms of how fashion functioned as rebellion.

Contrast

Contrast links items to show their differences. Rap musician Kendrick Lamar used contrast to explain what hip hop is to him when he accepted the award for best rap album at a Grammy Awards ceremony: "From the jump I thought it was about the accolades and the cars and the clothes. But it's really about expressing yourself and putting that paint on the canvas for the world to evolve for the next listener, the next generation after that, you know what I'm saying? Hip hop has done that for me."[1]

Credentials

Providing evidence of your background and experience with a subject shows your audience that your ideas are based on some expertise and accumulated experience. Credentials may include a discussion of your cultural background, years of relevant work experience, or other factors that suggest a personal knowledge of or connection to your topic. John Hickenlooper, who served as mayor of Denver and governor of Colorado, presented his credentials in a speech on the state of the state:

> As some of you know, I took what you might call an unconventional path into running for office. I started out here in Colorado as a geologist. During a downturn, everyone in our company got laid off. Next thing I knew I was making beer and starting a brewpub business. It turned out pretty well. But as every small business person knows, it's not easy out there, especially when bureaucracy gets in the way. I didn't run for public office until I was 50. Before that, I'd never run for anything. Not even in high school. I ran for public office as a small businessman. I thought government needed to operate with more common sense and less nonsense.[2]

Definitions

When defining something, you are establishing or identifying its essential qualities. Making use of definition to elaborate, you provide the meaning of a word or concept in terms the audience will understand. Several kinds of definitions are available if you choose to use this form of elaboration, including: (1) definition by authority; (2) definition by display; (3) etymological definition; and (4) operational definition.

Definition by Authority

Definition by authority is a definition offered by an expert on a subject. Karen Spence, wife of Vice President Mike Spence, defined *art therapy* in a presentation to the US Conference of Mayors. Spence is a teacher and painter who has been extensively involved in art-therapy initiatives, and art therapy is the cause she chose to champion during her time as Second Lady. She began with a definition of *art therapy* from a professional organization and then went on to elaborate on that definition from her own experience:

> As a Second Lady of the United States, I chose one initiative to champion, and it is art therapy. And I call my initiative—we call it—*healing with the heart.* Now art therapy—many of you know about art therapy in this room—but the definition, according to the American Art Therapy Association, is a mental health profession that uses the creative process of art making to improve and enhance the physical, mental, and emotional well-being of individuals of all ages. It is not arts and crafts. An art therapist, who has a minimum of a master's degree and frequently a doctorate degree, helps a client get to the root of his or her problem or issue and works the client through it with the use of art.[3]

Definition by Display

In definition by display, a word or idea is explained by pointing to something visible. A lawyer might use definition by display when showing a jury the position of wounds on a victim's hands and arms to help define the act of self-defense. An architect who shows a sketch of how a building will look after remodeling also is using definition by display.

Etymological Definition

An etymological definition explains the history, origins, or derivation of a word. In a presentation about digital avatars, you might cite the original meaning of the term—a Hindu concept referring to the manifestation of a god or the god's descent to earthly existence, typically as a divine teacher.

Operational Definition

An operational definition explains how something works or how it is operationalized or manifest in real life. In a graduation speech at Harvard University, author J. K. Rowling provided an operational definition of *failure*:

> Ultimately, we all have to decide for ourselves what constitutes failure, but the world is quite eager to give you a set of criteria if you let it. So I think it fair to say that by any conventional measure, a mere seven years after my graduation day, I had failed on an epic scale. An exceptionally short-lived marriage had imploded, and I was jobless, a

lone parent, and as poor as it is possible to be in modern Britain, without being homeless. The fears that my parents had had for me, and that I had had for myself, had both come to pass, and by every usual standard, I was the biggest failure I knew.[4]

Dreams

Dreams are considered by many audiences to be powerful sources from which to learn about and understand experience. Dreams can be defined in two ways, each of which can be used as a form of elaboration: (1) thoughts, images, or emotions that occur during sleep; and (2) strong desires, goals, or purposes.

Sleeping Dreams

In some cultures, the dreams experienced when sleeping are considered qualitatively more vital than waking events because they provide the opportunity to communicate with nonhuman and superhuman forms and to experience alternative realities. Further, dreams can point to and capture the essence of what is important to an individual or community. Even if you have not considered dreams in this way, you still can appreciate the fact that dreams can highlight and illustrate experiences in significant ways. Activist Sonia Johnson recounted a sleeping dream to illustrate the notion of trust:

> A woman in Missouri told me this dream. She was in a city, standing on top of a tall building, looking out upon other buildings as far as she could see. She was a country woman, uneasy amid all the concrete and steel, and longing for home.
>
> Gradually she became aware that to get home she would have to leap off the edge of the building. Looking down at the miniature cars creeping along the miniature street far, far below, she said to herself, "But that's ridiculous! I'll kill myself if I jump off here!" Still, the feeling persisted that if she didn't jump, she would never get home again. And the grief that overwhelmed her at the thought of being exiled forever from the grass and trees and fields of home became so much stronger than her fear of dying that she leapt.
>
> As she began to fall, a rope appeared before her; she reached out, grabbed it, and swung way out over the street. At the end of its arc, she knew that if she didn't let go, she would swing back to where she had been before and not be any closer to home. So she let go. As she began to fall again, another rope appeared. Grabbing it, she swung out to the end of its arc, and let go again.
>
> Trusting herself, letting go, reaching out, swinging out over the abyss, trusting, letting go, reaching out, she found her way home.[5]

Life Dreams

A future goal or desire is a second kind of dream, and these can be important sources of inspiration. Martin Luther King Jr.'s famous "I Have a Dream" speech is probably the best known example of the use of this kind of dream in a presentation. In the following paragraph, King introduced the idea of a dream, which would dominate the remainder of the speech:

> I say to you today, my friends, though, even though we face the difficulties of today and tomorrow, I still have a dream. It is a dream deeply rooted in the American dream. I have a dream that one day this nation will rise up, live out the true meaning of its creed: "We hold these truths to be self-evident, that all men are created equal."[6]

In accepting the *Sports Illustrated* Sportsperson of the Year Award, tennis champion Serena Williams referenced the day, when she was quite young, that she articulated out loud her dream to win the US Open:

> So I truly feel that that day changed my life. And now I had a goal, and I began to work toward that goal. And I believed one day I would stand on that court and hold that winner's trophy. And now I guess, thirty years later, I still have goals, and I still have dreams of winning. And this award makes me actually want to work harder to reach more goals. So I don't know if that is weird or not but when I get off here, I'm going home to start training because this is so awesome.[7]

Emotions

Although the emphasis on logic in contemporary Western culture often discourages speakers from considering emotions as a possible form of elaboration, emotions can be a powerful way to develop ideas. Human beings respond with their feelings as well as with logic to what happens in their lives. Emotions are aroused indirectly through means such as narration, vivid description, and display. Telling a story, describing something in great detail, and displaying an emotion yourself all invite identification with the emotion you want your audience to experience. Refugee advocate Melissa Fleming used the emotion of fear as a form of elaboration in her speech about a Syrian couple, Doaa and Bassem, who paid smugglers to take them to Europe on a boat crammed with 500 people. She described what happened on the fourth day of the journey:

> They were weak and weary. Soon they saw a boat approach—a smaller boat, 10 men on board, who started shouting at them, hurling insults, throwing sticks, asking them to all disembark and get on this smaller, more unseaworthy boat. The parents were terrified for their children, and they collectively refused to disembark. So the boat sped away in anger, and a half an hour later, came back and started deliberately ramming a hole in the side of Doaa's boat, just below where she and Bassem were sitting. And she heard how they yelled, "Let the fish eat your flesh!" and they started laughing as the boat capsized and sank.[8]

Exaggeration

Overstating a point can serve to elaborate an idea by making it striking and memorable. Exaggeration often is used in humorous presentations, after-dinner speeches, and roasts or on other ceremonial occasions. Exaggeration, as it is used in these settings, is not to be confused with the deliberate distortion of information or evidence. As a form of elaboration, exaggeration does not deal with actual facts as much as with the interpretation of ideas in a lighthearted way. "I'm so tired I could sleep for a year" is an example of exaggeration. Exaggeration or hyperbole is a favorite form of elaboration for President Donald Trump. Speaking at a rally in Nashville, Tennessee, about the opioid epidemic, he stated: "You go to the hospital, you have a broken arm; you come out, you are a drug addict with this crap."[9]

Examples

The example is a short illustration of a point. It is a specific illustration of a category of people, places, objects, actions, experiences, or conditions that shows the nature or character of that category. Governor Susana Martinez of New Mexico, in her state of the state speech, offered a series of examples to point to the strength of the New Mexican economy:

> On our watch, exports to Mexico are at an all-time high; we've been ranked number one in the nation in export growth. In Santa Teresa, our border port is thriving. New Mexico is poised to become a key trade route between the United States and Mexico, Central America, and South America. Our tax rate on manufacturing improved from third worst in the region to the best in the West. Even more promising, over the past year, we created 14,000 jobs, and our private sector grew at a rate of 2.4%—lifting us in the state-by-state rankings all the way to the 15th fastest-growing private sector in the country. And over the last year, we've seen New Mexico companies expand their workforce as we also welcome new companies here from around the world.[10]

Explanations

An explanation is a description of a term, concept, process, or proposal to make it clear and understandable. Mary Barra, CEO of General Motors, offered the following explanation of the Deferred Prosecution Agreement between GM and the US Attorney's office. The agreement was negotiated in response to GM's failure to recall cars with faulty ignition switches—switches that could shut off the engine while driving and prevent air bags from inflating:

> First, let's talk briefly about the agreement. The centerpiece is what's called a *Deferred Prosecution Agreement*. It means that the government agrees to *defer* prosecution of charges against GM related to the ignition switch for three years. After three years, if we meet all of the terms and conditions set by the government, federal prosecutors will seek to dismiss the charges and the matter will be *completely* closed. Among our obligations:

- The Agreement requires us to continue cooperating with the federal government and obey all laws;
- We are to work with the government to establish an independent monitor to review and assess our policies and procedures in specific areas relating to safety issues and recalls;
- And we must pay a $900 million financial penalty.[11]

Facts

Facts are statements that generally are accepted as true by a culture. They are pieces of information that are verifiable by direct observation, by reference to scientific findings, or because they are offered by individuals who are granted expert status on an issue. Israeli Prime Minister Benjamin Netanyahu used a series of facts in his presentation to the United Nations:

> Ladies and gentlemen, in this year of historic visits and historic anniversaries, Israel has so much to be grateful for. A hundred and twenty years ago, Theodor Herzl convened the First Zionist Congress to transform our tragic past into a brilliant future by establishing the Jewish state. One hundred years ago, the Balfour Declaration advanced Herzl's vision by recognizing the right of the Jewish people to a national home in our ancestral homeland. Seventy years ago, the United Nations further advanced that vision by adopting a resolution supporting the establishment of a Jewish state. And fifty years ago, we reunited our eternal capital Jerusalem, achieving a miraculous victory against those who sought to destroy our state. Theodor Herzl was our modern Moses—and his dream has come true. We've returned to the Promised Land; revived our language; in-gathered our exiles; and built a modern, thriving democracy.[12]

Figures of Speech

Figures of speech are unusual turns of language that can elaborate ideas in particularly vivid ways. Some of the most frequently used figures of speech are: (1) alliteration; (2) antithesis; (3) irony; (4) metaphor and simile; (5) oxymoron; and (6) personification.

Alliteration

In alliteration, initial or middle consonants are repeated in two or more adjacent words. In his acceptance address at the Democratic National Convention, President Bill Clinton incorporated several examples of alliteration with the letter *h* when he said, "Somewhere at this very moment a child is being born in America. Let it be our cause to give that child a happy home, a healthy family, and a hopeful future."[13] In his speech at the memorial service for those who died in a mass shooting on the Fort Hood military base in Texas, President Barack Obama used alliteration twice to honor those who were killed: "They are part of the finest fighting force that the world has ever known. They have served tour after tour of duty in distant, different, and difficult places."[14]

Antithesis

Antithesis involves the juxtaposition of opposing concepts—the contrast between contradictory ideas. Senator Hillary Clinton's keynote address to the Democratic National Convention made use of antithesis: "My mother was born before women could vote. My daughter got to vote for her mother for President."[15] In her eulogy for the musician Prince, Jane Clare Jones used a series of antithetical statements:

> He sang like an angel and a man possessed. He was reverence and sin. Confusion and commitment. Artifice and naked emotional exposure. He hated being stared at but wanted everyone to look at him. And when we looked, we were as awed as he wanted and needed us to be, and we offered up the love that he asked for and that he made, and for a long time it was enough, it was everything, and at the same time it was not and could never be enough.[16]

Irony

Irony occurs when saying the opposite of what is meant. A speaker, in other words, says one thing and means another. President Barack Obama, at a town-hall meeting in College Park, Maryland, used irony in describing negotiations around the federal debt: "Don't get me wrong, there's nothing I enjoy more than sitting, hour after hour, day after day, debating the fine points of the Federal budget with members of Congress. But after a while you do start feeling a little cooped up."[17] Irony also occurs when a sequence of events yields unexpected results. In a speech about personal safety, you might use the example of someone buying a gun for protection but being shot when a burglar finds the firearm and uses it.

Metaphor/Simile

A metaphor is a comparison in which something is spoken about in terms of something else. In his speech to the United Nations, Pope Francis used a metaphor comparing the accomplishments of the UN to lights in the darkness:

> Without claiming to be exhaustive, we can mention the codification and development of international law, the establishment of international norms regarding human rights, advances in humanitarian law, the resolution of numerous conflicts, operations of peacekeeping and reconciliation, and any number of other accomplishments in every area of international activity and endeavor. All these achievements are lights which help to dispel the darkness of the disorder caused by unrestrained ambitions and collective forms of selfishness.[18]

A simile involves a comparison introduced by either *like* or *as*. Fred Rogers, the host of the television show *Mr. Rogers' Neighborhood*, incorporated simile in his commencement address at Chatham University:

You know the motto on Chatham's seal: *Filiae Nostrae Sicut Antarii Lapides*. Well, the best translation I can come up with (thanks to several friends who remember their Latin better than I) is the following: "Our girls (our young women) are like support stones (like cornerstones)." What a great identity! Being a strong support to yourself and your neighbor—helping others win, too![19]

Oxymoron

An oxymoron is a form of antithesis in which words that normally would not appear together are paired. Putting opposites together in such a tight construction can be an effective form of elaboration. B. B. King's Blues Club in Memphis used the oxymoron "famous unknowns" as a label for the up-and-coming musicians who performed at the club. Walt Bresette used an oxymoron to close a speech to Green Party members, suggesting that to secure their rights, Native Americans must engage in "nonviolent ass kickin'."[20]

Personification

In personification, the speaker attributes human qualities to nonhuman objects or concepts. Upon his election as governor of Louisiana, Bobby Jindal provided an example of personification: "Today, we begin a new chapter in the history of Louisiana. I've said throughout the campaign that there are two entities that have the most to fear from us winning this election. One is *corruption* and the other is *incompetence*. If you happen to see either of them, let them know the party is over."[21]

Humor

Humor can function not just to entertain and amuse but also to develop and extend ideas. Humor is appropriate as a form of elaboration only when it is relevant to the idea you are developing. Television host Conan O'Brien, himself a graduate of Harvard University, made a humorous point about what lies ahead for graduates during his commencement address at Harvard:

> You see, you're in for a lifetime of "And you went to Harvard?" Accidentally give the wrong amount of change in a transaction and it's, "And you went to Harvard?" Ask the guy at the hardware store how these jumper cables work and hear, "And you went to Harvard?" Forget just once that your underwear goes inside your pants, and it's, "And you went to Harvard?" Get your head stuck in your niece's dollhouse because you wanted to see what it was like to be a giant, and it's "Uncle Conan, you went to Harvard!?"[22]

Myths

Myths are stories that explain the origins of practices, beliefs, institutions, or natural phenomena. They express fundamental social, cultural, and religious values important to a community. In testimony before the Supreme Court, Chief Weninock of the Yakimas told the story of the origins of Native Americans to develop the idea that they have legitimate claims to their traditional fishing places:

> God created the Indian Country, and it was like he spread out a big blanket. He put the Indians on it. They were created here in this Country, truly honest, and that was the time the river started to run. Then God created fish in this river and put deer in the mountains and made laws through which has come the increase of fish and game. Then the Creator gave us Indians Life; we walked, and as soon as we saw the game and fish we knew they were made for us.[23]

Narratives

Real or fictional narratives with characters, settings, plots, and dialogue can be used as forms of elaboration. You may use stories told by others or personal narratives, in which you recount your own experiences. This is the kind of narrative Meghan Markle, Her Royal Highness The Duchess of Sussex, used in a presentation to the United Nations conference on women:

> When I was just eleven years old, I unknowingly and somehow accidentally became a female advocate. It was around the same time as the Beijing conference, so a little over twenty years ago, where in my hometown of Los Angeles a pivotal moment reshaped my notion of what is possible. See, I had been in school watching a TV show in elementary school, and this commercial came on with the tag line for this dishwashing liquid, and the tag line said, "Women all over America are fighting greasy pots and pans." Two boys from my class said, "Yeah, that's where women belong, in the kitchen." I remember feeling shocked and angry and also just feeling so hurt; it just wasn't right, and something needed to be done. So I went home and told my dad what had happened, and he encouraged me to write letters, so I did—to the most powerful people I could think of.
>
> Now my eleven-year-old self worked out that if I really wanted someone to hear me, well then I should write a letter to the First Lady. So off I went, scribbling away to our First Lady at the time, Hillary Clinton. I also put pen to paper, and I wrote a letter to my news source at the time, Linda Ellerbee, who hosted a kids news program, and then to powerhouse attorney Gloria Allred because, even at eleven, I wanted to cover all my bases. Finally, I wrote to the soap manufacturer. And a few weeks went by and, to my surprise, I received letters of encouragement from Hillary Clinton, from Linda Ellerbee, and from Gloria Allred. It was amazing. The kids news show, they sent a camera crew to my home to cover the story, and it was roughly a month later when the soap manufacturer, Procter & Gamble, changed the commercial for their ivory clear dishwashing liquid. They changed it from "Women all over America are fighting greasy pots and pans" to "People all over America . . . ." It was at that moment that I realized the magnitude of my actions. At the age of eleven, I had created my small level of impact by standing up for equality.[24]

Participation

Audience participation is an invitation to the audience to respond verbally during the course of the presentation. This form of elaboration allows you to use the ideas, comments, or responses of the audience to develop your ideas. More often, it is simply a way for your audience to interact with you and engage the presentation. Audience participation assumes a variety of forms: (1) call/response; (2) discussion; and (3) testimonials.

Call/Response

Call/response is a pattern of spontaneous vocal and nonverbal responses from listeners that acknowledge a speaker's statements and testify to the impact of the message. Call/response functions, much as applause does, as a form of affirmation, support, and encouragement. It tells you when the audience is with you and when you can move to a discussion of your next idea. Although you cannot rely on your audience to offer encouraging remarks, such encouragement can function as a powerful form of elaboration and affirmation of your ideas if it occurs.

Call/response patterns can be formulaic or improvised by the audience. Denver Broncos fans use call and response when one group in the stadium yells *Go!* and another group answers *Broncos!* Participants at a campaign rally might spontaneously call out *I hear you* to signal their agreement with the candidate. Supporters of President Donald Trump often yell *build that wall* at rallies and events to signal their encouragement of and support for his wall at the United States-Mexico border. An audience might urge a speaker to continue in a particular direction by shouting *take your time, work it, amen,* or *hallelujah.* Nonverbally, audience members might offer encouragement by waving their hands in the air, whistling, jumping up and down, or clapping. In one of Karen's presentational speaking classes, some of her students made signs that read, *You're doing great, Keep it up, We're with you,* which they held up during students' presentations. On any given day, no one knew who had the signs or if and when they would appear, but they were a delightful form of encouragement throughout the semester.

Discussion

Discussion is the informal exploration of a question or issue by at least two individuals. If your goal is discovering knowledge and belief, discussion is a necessary form of elaboration, although it can be part of any presentation. Most interviews and informal conversations naturally take the form of a discussion, with all participants sharing ideas and responding to the thoughts of others. Managing a discussion is described in greater detail in chapter 2 in the discussion of the interactional goal of discovering knowledge and belief.

Testimonials

Another form of audience response that can be used to develop ideas is asking audience members to offer examples from their own lives. Such testimonials can include stories told by participants in meetings of Alcoholics Anonymous or other support groups, for example. Religious revivals sometimes make use of testimonials to help secure new converts, and the testimony of witnesses in courts of law is another example of this form of elaboration. In her acceptance speech for best actress at the Academy Awards ceremony, Frances McDormand asked all the women who had been nominated to stand as testament to the abundance of female talent available in the film industry:

> If I may be so honored to have all the female nominees in every category stand with me in this room tonight, the actors—Meryl [Streep], if you do it, everybody else will, c'mon—the filmmakers, the producers, the directors, the writers, the cinematographers, the composers, the songwriters, the designers. C'mon! Okay, look around everybody. Look around, ladies and gentlemen, because we all have stories to tell and projects we need financed. . . . Invite us into your office in a couple days, or you can come to ours, whatever suits you best, and we'll tell you all about them.[25]

Poetry

Poetry is the use of meaning, sound, and rhythm in language, chosen and arranged to create a concentrated image of a particular condition or experience. A poem by US poet laureate Tracy Smith could be used in a presentation to describe the experience of living paycheck to paycheck:

> When some people talk about money
> They speak as if it were a mysterious lover
> Who went out to buy milk and never
> Came back, and it makes me nostalgic
> For the years I lived on coffee and bread,
> Hungry all the time, walking to work on payday
> Like a woman journeying for water
> From a village without a well, then living
> One or two nights like everyone else
> On roast chicken and red wine.[26]

Presentational Aids

Presentational aids are materials that supplement spoken words by providing visual and/or audio elaboration. Charts, graphs, photographs, sketches, and cartoons are visual, while audio aids include music, recorded conversations, and other sounds that elaborate your ideas. In all likelihood, you will make considerable use of formats that combine audio and visual components—video clips and PowerPoint slides, for example. In a presentation about the origins of the universe, you might show pictures from the Hubble Space Telescope that helped document the Big Bang and established more precisely the age of the planet. We deal with presentational aids more extensively in chapter 9, so be sure to review that chapter if you plan to use them as a form of elaboration.

Proverbs

Proverbs are succinct cultural sayings that express obvious truths and capture audience members' experiences. At a joint press conference with Mexican President Felipe Calderón, President Barack Obama used a proverb to describe the relationship between the United States and Mexico:

> This is the progress that we've made today. It's progress that calls to mind a Mexican proverb that I am told says, "Tell me who you walk with, and I will tell you who you are." Mr. President, the United States is proud to walk with Mexico. And through our work, we're reminded again of who we are—which is two neighbors, two partners bound by a common vision of prosperity and security for both our people.[27]

Puns

Puns are plays on words based either on different words that sound alike or on various meanings of the same word. In a presentation about her work, visual artist Janet Hughes used puns on the word *read* to describe what it meant to her to be included in a special exhibition. (Hughes's presentation is one of the sample presentations at the end of the book.)

> She was well read.
> She became widely read.
> She painted the town
> The picture
> And her lips.
> Her lips were read.
> Her lips were red.[28]

Taylor Mali, in his TED Talk entitled "What Teachers Make," used a pun as his major form of elaboration. He recounted what he would have liked to reply to a lawyer at a dinner party who suggested that those who choose teaching as a career are not likely to be able to teach students anything because teachers are so poorly paid. The lawyer turned to him and asked, "You're a teacher, Taylor. Come on, be honest. What do you make?" His reply puns on the word *make*: "I make kids wonder, I make 'em question, I make 'em criticize, I make 'em apologize and mean it. I make 'em write, write, write. And then I make 'em read. I make 'em spell." He concludes with: "Teachers make a goddamn difference. Now what about you?"[29]

Questions

Questions can be used to develop an idea by encouraging listeners to think about the idea and to become mentally engaged in the subject matter. Three common kinds of questions are: (1) rhetorical questions; (2) substantive questions; and (3) questions of facilitation.

Rhetorical Questions

Rhetorical questions are those a speaker asks and wants the audience to answer mentally. They are designed to stimulate audience members to think about the subject. Maddie Poynter, speaking as part of the Bully Project Movement, incorporated into her presentation a series of rhetorical questions:

> If someone is alone on the playground, will you offer to be his friend? If someone gets pushed down, will you lift them back up? If a friend is sad because of a mean text or message, will you send some kind words to make her smile? If someone puts you down, will you believe them or choose to believe in yourself?[30]

Substantive Questions

Substantive questions are those that you as speaker both ask and answer or ones you expect your audience to answer out loud. Author Alice Walker, in a speech to the Midwives Alliance of North America shortly after the terrorist attacks of September 11, 2001, used a substantive question to talk about those who would engage in such acts: "What is the story whose fiery end I am witnessing?" She answers her own question:

> This was an act by a man who did not believe in the possibility of love, or even common sense, to transform the world. I can easily imagine there will be thousands like him born in our time, that from the roots of this one man's story, they will come to birth practically every minute, and our government will not be remotely able to "smoke" all of them "out of their holes."[31]

Questions of Facilitation

Questions of facilitation help manage group interactions. They are used to enable all perspectives to be heard by keeping the discussion on track and preventing any single individual from monopolizing the conversation. A more complete discussion of the use of these questions is offered in chapter 2 in the section about the interactional goal of discovering knowledge and belief.

Quotations

When a quotation is used as a form of elaboration, a speaker uses the words of others to develop and extend an idea. A quotation may draw its effectiveness from the content of the quotation, from the eloquence of the ideas expressed, or from the reputation or expertise of the person who is quoted. When she accepted a lifetime achievement award from the Genesis Foundation in Tel Aviv, Israel, Supreme Court Justice Ruth Bader Ginsburg quoted Anne Frank to her audience:

When I became active in the movement to open doors to women, enabling them to enter occupations once closed to them—lawyering and judging, bartending, policing, and firefighting, for example—I was heartened by the words of a girl of my generation. She wrote: "One of the many questions that have often bothered me is why women have been, and still are, thought to be so inferior to men. It's easy to say it's unfair, but that's not enough for me; I'd really like to know the reason for this great injustice! Men presumably dominated women from the very beginning because of their greater physical strength. . . . Until recently, women silently went along with this, which was stupid, since the longer it's kept up, the more deeply entrenched it becomes. Fortunately, education, work and progress have opened women's eyes. In many countries they've been granted equal rights; many people, mainly women, but also men, now realize how wrong it was to tolerate this state of affairs for so long. . . . Yours, Anne M. Frank." This insightful comment was one of the last entered in her diary.[32]

Repetition and Restatement

In repetition, the same words or phrases are repeated several times; in restatement, an idea is repeated using different words. Both forms of elaboration function to reinforce an idea. In her speech at the Women's March on Washington, civil rights activist Angela Davis used repetition to reinforce the notion of resistance:

> We dedicate ourselves to collective resistance. Resistance to the billionaire mortgage profiteers and gentrifiers. Resistance to the health care privateers. Resistance to the attacks on Muslims and on immigrants. Resistance to attacks on disabled people. Resistance to state violence perpetrated by the police and through the prison industrial complex. Resistance to institutional and intimate gender violence, especially against trans women of color.[33]

Rhythm and Rhyme

In rhythm and rhyme, words and phrases are chosen for their sound effects. Rhythm is the arrangement of words to achieve a regular recurrence of beat or accent, while rhyme involves words that correspond with one another in terms of ending sounds. In this form of elaboration, the sounds of the words develop the idea the speaker wants to convey. Many forms of elaboration, such as alliteration and repetition, rely to some degree on the sounds of words, but in rhythm and rhyme, the sounds of the words are emphasized as much as—if not more than—their content. Rap artists, of course, are known for their ability to combine rhythm and rhyme, exemplified by the rapper Drake in his song "Is There More":

> Too many lyrics 'bout houses and loot
> Too many Walt Disney characters, mouses and goofs

I mean you know I love a challenge, but challenged by who?
I'll let you bring a thousand recruits
My peers are a talented group
But even if you take all their statistics and carry the two
Even if you rounded up the numbers and rounded the troops
There's still nothing they could really do
It's too bad reality checks don't cover the balances due
Whenever it's time to recoup.[34]

Rituals

Rituals are established forms or systems of rites in which members of a community participate to commemorate an important event or occasion. Often handed down from generation to generation, rituals and ceremonies function to connect community members with their heritage, their community, their country, or the cosmos. Through that connection, rituals generate feelings of power, wholeness, and community. Induction ceremonies of all kinds usually involve rituals. Author Diane Stein often uses rituals in her workshops designed to create changes in consciousness. In her croning ritual, for example, a woman who is undergoing a transition—menopause, retirement, or her last child's departure from home, for example—is given tangible or verbal gifts by each of those present.[35] Speakers who ask listeners to join them in reciting a familiar credo or pledge also are using ritual as a form of elaboration.

Sensory Images

Sensory images are words or phrases that communicate feelings and perceptions through one or more of the five senses—sight, smell, sound, taste, and touch. In his address after receiving the Nobel Prize in Literature, Patrick Modiano made use of visual images to describe the novelist's task: "Yet it has to be the vocation of the novelist, when faced with this large blank page of oblivion, to make a few faded words visible again, like lost icebergs adrift on the surface of the ocean."[36]

Statistics

Statistics are numerical data designed to show relationships between or among phenomena. The relationship expressed can emphasize size or magnitude, establish trends such as increases or decreases in a particular population, or make comparisons. In a presentation about homelessness, statistics might be used to show the extent of the problem: "According to the US Department of Housing and Urban Development, there were roughly 554,000 homeless people living somewhere in the United States on a given night last year. A total of 193,000 of those people were 'unsheltered,' meaning that they were living on the streets and had no access to emergency shelters, transitional housing, or Safe Havens."[37]

Understatement

In understatement, the speaker states an important point in a restrained style. The low-key nature of the understatement highlights its importance. In her speech to the Democratic National Convention, Michelle Obama used understatement to talk about the relationship between her husband and brother: "As you might imagine, for Barack, running for President is nothing compared to that first game of basketball with my brother Craig."[38] Captain Eric Moody was flying a plane from London to Auckland, New Zealand, when the plane flew into a cloud of volcanic ash and all four engines failed. He made the following understated announcement to the passengers: "Ladies and gentlemen, this is your captain speaking. We have a small problem. All four engines have stopped. We are doing our damnedest to get them going again. I trust you are not in too much distress."[39]

Visions

Visions are valuable sources of power, energy, and insight that may be used to elaborate ideas. Visions are of two types: (1) religious or spiritual visions; and (2) visionary statements about the future.

Spiritual Visions

A vision in the spiritual sense is a mystical experience that involves seeing something supernatural or prophetic. In this context, visions function as vehicles through which special powers or insights are made available to those who experience them. An example is the story of how the Lady of Guadalupe, also known as the *Virgin of Guadalupe*, appeared to Juan Diego near Mexico City in December of 1531. As proof of her presence, she made red roses appear for him to pick, and when he brought them to the bishop, her image was visible on Diego's cloak. In certain cultures, sharing a vision of this type is an especially meaningful form of elaboration because of shared beliefs about the power of the source.

Secular Visions

In secular contexts, visions capture and embody the ideals or desired future state of an individual, group, or nation. State-of-the-union addresses envision a country's future for the year to come. Lady Gaga proposed an alternative vision to "don't ask, don't tell," the policy barring gay men and lesbians from serving openly in the military:

> Doesn't it seem to be that "don't ask, don't tell" is backwards? Doesn't it seem to be that, based on the Constitution of the United States, that we're penalizing the wrong soldier? . . . I am here today because I would like to propose a new law; a law that sends home the soldier that has the problem. Our new law is called "if you don't like it, go home." A law that discharges the soldier with the issue, a law that discharges the soldier with the *real* problem, the homophobic

soldier that has the real negative effect on unit cohesion. A law that sends home the homophobe, a law that sends home the prejudiced. A law that doesn't prosecute the gay soldier who fights for equality with no problem, but prosecutes the straight soldier who fights against it.[40]

The list in this chapter provides some suggestions for ways to elaborate the ideas of your presentation. Your own processes of invention will generate others as you work to develop the main ideas of your presentation. Your next task is to develop an introduction and a conclusion that complete the frame of your presentation.

7

$$\overline{}\sim\!\!\!\longrightarrow$$

Beginning and Ending

Now that you have selected the basic structure of your presentation and the forms of elaboration for amplifying your main ideas, your next step is to develop an introduction and a conclusion. Because your ideas often change extensively as you work to put them into an organizational structure, you want to wait until you have prepared the body and main ideas before you decide how you want to start and end your presentation.

THE INTRODUCTION

The introduction is a critical part of your presentation because it is where you have your first opportunity to invite your audience to see the world as you see it. You offer your audience a glimpse of your perspective and how you will be approaching it. By the end of your introduction, your audience should know the subject of your presentation and your interactional goal(s). Your audience also will have begun making assessments about you as a speaker, and you want them to see you as someone with whom they want to continue to interact.

The introduction not only gives the audience information about you and your topic but also begins the process of establishing the conditions of safety, openness, freedom, and value for your audience. Everything you do in your introduction should communicate to your audience members that you want them to feel comfortable and free to choose whether and how to make use of new ideas that emerge in their interaction with you. Communicating genuine warmth as part of an introduction is likely to put your audience members at ease and encourage them to continue listening. Similarly, when you are energetic about the ideas of others, you communicate that you value diverse perspectives. Carefully considering how you introduce your presentation is important, then, because it makes a difference in how the entire presentation is received.

You may have been told that introductions should be dramatic and exciting or that you should tell a joke to get the attention of audience members. By using such openings, you signal to your audience members that you do not believe they are interested in your topic or are able to be attentive listeners. Instead, you suggest they need to be startled, cajoled, or humored into listening to you. We have seen presentations where students began by pulling out a gun and pointing it at the audience, riding a motorcycle into the classroom, or jumping out of a second-story window. In every case, these actions only scared audience members and left them unable to focus on the topic of the presentation itself. Similarly, a joke, especially if it is unrelated to your topic, takes audience members' attention away from the subject of your presentation.

Even interested audience members, however, may not be fully present mentally for a variety of reasons as you begin your presentation—perhaps they are talking with a colleague, texting, or thinking about their own upcoming presentations. There also will be times when you must speak to a captive audience—one that is required to be there for some reason. A supervisor may have required the members of your audience to attend a seminar in which they are not very interested, your audience members may be attending a conference presentation and discover that a particular presentation is not what they thought it would be, or you may be giving a history lecture to seniors in their final week of high school. In these instances, we still do not recommend a startling statement or a joke for your introduction. The most effective introduction in this situation is one that connects the topic to the audience in a way that is engaging, specific, and perhaps personal. Telling a story in some detail, for example, about something that happened to you that is directly relevant to audience members might be a good way to begin in these instances.

There are many different ways to begin a presentation. Below are descriptions of some commonly used types of introductions. You do not need to select an introduction only from this list; often, your subject matter will suggest an introduction unique to your presentation. You also might find that there are times when a combination of several different types of introductions is the best way to open your presentation. As with the list of organizational patterns, these are arranged in alphabetical order because we do not want to privilege some over others. We hope you will consider all possible introductions for a presentation rather than selecting the first one that seems appropriate.

Narrative

In a narrative or story that functions as an introduction, you describe a particular incident and furnish specific details about the characters, actions, and settings involved. For example, Supreme Court Justice Sonia

Sotomayor's opening statement at her confirmation hearing began with a narrative about her life:

> The progression of my life has been uniquely American. My parents left Puerto Rico during World War II. I grew up in modest circumstances in a Bronx housing project. My father, a factory worker with a third grade education, passed away when I was nine years old. On her own, my mother raised my brother and me. She taught us that the key to success in America is a good education. And she set the example, studying alongside my brother and me at our kitchen table so that she could become a registered nurse.
>
> We worked hard. I poured myself into my studies at Cardinal Spellman High School, earning scholarships to Princeton University and then Yale Law School, while my brother went on to medical school. Our achievements are due to the values that we learned as children, and they have continued to guide my life's endeavors. I try to pass on this legacy by serving as a mentor and friend to my many godchildren and to students of all backgrounds.[1]

Poem

When you use a poem to introduce your presentation, the concentrated imagery and rhythmic use of language combine to evoke a powerful introduction to the main idea of the presentation. An excerpt from the poem "Introduction to Poetry" by Billy Collins could be used, for example, in a presentation to English teachers about teaching poetry:

> I ask them to take a poem
> and hold it up to the light
> like a color slide
> or press an ear against its hive.
>
> •   •   •   •   •   •   •   •
>
> But all they want to do
> is tie the poem to a chair with rope
> and torture a confession out of it.
> They begin beating it with a hose
> to find out what it really means.[2]

Presentation of Basic Theme

You may decide that explicitly stating your primary idea or theme is the best way to introduce your presentation. Jessica Jackley, cofounder of the lending agencies Kiva and Profounder, used this kind of opening in her presentation, "Poverty, Money—and Love": "The stories we tell about each other matter very much. The stories we tell ourselves about our own lives matter. And, most of all, I think the way that we participate in each other's stories is of deep importance."[3] (Jackley's presentation is one of the sample presentations at the end of the book.)

Question

Questions can function as introductions, just as they can serve as forms of elaboration. An introduction that features questions can consist of: (1) a rhetorical question or questions; or (2) a substantive question or questions.

Rhetorical Question

Rhetorical questions are ones you expect your audience to answer mentally. Such questions require audience members to engage the material by answering the questions for themselves. A presentation welcoming a new group of camp counselors, for example, could begin with this series of rhetorical questions:

> So why do we do it?
> What *good* is it?
> Does it teach you anything
> Like determination? Invention? Improvisation?
> Foresight? Hindsight?
> Love?
> Art? Music? Religion?
> Strength or patience or accuracy or quickness or tolerance or
> Which wood will burn and how long is a day and how far is a mile
> And how delicious is water and smoky green pea soup?[4]

Substantive Question

Your presentation can begin with an actual question you expect the audience to answer. In a presentation about the drawbacks of technology, you might ask your audience members to raise their hands if they have upgraded a computer within the last year. By answering your question, they become involved in your subject and begin to anticipate your presentation.

Quotation

When a quotation is used to start a presentation, you use a statement made by someone who has addressed your topic in a particularly eloquent way. As speaker of the House of Representatives, Nancy Pelosi incorporated Helen Keller's language to begin a presentation at the unveiling of a statue of Keller in the Capitol Rotunda: "As Helen Keller said: 'My sympathies are with all who struggle for justice.' In her lifetime, Helen Keller worked for opportunity for people with disabilities, for racial equality, and for the rights of women."[5]

Reference to Speaking Situation

Another way to begin a presentation is by mentioning or referring to any of the components of the speaking situation: (1) audience; (2) occasion; (3) place; or (4) self.

Reference to Audience

When beginning with a reference to your audience, you focus on special attributes that characterize your audience. When Dan Rather retired as a CBS newscaster, he opened his sign-off with a reference to his audience:

> We've shared a lot in the 24 years we've been meeting here each evening, and before I say good night, this night, I need to say "thank you." Thank you to the thousands of wonderful professionals at CBS News, past and present, with whom it's been my honor to work over these years. And a deeply felt thanks to all of you who have let us into your homes, night after night. It has been a privilege, and one never taken lightly.[6]

Reference to Occasion

A reference to the occasion uses the purpose for gathering as a shared starting point. The Reverend Al Sharpton began his eulogy for Michael Jackson with a reference to the occasion: "All over the world today, people are gathered in love vigils to celebrate the life of a man that taught the world how to love."[7]

Reference to Place

Referring to the site where you are presenting is another possibility for your introduction. Joe Kennedy III, member of the US House of Representatives, referenced place in his Democratic rebuttal to the state of the union address:

> Good evening ladies and gentlemen. It is a privilege to join you tonight.
>
> We are here in Fall River, Massachusetts—a proud American city, built by immigrants.
>
> From textiles to robots, this is a place that knows how to make great things.
>
> The students with us this evening in the auto shop at Diman Regional Technical School carry on that rich legacy.
>
> Like many American hometowns, Fall River has faced its share of storms. But people here are tough. They fight for each other. They pull for their city. It is a fitting place to gather as our nation reflects on the state of our union.[8]

Reference to Self

You may decide to begin your presentation with a reference to yourself as the speaker. You might discuss yourself as a representative of a particular category of individuals whom you will discuss in your presentation, or you might highlight a quality or experience you bring to the speaking situation. Imre Kertész, accepting the Nobel Prize in Literature, opened with a reference to himself:

> I must begin with a confession, a strange confession perhaps, but a candid one. From the moment I stepped on the airplane to make the journey here and accept this year's Nobel Prize in Literature, I have been feeling the steady, searching gaze of a dispassionate observer on

my back. Even at this special moment, when I find myself being the center of attention, I feel I am closer to this cool and detached observer than to the writer whose work, of a sudden, is read around the world. I can only hope that the speech I have the honor to deliver on this occasion will help me dissolve the duality and fuse the two selves within me.[9]

The introduction to your presentation is critical because it not only introduces your audience to your topic and your perspective on that topic but also establishes the tone of the entire presentation. As a result of what you say in the introduction, your audience members will decide whether to continue listening, whether they want to continue interacting with you, and whether they feel safe and valued and able to discuss and consider a variety of perspectives with you.

THE CONCLUSION

The conclusion of your presentation provides a final opportunity to leave your audience members with your perspective clearly in mind. This is one last place in which to communicate the overall vision of your presentation. The primary function of the conclusion, then, is to reemphasize the main idea or gist of your presentation. To accomplish this function, your conclusion needs to be consistent with the tenor of the rest of the presentation—using the same tone to enact the qualities and conditions you have been seeking to create. Changing tone drastically at this point is jarring for the audience because it is unexpected. For the same reason, the conclusion is not the place to introduce new ideas. Doing so can detract from audience members' understanding and retention of your central idea. Think of the conclusion as a place for summarizing, emphasizing, and highlighting the main ideas you offered earlier in the body of your presentation.

A second function of the conclusion is to convey to the audience what you would like to have happen next in the interaction. If you want to convey a sense of finality and signal that there will not be questions, conclude in a way that communicates closure. Quotations and poems often are used as endings when a speaker wants to conclude with finality. You would not call for questions if time is limited, if the group is extremely large, or if a call for questions is inappropriate for the occasion—a toast at a wedding or a eulogy at a funeral, for example.

On the other hand, if you want to encourage the participation of audience members following your presentation, signal that now is the time for them to speak by using a conclusion that is open and tentative. At the end of your prepared remarks, pause briefly and then call for questions. If you want the audience to do something specific—sign a petition or gather in small groups, for example—this is the time to make that request or, if already made, to reinforce that request.

Conclusions assume a variety of forms. Some of the most common types are listed below. As with the options for introductions to a presentation, these are only some of the kinds of conclusions possible. We hope they will stimulate your thinking so that you construct conclusions that effectively summarize your presentation and signal what you expect to happen next. Again, the patterns are arranged in alphabetical order so as not to privilege some over others.

Call to Action

With some interactional goals, a challenge to the audience to take some kind of action is an appropriate conclusion. LeBron James ended his speech at an Excellence in Sports Performance Yearly Award (ESPY) ceremony with a call to action: "Let's use this moment as a call to action for all professional athletes to educate ourselves, explore these issues, speak up, use our influence and renounce all violence. And most importantly, go back to our communities and invest our time, our resources, help rebuild them, help strengthen them, help change them. We all have to do better."[10]

Pledge

A pledge is a promise that something will happen or a commitment to undertake certain actions. Concluding your presentation with a pledge can signal your dedication to a proposal or a cause. In President Barack Obama's farewell speech at the end of his presidency, he offered a pledge: "My fellow Americans, it has been the honor of my life to serve you. I won't stop; in fact, I will be right there with you, as a citizen, for all my days that remain."[11]

Poem

Just as poems work well in introductions, they also function well in conclusions. "Whatif," by children's book author Shel Silverstein, could be used to conclude a presentation about how the things many people worry about always appear worse at night:

> Last night, while I lay thinking here,
> some Whatifs crawled inside my ear
> and pranced and partied all night long
> and sang their same old Whatif song:
> Whatif I'm dumb in school?
> Whatif they've closed the swimming pool?
> Whatif I get beat up?
> Whatif there's poison in my cup?
>
> • • • • • • • •
>
> Whatif the fish won't bite?
> Whatif the wind tears up my kite?

Whatif they start a war?
Whatif my parents get divorced?
Whatif the bus is late?
Whatif my teeth don't grow in straight?
Whatif I tear my pants?
Whatif I never learn to dance?
Everything seems well, and then
the nighttime Whatifs strike again![12]

Prayer

Prayers are entreaties, supplications, or requests directed to a supreme being. Prayer makes an effective conclusion if your audience members align with your spiritual tradition. It often is used in a presentation to a group that needs to make an important decision or to cope with a difficult situation. Facebook CEO Mark Zuckerberg ended his commencement address at Harvard University with a prayer:

> Before you walk out those gates one last time, as we sit in front of Memorial Church, I am reminded of a prayer, *Mi Shebeirach*, that I say whenever I face a challenge, that I sing to my daughter thinking about her future when I tuck her into bed. It goes: "May the source of strength, who blessed the ones before us, help us find the courage to make our lives a blessing." I hope you find the courage to make your life a blessing.[13]

Quotation

You can use an eloquent statement made by someone else as a conclusion, just as you can use it as an introduction. Senator Jeff Flake of Arizona, in describing his decision not to seek reelection, quoted President Abraham Lincoln in his conclusion:

> I will close by borrowing the words of President Lincoln, who knew more about healthy enmity and preserving our founding values than any other American who has ever lived. His words from his first inaugural were a prayer in his time and are now no less in ours: "We are not enemies, but friends. We must not be enemies. Though passion may have strained, it must not break the bonds of our affection. The mystic chords of memory will swell when again touched, as surely as they will be, by the better angels of our nature."[14]

Reference to Introduction

A reference back to the introduction of your presentation provides a sense of completeness to the main ideas you have developed. Christine Keen, issues manager for the Society for Human Resource Management, began a presentation with a reference to a Chinese proverb: "The Chinese have a curse: 'May you live in interesting times.' And these certainly are interesting times. American business and American society are undergoing dramatic changes, and human resources sits right at the crossroads of these changes." To close, she referred back to her opening proverb: "For at least the next decade, then, we will all live in interesting times. And it's up to us to determine if that's a curse or a blessing."[15]

Reference to Speaking Situation

You can conclude your presentation by reminding audience members of important elements of your presentation by referencing: (1) audience; (2) occasion; (3) place; or (4) self.

Reference to Audience

A reference to the audience in a conclusion highlights the importance of the audience to the interaction. At a freedom rally in Prescott, Arizona, sponsored by the Tea Party, Vietnamese immigrant Quang Nguyen ended with a reference to his audience:

> At this time, I would like to ask all the Vietnam veterans to please stand. I thank you for my life. I thank you for your sacrifices, and I thank you for giving me the freedom and liberty I have today. I now ask all veterans, firefighters, and police officers to please stand. On behalf of all first generation immigrants, I thank you for your services, and may God bless you all.[16]

Reference to Occasion

If the occasion on which you are speaking is significant, referring to that occasion leaves your audience with a clear sense of the significance of your presentation in relation to that event. Actor, producer, and writer Mindy Kaling, who herself graduated from Dartmouth College, closed her commencement address to Dartmouth graduates with a reference to the occasion:

> I've covered a lot of ground today; not all of it was serious. But I wanted to leave you with this: I was not someone who should have the life I have now, and yet I do. I was sitting in the chair you are literally sitting in right now and I just whispered, "Why not me?" And I kept whispering it for seventeen years; and here I am, someone that this school deemed worthy enough to speak to you at your commencement.
>
> Don't let anyone tell you that you can't do something, but especially not yourself. Go conquer the world. Just remember this: Why not you? You made it this far.
>
> Thank you very much, and congratulations to the class of 2018.[17]

Reference to Place

A reference to place is an appropriate ending to a presentation given at a significant location. Speaking in Cairo, Pope Francis made reference to Egypt to conclude: "It is my hope that this noble and beloved land of Egypt, with God's help, may continue to respond to the calling it has received to be a land of civilization and covenant and thus to contribute to the development of processes of peace for its beloved people and for the entire region of the Middle East."[18]

Reference to Self

In a case where you were selected as the speaker because of certain accomplishments, a reference to self is an appropriate conclusion. President Barack Obama, speaking on Father's Day, ended with a reference to himself as a father:

> Over the course of my life, I have been an attorney, I've been a professor, I've been a state senator, I've been a US senator—and I currently am serving as President of the United States. But I can say without hesitation that the most challenging, most fulfilling, most important job I will have during my time on this Earth is to be Sasha and Malia's dad.[19]

Rhetorical Question

A rhetorical question—a question you expect your audience to answer mentally—is a good conclusion because it leaves the audience thinking about the subject of the presentation. In his commencement address at Princeton University, Amazon CEO Jeff Bezos ended with two rhetorical questions: "Tomorrow, in a very real sense, your life—the life you author from scratch on your own—begins. How will you use your gifts? What choices will you make?"[20]

Song

Singing a song and/or asking the audience to join in the singing of a song can be a particularly vivid and powerful way to conclude a presentation. A speaker might ask an audience of union members to join in the singing of "I Dreamed I Saw Joe Hill Last Night" to remind them of the strength and tenacity of labor movements. President Barack Obama used song as a conclusion at the funeral for the Reverend Clementa Pinckney, one of the victims of a church shooting in Charleston, South Carolina. The theme of his presentation was grace, and to end, he began singing "Amazing Grace," and the other mourners at the funeral joined in.[21]

Summary of Basic Theme

In a conclusion that summarizes your basic theme, you emphasize the primary idea of the presentation. In his address after receiving the Nobel Prize in Literature, Mo Yan referenced his role as storyteller—the basic theme of his presentation: "I am a storyteller. Telling stories earned me the Nobel Prize in Literature. Many interesting things have happened to me in the wake of winning the prize, and they have convinced me that truth and justice are alive and well. So I will continue telling my stories in the days to come."[22]

Summary of Main Ideas

In this type of conclusion, you reiterate your major ideas rather than restate the overall theme of your presentation. You list the main points of your presentation so that your audience members can remember them easily. In a presentation in which she encouraged her audience members to find and follow their passions, hypnotherapist and coach Lindsay Cook ended with a summary of her four main points: "Follow your dream. Trust your instincts. Find that something you can believe in passionately, and give it your all. Do what you love."[23]

The conclusion, like the introduction, is crucial to the overall impact of your presentation. Your conclusion offers your audience a reminder of the gist of your message and its main ideas and provides you with a final opportunity to create an environment of safety, openness, freedom, and value. The conclusion also indicates to your audience that you are closing. It either provides a sense of finality or suggests that now is the time for the audience to assume a larger role in the interaction. Having developed your introduction and conclusion, you now will devise the transitions that will enable you to move from one part of your presentation to the next and from one idea to another.

8

Connecting Ideas

The process of connecting ideas involves the use of transitions that enable you to link the various parts of your presentation together. Your task now is to communicate the frame or form you have created to your audience members by providing them with guideposts as you move from one idea to the next.

You cannot assume that your listeners will grasp the organization of your presentation that is so obvious to you. As your listeners process your ideas, there is much that can keep them from coming to the same understanding of your frame as you have. They are forgetting much of what you say simply because the short-term memory can handle only a limited number of new inputs at one time. They are consolidating information into manageable and retainable chunks. They are fitting your new information into a context or framework with which they are already familiar, and it may not be the one you envision. They are developing expectations and making predictions about what will come next in your presentation. They are drawing inferences and developing new ideas from the ideas you discuss. In general, they are using your ideas to build an organizational structure of their own. And all of this is compounded by their fading in and out, attending to your presentation and then thinking of other things. You can increase the possibility of a common structure by using transitions to provide explicit cues about the organization of your presentation.

Some speakers concentrate so hard on preparing each segment of a presentation—the introduction, the body, and the conclusion—that they forget to think about how they will move from each of these sections to the next. Consequently, their transitions are rough or nonexistent. If you haven't made decisions about how to move from one point to the next, you might find yourself saying *uh* and then launching into your next point. You also might end up using the same transition over and over, such as *next* or *another point is*. You want to think deliberately about your transitions—and perhaps even to write them out in your notes—so that they help promote rather than detract from the perspective you are offering in your presentation.

FUNCTIONS OF TRANSITIONS

The purpose of transitions is to link the various parts of your presentation—to make clear the connections between sections. Transitions are structural guideposts that orient listeners to your frame and direct them to the next point or section of your presentation. The transitions in a presentation fulfill three major functions: (1) remind and forecast; (2) keep listeners on track; and (3) communicate safety, openness, freedom, and value.

Transitions Remind and Forecast

A significant function of transitions is to remind and forecast. Use a transition to summarize or restate the point you have just discussed and to preview what will happen next in the presentation. Transitions let your audience know where you have been and where you are going. Consequently, they orient audience members to where you are within your larger organizational structure.

Transitions Keep Listeners on Track

A second function of transitions is to help your audience stay on track. Transitions help reorient audience members who may have become so focused on a specific idea that they've missed part of your presentation. Other listeners might have become distracted—by something else happening in the room or a text coming in on their phones, for example—and stopped listening. Transitions provide a means for these audience members to start attending to the presentation again.

Transitions Communicate Safety, Openness, Freedom, and Value

Transitions serve a third function—helping you create the kind of speaking environment in which everyone can consider all perspectives fully. Transitions help an audience feel safe because you are providing clear signals about the structure of your presentation and its progression. Audience members will not be surprised by where you are going if you offer frequent internal indicators of your structure. They also will feel valued because you have taken the time to include connections that make listening easy for them.

The use of transitions enhances the conditions of freedom and openness. Transitions demonstrate to your audience that you truly want them to understand the perspective you are offering and to be able to consider it as a viable option. If audience members are confused about what you are proposing because you have not taken the time to make the connections among the ideas in your presentation clear, they will be unable to give your presentation complete consideration. When you make deliberate choices about your transitions, the audience is more likely to perceive, understand, and appreciate the presentation and the coherence you have given it.

FORMS OF TRANSITIONS

Transitions can assume a variety of forms, including: (1) paragraphs; (2) sentences; and (3) words and phrases. In each case, transitions assist your listeners in following your structure or frame as you move from one idea to the next. The type of transition you choose will depend on what you need to accomplish with the transition. The type also may depend on the length of your presentation. In a very short talk, for example, you do not have time to make use of a paragraph as a transition and will want to use a word or sentence instead.

Paragraphs

Paragraphs are the longest kind of transition or form of connection in a presentation. They most often are used in two places. One is between the major sections of the presentation—between the introduction and the body and between the body and the conclusion. Transitional paragraphs also can be used between main ideas within the body of the presentation itself. In each case, the paragraph contains some combination of summarizing and forecasting.

At times, your transition paragraph will consist primarily of a summary and a short forecast or preview. This transitional arrangement most often is used when the ideas offered are complicated or new to the audience, and a summary of them is necessary if audience members are going to be able to move with you to the next set of ideas. Perhaps you have been discussing the virtues and limitations of various security systems for the networked computers in your office. Because the systems are complex, a summary of the strengths and weaknesses of each system will be helpful to your audience before moving to your next main idea, which is the need to make a decision about security quickly. A transition that focuses on summary also could be used when the ideas you are offering are novel for an audience. If you are discussing reasons why your audience of parents should consider sending their children to a new charter school—something they have not considered before—reiterating the benefits of this kind of education may be the most helpful transition for your audience.

In other cases, the paragraph of connection consists of a short summary and a much lengthier forecast. This kind of transition paragraph is used when you are most concerned with focusing your audience's attention in a new direction. If you are using the organizational pattern of elimination, for example, you might choose this kind of transition as you move from your introduction to the body of your presentation. In your transition, you alert listeners to the fact that you will be describing various solutions, ending with the one you believe is most desirable. Similarly, if you are describing multiple perspectives in your presentation, you might want to devote the bulk of your transition paragraph to forecasting to ensure that your audience members understand that this is the approach you will be taking.

Sometimes, the transition paragraph is fairly balanced between restatement and forecasting. You might use a couple of sentences to summarize and a couple of sentences to preview where you are heading next. In a presentation to the International Consumer Electronics Show, Microsoft CEO Bill Gates used a transition paragraph balanced between summary and forecast to move between the introduction and the body of his presentation: "So what are the fundamental hardware trends? You know, consumer electronics historically have been mostly about hardware. How is that changing? Well, first and foremost we have the continued truth of Moore's Law. It may not last forever, but for the next decade we're certainly going to get this doubling in power every 18 months to two years."[1] Gates then went on to discuss the impact of Moore's Law on the computer industry.

Sentences

When sentences serve as transitions, they most often are used to move between major segments of a presentation and between main ideas in the body of a presentation. This kind of transition can be a single sentence or a couple of sentences. The sentence that moves between segments of a presentation contains both a reference to the previous section and a preview of what will follow in the next section. President Barack Obama used such a sentence transition in a speech on immigration at American University. The focus of one section of his speech was on challenges in contemporary times, and the next section dealt with immigration reform. His transition between the two was, "Immigration reform is no exception."[2]

A sentence that moves between main ideas also can contain both restatement and forecast. In a presentation about an upturn in the economy, you could use a sentence to transition from the main idea about financial indicators pointing to economic growth to the next main idea that such growth is easier to recognize on the local level: "But indicators of growth at the national level are impersonal and abstract. We can also see evidence of the economy's recovery in the story of our own city."

Rhetorical questions often are used as sentence transitions because the question format invites audience members to consider possible answers, which are the subject of the next section. In his commencement address at the University of Texas, Naval Adm. William McRaven used a rhetorical question to move from his introduction into the body of his speech:

> But changing the world can happen anywhere and anyone can do it. So, what starts here can indeed change the world, but the question is . . . what will the world look like after you change it? Well, I am confident that it will look much, much better, but if you will humor this old sailor for just a moment, I have a few suggestions that may help you on your way to a better world.[3]

Your thesis statement can serve as a transition sentence because it fulfills the summarizing and previewing functions of a transition. The thesis statement is often placed at the end of the introduction, where it leads from the preliminary material to the body of the presentation. Comedian Jimmy Fallon, speaking at the Marjorie Stoneman Douglas High School graduation a few months after the shootings there, began his presentation by describing how the graduates would now be adults, not classmates. He then used his thesis statement to transition into the main points of his address: "So before you go, I want to share a few thoughts with you. Not advice, necessarily, just a few things I learned that helped me along the way." He then shared with the graduates five things he had learned and hoped they would remember and do.[4]

Words and Phrases

Phrases or single words also can function as transitions. Because these are brief, they most often are used to move between forms of elaboration rather than between major segments or main ideas of the presentation. These kinds of transitions typically include words such as *similarly, likewise, in addition,* and *in comparison.* To move between two examples of overspending in a company, you might say, "Similarly, we can see another instance of overspending in the parts department."

Some transitions indicate a causal relationship between forms of elaboration, indicated by phrases such as *therefore, as a result,* and *consequently.* With the topic of overspending, you might move from making a point about bad accounting practices—an explanation—to a metaphor by means of a transition that stresses a causal connection: "As a result of bad accounting practices, we now find ourselves in hot water."

Other transition words or phrases focus on summary. Words such as *finally, in summary,* and *as we have seen* are examples of transitions of this type. For a presentation in which you have offered a problem-solution approach, for example, you might begin your conclusion by saying, "As we have seen, the problem of overcrowding in schools will not be fixed overnight."

As a speaker, you might be tempted to overuse certain transitions because they are familiar. Consequently, they have lost much of their impact. Many speakers use *next, furthermore,* or numbers (*first, second, third*) as transitions. They also use *in conclusion, I would like to say* as a way to move into their conclusions. Rather than serving as effective transitions, these do little more than tell your audience that you didn't take the time to think of a transition that effectively allows you to move from one idea to another. Saying *I see that my time is up* is equally unimpressive. Rather than assisting your audience in moving between segments of your presentation, you let time—or, more precisely, the lack of it—provide your transition. Transitions should be designed carefully to assist your audience in moving with you among the segments, main ideas, and forms of elaboration in your presentation. They should not be fillers you insert because you did not take the time to do the kind of planning your subject and your audience deserve.

Transitions provide your audience with crucial cues about the world you are creating with your presentation. As you incorporate explicit cues about the frame or structure into your presentation, you encourage your listeners to understand your perspective fully. In finalizing your transitions, the process of developing your presentation is complete, and you are ready to work on the most effective way to deliver it.

9

Delivering

Delivering your presentation is the final step in the process of preparing a presentation. Delivery means using your body and other presentational aids to help express the ideas that make up the content of your presentation. The various components of delivery—mode of presentation, speaking notes, time limits, practice, bodily elements, and presentational aids—can be thought of as tools to facilitate the full presentation of your perspective and to provide opportunities for transformation for your audience.

FUNCTIONS OF DELIVERY

The elements of delivery perform two primary functions for your presentation. Delivery assists you in the creation of an environment of safety, openness, freedom, and value. When your posture, gestures, and facial expressions communicate warmth and a genuine interest in audience members rather than combativeness, aloofness, or superiority, you are more likely to create an environment in which transformation is possible. When you use presentational aids thoughtfully and carefully, you communicate that you value audience members and their capacity for understanding.

A second function of delivery is that it offers an additional means for you to give full expression to your perspective. The more attractive and appealing your perspective is because of how it is delivered, the more likely it will be accorded full consideration by those in your audience. Many elements of delivery communicate your message to your audience visually and thus reinforce what you are saying verbally. Audience members are able to remember your perspective more easily because they have been able to process it using more than one sensory channel.

117

COMPONENTS OF DELIVERY

Factors to consider in delivering your ideas include: (1) mode of presentation; (2) speaking notes; (3) time limits; (4) practice; (5) bodily elements; and (6) presentational aids. You have a great deal of freedom in how you combine the various components of delivery, but you always want to be guided by your interactional goal; your audience; and your desire to create an environment of safety, openness, freedom, and value.

Mode of Presentation

One of the first choices you make when considering how best to use the delivery options available to you is mode of presentation. The four options available to you are: (1) extemporaneous mode; (2) manuscript mode; (3) memorized mode; and (4) impromptu mode.

Extemporaneous Mode

The mode of presentation you are likely to use for most formal speaking situations is the extemporaneous mode. In this mode, you speak from notes of some kind, and not everything you plan to say is written out in those notes. This means that each time you give the presentation, it will be different. This mode of presentation allows you to present your ideas in a careful and thoughtful way while doing so in a conversational tone. Perhaps most important, an extemporaneous delivery enables you to adjust your presentation to your audience members—explaining something further if audience members seem confused, for example, or acknowledging that their views on an issue are encouraging you to think about it in new ways.

Manuscript Mode

Sometimes, you will choose to write your presentation out completely and to read from a text. The manuscript mode is used if there are strict time limits or when the wording of the ideas in your presentation is critical and you want to make sure you deliver the presentation you want to deliver. This mode has the advantage of allowing you to present your ideas exactly as you have planned, using the precise language you intended. Generally, however, the disadvantages of this mode outweigh its advantages. Because your entire presentation is written out in advance, your ideas are more likely to be phrased in a written style, which is more formal and less conversational than your natural oral style. You also cannot adapt to your audience as easily during the presentation. Whatever happens in the course of the interaction, your inclination is to continue reading your manuscript no matter how the audience is responding.

If you choose to use a manuscript, begin by converting the written style into a conversational one, which will help you sound as though you are speaking your presentation rather than reading it. Read the manuscript out loud and change formal language such as *do not* to more conversational constructions such as *don't*. Change passive voice to active voice—*I researched this topic extensively* rather than *this topic has been extensively researched*. Make your presentation, in other words, sound like you talk. As you practice speaking from the manuscript, think about your ideas as you say them and remind yourself of the feelings and emotions that led you to express ideas in particular ways. Don't be afraid to deviate from the manuscript if something occurs to you or you want to respond to the audience during the presentation.

Memorized Mode

The popularity of TED Talks has made many speakers believe in the need to memorize presentations because that is what TED speakers typically do. We do not recommend memorizing presentations, however, because having to produce your speech from memory just adds another layer of speech anxiety to a speaking situation. In addition, such presentations often sound memorized, and you are unwilling or unable to adapt to the audience and situation because you are afraid of what will happen if you get off script. If, for some reason, you must memorize a presentation because notes would be inappropriate, think about the words as you are saying them so they sound fresh, lively, and not memorized.

Impromptu Mode

Impromptu speaking is the mode of presentation you use most often—when you speak in class, offer your ideas at a staff meeting, or explain how your current project is progressing in response to a question from your supervisor. In this mode, you speak with little or no planning or preparation, forming your presentation at the time that you speak. There will be times, however, when you are asked to speak impromptu in more formal situations—to give a toast at a wedding, to say a few words at a memorial service, to accept an award, or to introduce someone, for example. Remember that you have been asked to speak because of your expertise or special connection to the occasion, so responding appropriately probably will not be difficult in these situations. If you have time, find a quiet place to think for a few minutes and develop a few main points that can serve as the basic structure for your presentation. You then can elaborate on each of the points as you speak, using a story, a fact, an example, or other form of elaboration.

Speaking Notes

Your choice of notes is an important element in creating a situation in which you feel comfortable presenting your ideas. Although you may have been told at some time to use note cards, they often are not practical for an extensive presentation where you need to present a great deal of information. You may find that using several sheets of paper rather than note cards works better in that you aren't creating a distraction for your audience by continuously shuffling through a stack of cards.

Another advantage of larger sheets of paper over note cards is that, if you are using a lectern, an 8½″ × 11″ sheet of paper will sit higher on the stand than will a note card, making it is easier for you to glance down and find your place. Do not display your notes on your laptop computer, iPad, or cell phone. You will not be able to maintain eye contact with your audience because your eyes will be on the screen, and your frequent clicking or swiping to scroll to the next page will be distracting to both you and the audience.

You will find that certain approaches to notes work better for you than others. Your notes may consist of a list of key ideas, major points of elaboration, and transitions. Someone else may prefer a formal outline or a visual diagram. Whatever format you choose, your notes should be easy for you to read. Typing your notes rather than handwriting them, double or triple spacing them, and using a large and bold font can make them easy to see as you glance back and forth between the notes and your audience.

You also might find that writing notes to yourself about aspects of delivery you want to be sure to remember is helpful. If you tend to talk fast during presentations, for example, you might want to write *SLOW DOWN* in bold, colorful letters at the top of each page of notes. Write *MOVE* on your notes to encourage you to move out from behind the lectern and to use appropriate gestures. If you have a tendency to play with your hair, use a notation such as *HAIR* to remind yourself to manage this problematic element of delivery.

Time Limits

When you are asked to speak, you most likely will be given a length of time for your presentation. Perhaps you are speaking at a luncheon meeting and are scheduled to talk for 20 minutes, or perhaps you are lecturing to a class that meets for 50 minutes. Staying within the time frame available is critical because time limits create expectations on the part of the audience, and audience members can become irritated and restless if you violate those limits. Acceptance speeches at the Academy Awards are examples of a situation in which maintaining strict time limits is important if the ceremony is to end at a reasonable hour. By staying within the time limits you are given, you will be communicating that you are considerate of your audience members' needs and interests.

Paying close attention to time constraints also means you need to consider carefully what to leave in and what to take out according to the amount of time available. When you refuse to cut a presentation down to fit a time limit, you are forced to talk very fast or go overtime to cover all of your ideas. This approach works against accomplishing your goal of giving full expression to your perspective. Attending to time limits, then, not only communicates to your audience members that you are respectful of their time, but it also helps you focus your perspective so that you can offer it as fully as possible in the time available.

Practice

Unless you are giving an impromptu presentation, you want to practice extensively. Practice facilitates the full articulation of your perspective and the creation of an environment of safety, openness, freedom, and value. Try to practice under the most realistic conditions possible. You may find that practicing in front of real people—someone such as your roommate or partner—is helpful. The feedback of a live audience better approximates what you will experience in front of your audience during the actual presentation. If you will be standing to give your presentation, stand up to practice it. Each time you practice, deliver your presentation all the way through without stopping. If you stumble over a word or an idea, don't start the presentation over. Instead, think about what you would do if that happened in front of your actual audience, and go on from there. We suggest practicing in front of a mirror a time or two and, if possible, recording one of your practice sessions, both of which will show you the general impression created by your presentation and whether you have gestures or vocal dysfluencies that distract from the presentation of your ideas.

Practice, then, is a major factor in your ability to create a potentially transformative environment and to ensure that your perspective is presented fully. For a major presentation, practice your talk at least once and even twice a day for the week or so before the presentation. Every presentation, no matter its length, deserves at least five or six practice sessions. The more times you give your presentation, the more familiar and comfortable you are with it, and the more confident you can be that your delivery will enhance rather than detract from the full articulation of your perspective.

Bodily Elements

Elements of your body that contribute to or detract from the delivery of your presentation include voice, movement, and personal appearance. **Voice** includes the factors of volume, rate, pitch, and pausing. Volume is the degree of loudness or intensity of sound, and rate is the speed at which you speak. Pitch is the tone or register of vocal vibration, and pausing is the length of time between words or sentences.

Various other aspects of your body also can assist you in offering your perspective. **Movement** involves posture, gestures, facial expressions, and general bodily movement. Posture is how you carry your body, and gestures are movements of your hands, arms, body, and head. Facial expressions are the use of the face and eyes to communicate, and movement includes the general actions of your body, such as when you walk, stand, or sit.

Personal appearance is another way in which your message is delivered. Hairstyle, clothing, jewelry, accessories such as scarves or ties, and tattoos are other aspects of personal appearance available for decorating your body that can affect how your presentation is received. Personal hygiene, which concerns issues of health, cleanliness, and neatness, is another element of personal appearance that impacts delivery.

We cannot offer you specific guidelines for using bodily elements in delivery because what is appropriate in one situation is inappropriate in another. We want you to consider all bodily elements as resources to use in your presentations in ways that fit the subject, occasion, audience, and your own speaking style. In some instances, you will need to stay behind the podium to speak because the microphone is fixed to the podium. For other presentations, you will want to make use of movement and gestures, walking around the room to engage the audience more fully. In some presentations, you will want to sit, either because your audience is seated in a circle or because you are speaking to just one person. On other occasions, you will need to speak loudly in order to be heard and will need to stand in order to be seen.

Eye contact is another aspect of delivery where the same rules do not apply across all speaking contexts. Although many audiences in the United States expect eye contact, you might find yourself speaking to individuals from a culture in which direct eye contact is regarded as insulting or disrespectful. In such a case, you would avoid extensive eye contact and might choose to move around the room, glancing at various places as you talk so that you generally avoid looking directly at the audience. You also could look at groups of people in the audience rather than focusing on individual audience members, or you could look down at your notes more often than you normally would to minimize eye contact. Only you can decide which of the resources of bodily elements you need to engage and how, and you will make that decision by analyzing the speaking environment, as we asked you to do in chapter 3.

Presentational Aids

Presentational aids are any audiovisual aids you use to supplement the content of your presentation, and many options are available for this purpose. Some aids are exclusively visual. **Objects,** for example, are aids that you show to your audience to illustrate some feature of your presentation. If you choose to show a fossil to explain plant life in an earlier geologic period or a quilt made by your grandmother in a presentation on sewing, you are using an object as a presentational aid. A three-dimensional representation of something such as a building makes use of a **model** and might be used in a presentation about architecture or the revitalization of a neighborhood. **Diagrams** show how something works, and you might choose to use them to show how the funds raised in a crowdsourcing campaign are being spent. **Graphs** and **charts** show information in numerical form. Graphs often are used to show relationships among components. For a presentation on water conservation, you might use a graph that shows how conservation has reduced water use over the past five years. Charts also organize information in a visual format. To discuss where layoffs may occur in a company, an organizational chart would be useful in your presentation. **Maps** display geographical areas. You could use a map of the United States in a presentation about college recruitment to show how your university draws students from all 50 states. **Pictures,** which include paintings and photographs, are two-dimensional representations of people, places, and things. A photograph of a street scene in Beijing could be used to illustrate the increase in automobile traffic in China. With many of these presentational aids, you have a choice not only about what kind of visual aid to use but also how to present or display it. Diagrams or graphs, for example, can be displayed via computer-generated slides, flip charts, chalkboards, whiteboards, posters, or handouts.

Other forms of presentational aids are available that involve both audio and visual elements. **Audio and visual clips**—short recordings of music, sounds, and speech or excerpts from movies, television, radio, and videos—are another option for presentational aids. Playing a segment of a dashcam video that shows a wildfire in California is an example of the use of an audiovisual clip as a presentational aid. Don't forget that you also can use members of your audience as visual aids—you can ask audience members to join you at the front of the room and use their clothing, height, or other characteristics to illustrate points in your presentation. You could also line audience members up in a certain way or ask them to hold up signs you have created as visual aids. Of course, you never want to force audience members to serve as visual aids for you if they are shy or reluctant to do so. If you plan to make use of audience members as visual aids, ask for volunteers before you begin so there will be no moments of discomfort as you try to solicit volunteers in the course of your presentation.

Regardless of the kinds of presentational aids you select, they should be supplemental. They should elaborate on ideas in the presentation but should not constitute the presentation itself. If you discover that your video clip consumes over half of your presentation, you need to cut it down so that it becomes a form of elaboration for a point you are making. Likewise, a presentation that consists solely of showing PowerPoint slides and reading each one aloud is a presentation in which the aid has become the presentation. You also need to be prepared in case your presentational aids fail or are not available. Perhaps the computer does not work, or you accidentally leave your handouts at home. If you can give the presentation without any aids at all and it still makes sense, you will be prepared for any contingency and can be confident that your presentation is more than a presentational aid.

Presentational Software
Despite the abundance of different media available for presenting audiovisual aids, most speakers use only one form—PowerPoint soft-

ware. (Apple's Keynote is similar, but PowerPoint dominates in terms of presentational software, so we will concentrate our discussion on it.) The typical presentation today consists of a speaker presenting slides with bulleted lists often illustrated by images or graphics. These kinds of PowerPoint presentations are so universal that you might think using such software is the only way to give a presentation. Because of the pervasiveness of this mode of presentation, we want to spend more time on it than on other kinds of visual aids.

Think about when you are in an audience and a speaker is using PowerPoint in the standard way—showing slides with bullet points and reading the slides to the audience. If you are like many audience members, you find such presentations to be "mind-numbingly dull"[1] and something to be endured rather than serving as an invitation to understand the speaker's perspective. If this is your reaction, you are not alone. General David Petraeus, whose military career has included overseeing the wars in Iraq and Afghanistan, says that sitting through PowerPoint briefings is "just agony."[2] Seth Godin, author of *Really Bad PowerPoint*, says that "almost every PowerPoint presentation sucks rotten eggs."[3]

Audiences often react negatively to PowerPoint presentations because they have been exposed to so many routine, uninspired examples. As a speaker, then, you are faced with a dilemma. You may be expected to use PowerPoint (or believe it is expected of you), but, at the same time, you know that you risk losing the attention of the audience during PowerPoint presentations. In the next section, we'll consider some of the problems with Power Point and some ways to address them.

Problems with PowerPoint Software. The fact that using PowerPoint software may encourage audiences not to pay attention to your presentation is a major difficulty, but there are other problems as well. PowerPoint software contains biases that may not enable you to present your perspective effectively. Journalist Franck Frommer calls such biases the "PowerPointing of minds."[4] These biases or ideological underpinnings affect not only the nature of your presentation but the kind of thinking and understanding in which audience members engage as a result of the presentation. As artist and musician David Byrne explains, PowerPoint appears to be a neutral tool, "unbiased and free of any leanings one way or another."[5] But, in fact, PowerPoint has

> been designed assuming, a priori, a specific world view. The software, by making certain directions and actions easier and more convenient than others, tells you how to think as it helps you accomplish your task. Not in an obvious way or in an obnoxious way or even in a scheming way. The biases are almost unintentional, they are so natural and well-integrated. . . . You are thus subtly indoctrinated into a manner of being and behaving, assuming and acting, that grows on you as you use the program.[6]

Rhetoric professor Jens Kjeldsen makes a similar point: "The problem lies in *PowerPoint's cognitive style*, for the software forces us to speak and think in particular ways. Like all tools—and media—it has constraints, certain possibilities and limitations."[7] Edward Tufte, a former professor of political science, statistics, and computer science at Yale University and the author of books such as *Envisioning Information*, makes the same point: "PowerPoint comes with a big attitude."[8]

One bias inherent in PowerPoint software is that it does not allow you to present detailed or sophisticated information to your audience. As Kjeldsen explains, "The software makes us think and speak in isolated blocks, instead of in coherent context, totalities, narratives or linear reasoning."[9] The lists of short phrases it requires—the power points—do not allow for the development of a complicated argument. Because PowerPoint software organizes all content into lists, you are not able to present complex relationships among items. Instead, the evidence is sliced and diced "into arbitrary compartments," short circuiting the capacity to think in sophisticated ways.[10] Material that does not fit easily into lists may be omitted by speakers as a result. Clifford Nass, a professor of sociology at Stanford University, told about how he decided not to include a book in a course because its content did not align with the format required by PowerPoint:

> I hate to admit this but I actually removed a book from my syllabus last year because I couldn't figure out how to PowerPoint it. It's a lovely book called *Interface Culture*, by Steven Johnson, but it's very discursive; the charm of it is the throwaways. When I read this book, I thought, my head's filled with ideas, and now I've got to write out exactly what those ideas are, and they're not neat.[11]

Eventually, he abandoned the effort to teach the book because every time he tried to capture its content in bullet points, he realized that it wasn't quite right.

PowerPoint also diminishes audience members' ability to reason in sophisticated ways because it does not allow for the presentation of extensive data in graphics and tables. Sizeable graphs and tables must be broken up and spread over many different slides, making their use for analysis and evaluation difficult. These problems are magnified because PowerPoint slides do not give you much working space. Only about 40% of a slide is available for you to use for your content, and the remaining space is devoted to bullets, frames, visual images, and branding.[12] The result, according to many studies, is superficial, simplistic thinking and the stifling of "critical thinking and thoughtful decision making."[13]

Another bias in PowerPoint software is that it makes information more difficult to remember. In a study in which some audience members were shown a graphic representation of a business strategy and others were shown a version of the strategy in bullet points (the kind commonly used in PowerPoint), those who saw the image paid significantly more attention to the presentation and remembered the strategy better afterwards.[14] Studies done on the use of PowerPoint in education have generated similar results. In one study of university lecture courses, students had a difficult time summarizing course content that relied heavily on PowerPoint compared to traditional note taking.[15] In another study, those who were exposed to conventional lecture/discussion sessions remembered more of the material and had more positive attitudes toward it than did those who had learned via PowerPoint.[16]

The sharing of perspective that takes place is one sided with PowerPoint, which is another ideological bias that underpins the software. PowerPoint imposes an authoritarian presenter-audience relationship on the interaction instead of encouraging an exchange of ideas between the speaker and the audience. You as the speaker dominate the audience with your ideas because PowerPoint doesn't encourage you to ask questions, to get ideas from audience members, or to improvise. This is because a PowerPoint presentation locks you into a path that disregards any input other than the presentation as you have prepared it. This means you cannot easily skip points in the presentation that are no longer appropriate or relevant because skipping slides makes any improvisation you do obvious.[17] Finally, the fact that, with PowerPoint, the lights are usually dimmed and everyone is looking at the screen means that there is little possibility of interaction between you and audience members because you can't see them, and they can't see you. A dark screen means that the audience can space out entirely—think about other things, sleep, even—because neither the audience nor the speaker is visible.

Furthermore, PowerPoint software is biased against speaker preparation. With PowerPoint, speakers do not feel the need to prepare, practice, or use notes for their presentations because they can count on reading the slides they are showing, much as if they were using a teleprompter. When speakers rely on PowerPoint slides rather than developing and practicing a carefully crafted presentation, they are less likely to think about how to create an environment in which audience members are engaged and interested in sharing their perspectives. When speakers recycle their PowerPoint slides from other presentations in the hopes of saving preparation time, matters only get worse—the speaker has not taken the time to create slides that work for the specific audience, topic, occasion, and time limit.

Using Presentational Software Effectively

Let's assume you have thought carefully about the problems inherent in PowerPoint presentations and have decided that you still want to use presentational software. Various options are available to you to circumvent some of the problems inherent in PowerPoint: (1) develop your ideas before using the software; (2) pay attention to design principles;

(3) keep the focus on you; (4) develop a backup plan; and (5) consider options other than PowerPoint software.

Develop your ideas before using the software.   Develop your key ideas before you touch your software. You might be tempted to make the software your major concern in the preparation process for your presentation, immediately starting to lay out slides. When you do this, though, you tend to "get bogged down in what the presentation looks like much too soon," and the templates can take you in directions you may not want to go.[18] As Nancy Duarte, CEO of a presentation-design firm, explains, "Presentation software was never intended to be a brainstorming tool or drawing tool. The applications are simply containers for ideas and assets, not the means to generate them."[19] Your focus should not be on your slides at this point in the process: "As speakers, we should not be thinking of how to fill in a template. We should be thinking of purpose, goals and means. What do we want to achieve? How can we best achieve it?"[20]

Use some system other than PowerPoint software to create the ideas for your presentation. Brainstorm as many possible ideas for your presentation as you can, letting the ideas flow, capturing them using words, diagrams, and images. You may find it useful to not use your computer at all but to work on paper, a whiteboard, a blackboard, large sheets of paper, or sticky notes. If you like to use mind maps, concept maps, or idea webs to outline your ideas visually, a good tool is Inspiration software (Inspiration.com). At the end of this brainstorming session, identify the one key idea that is central from the point of view of the audience and go from there to develop the main ideas that you will use to elaborate that idea. This is the process outlined in chapter 4, the chapter on focusing. Only after you have developed your thesis, main ideas, and many of your forms of elaboration is it appropriate to think about whether or not you will use PowerPoint or a similar presentational software.

Pay attention to design principles.   If you have decided you want to use PowerPoint, carefully consider the design of your slides. Many books are available that will help you develop slides that meet the criteria for good presentation design, including *The Non-Designer's Presentation Book* by Robin Williams, *Presentation Zen* by Garr Reynolds, and *Beyond Bullet Points: Using PowerPoint to Tell a Compelling Story that Gets Results* by Cliff Atkinson. At the very least, you'll want to pay attention to two key design principles—the signal-to-noise ratio and the picture-superiority effect.

The **signal-to-noise ratio** is the ratio of relevant to irrelevant elements in a slide or other display. You want to have a high signal-to-noise ratio in your slides, which means that most items on your slides are directed toward support of your message and not toward extraneous or decorative design elements. To achieve a high signal-to-noise ratio, make sure everything on your slides clearly supports and develops your message, and remove anything that compromises or detracts from it so there is "as little degradation to the message as possible."[21] One of the biggest mistakes that speakers make is to use every inch of space on a slide, "filling it up with text, boxes, clip art, charts, footers, and the ubiquitous company logo."[22]

If you include things that have nothing to do with your presentation in your slides, you distract from what you want your focus to be. To have no graphics at all is better than showing irrelevant words, lines, shapes, symbols, and logos that take the viewer's mind in the wrong direction. The more irrelevant items you add to slides, the more difficulty your audience will have trying to combine the pieces of your presentation into a coherent whole.

Another way to be sure that you have an appropriate signal-to-noise ratio is to make your photographs and video clips relevant. Don't use them just because you think they are cool or beautiful or funny. Be careful, too, with animation or movement on your slides. Movement creates a focal point and calls attention to itself, so only animate when you have something special on which you want the audience to focus. Some good advice regarding relevance is this: "Away with everything just meant to be a little amusing and diverting. Away with irrelevant pictures and dingbats, disturbing animations and sounds without function."[23]

A second key design principle, the **picture-superiority effect,** says that pictures are remembered better than words, especially when people are exposed to information for a short amount of time. As much as possible, use images on your PowerPoint slides to improve your audience's understanding of your perspective. Replace words with photographs or other appropriate images or graphics whenever possible. A PowerPoint presentation is not a document, so your slides should not resemble printed matter. If you do use text on a PowerPoint slide, do not use more than five lines; one to three lines is ideal. In general, there should be no more than seven words per line, and you will want to use at least a 24-point font. Your projected slides should be as visual as possible and support your points quickly, efficiently, and powerfully, with the verbal content of your presentation coming primarily from your spoken words.

Because you are emphasizing visuals in your PowerPoint slides, be sure to use good images instead of cheesy clip art. There are a number of places where you can get free or inexpensive professional-quality illustrations and photographs. The following sites offer free images. As you know, options available on the web are constantly changing, so watch for other good sources of images.

- Library of Congress: loc.gov/library/libarch-digital.html
- Pixabay: pixabay.com
- Public Domain Review: PublicDomainReview.org
- Dreams Time Stock Photos: www.dreamstime.com
- Everystockphoto search engine: www.everystockphoto.com

- Image After: www.imageafter.com
- Morgue File: www.morguefile.com
- Stock.xching: www.sxc.hu

Keep the focus on you. As you deliver your presentation, keep the focus on you. If audience members are not engaged with you, they are less likely to understand the perspective you are presenting, and you will have less opportunity to understand their perspectives. The focus will not be on you if you are glued to your laptop and continually look down to change your slides or if you walk back to the computer to change slides every few minutes. To keep the audience's focus on you, use a remote control. A remote allows you to move closer to all the members of your audience.

Another way to keep the focus on you is to keep the lights on in the room when you are speaking. You've undoubtedly had the experience, when a presentation is about to begin, of the speaker asking, "Could someone get the lights, please?" The room goes dark, except for the light reflecting off the screen, and the presenter disappears. The more lights you can keep on during your presentation, the better. Much of your message comes from your nonverbal behavior. If the audience can't see you, an important connection is lost.

Given the choice of looking at the speaker or a slide, audiences usually will choose the slide. To bring audience members' attention back to you, use the letter B key. Press it once while in SLIDE SHOW mode; the screen will go black, and audience members will turn their attention back to you. Press it again, your slide will reappear, and they will redirect their attention back to the screen.

Develop a backup plan. Don't forget to have a backup plan. If you are bringing a presentation on your laptop, have a copy on a portable drive with you as well. If you send your presentation in advance, bring an extra copy in case the presentation was corrupted in the transfer or if there are compatibility issues with the equipment in the room where you are presenting. If the technology in the room fails completely, be prepared to give your presentation without any visual support.

Consider options other than PowerPoint software. PowerPoint slides are not your only option for including visual material in your presentation. Many other options are available, and new software is being developed all the time. One alternative is Prezi (Prezi.com), a free presenting application that allows you to zoom in and out of images and to create presentations that flow like a movie. Students and professors have access to the educational version of Prezi, which has slightly better features than the basic free edition.

Although PowerPoint is the first thing many people think of when they are asked to give a presentation, not all information is suited to digital presentations. Don't forget that presentational aids can include many different kinds of visual formats. Think about the other alternatives that you have available so you can select the best method for presenting your information. The method you choose depends on factors such as the number of people in the audience, the size of the room, how much time you have, and whether you want to engage your audience in a discussion.

Handouts are one alternative. When they have a handout, audience members can easily follow along with your presentation, and they can take notes on the handout and bring it home with them. As presentation designer Robin Williams notes, what the audience members see on the screen is temporary, and "there is no guarantee they will remember it correctly; what you give them to take back to the office is permanent."[24] If you are speaking in a large room, some people might not be able to see your slides. A handout is the perfect solution to both of these problems. Handouts can range from an outline of key points in your presentation to a table of data that is difficult to present in PowerPoint to a more detailed document. A handout also allows you to provide your audience with your contact information, additional resources, or web addresses.

You might have heard the rule that you should never pass out handouts at the beginning of a presentation because audience members will read the handout and not pay attention to you. Certainly, if you give people a handout, they will read it the first moment they are bored with your presentation. Remember, though, that your audience members already have all sorts of ways to distract themselves other than with your handout. Their smartphones and other mobile technologies give them access to the Internet, email, and Twitter and to work responsibilities, school assignments, games, and movies. They also probably have paper and pens that they can use for making a grocery list or doodling. They also can distract themselves simply by thinking about things unrelated to your presentation. A handout at least keeps the audience focused temporarily on your topic.

To prevent your handout from being too much of a distraction, distribute it, if possible, at the moment in your presentation when you want to make use of it (you might ask someone in the audience to help you pass it out). Another option is to distribute it at the end of your presentation as a summary of your major points. Timing the distribution of your handout helps keep audience members focused on you and provides them with one less potential distraction. Williams summarizes the benefits of a good handout: "Your thoughtfully created handout tells me you respect me enough to have created it for me, and that in turn makes me pay a little more attention."[25]

Remember, too, that you don't have to choose between slides and handouts—consider using a mixture of both. You can use slides for most of your presentation but occasionally stop to distribute handouts with more detailed data. Another option—one that works particularly well for a presentation where your interactional goal is to discover knowledge and belief—is to begin with a short briefing paper or technical report that everyone reads at the beginning of your presentation (people can read three or four times faster than presenters can talk). Following the reading period, you can lead a discussion on the material in the document.[26] This is, in fact, what Jeff Bezos does in meetings with his senior team of executives at Amazon. He banned PowerPoint presentations and instead asks executives who have ideas they want to propose to the team to write a four-to-six-page memo called a *narrative,* which, as Bezos explains, has "real sentences, topic sentences, verbs and nouns . . . not just bullet points." At the beginning of the meeting, everyone spends 20 minutes reading the narrative in a kind of "study hall," which is then followed by a discussion of the idea in detail. Bezos believes that the narrative handout forces better thought and better understanding of the proposed idea than a PowerPoint presentation does.[27]

TWIRKS

Although there are no absolute rules for the use of elements of delivery, there is a category of elements or conditions called *twirks* that can interfere with delivery. *Twirk* is an arcane word that linguist Suzette Haden Elgin discovered and uses to refer to *"a feature of language behavior which attracts so much attention to itself that it outweighs both the content and the form of the speech."*[28] There is, of course, a contemporary definition of *twirk*—an explicit and sexually provocative dance—but we will use it the way Elgin does because it provides an easy way to talk about potential problems with delivery. According to Elgin, a twirk is anything that provokes a reaction not based on the content of your presentation. It is a distraction either because it is so striking or unusual or because it is repeated with such frequency. Elgin offers the following example of a twirk:

> Suppose you make an interesting, rational, and compelling speech, and you do that while wearing a purple velvet floppy hat with rabbit ears and scarlet satin roses. Then that hat is a *twirk*—and it will seriously interfere with the manner in which your speech is heard and understood by your audience. You could be the greatest orator since Demosthenes, and that hat would still undercut you and cancel out the power of your words and all the nonverbal communication that went with them.[29]

Any element that calls attention to itself rather than to your perspective is a twirk.

Elements that are distracting or sustained have the potential to interfere with the full presentation and reception of your perspective because they dominate audience members' attention and make fulfilling the functions of your presentation difficult. Analyze all aspects of your planned delivery to discover and eliminate the twirks that could hinder the transformative possibilities for your particular audience. No object or condition is in itself good or bad, positive or negative. Something only becomes a twirk when it interferes with the reception of your message.

Some twirks that are most likely to affect a speaking presentation involve: (1) communication anxiety; (2) language; (3) clothing and adornment; (4) physical conditions; and (5) presentational aids.

Communication Anxiety

When you become so nervous that it interferes with your ability to present your perspective effectively, you are experiencing communication anxiety or stage fright, and your anxiety will function as a twirk. When you perceive that you are in a challenging, frightening, or new situation, your body responds by producing adrenaline. Adrenaline sets you up to respond by "fight or flight," but in a communication situation, of course, you can do neither, so the adrenaline in your body seeks some kind of release. Adrenaline manifests in symptoms often associated with communication anxiety, such as a dry mouth, an accelerated heartbeat, shaking hands and knees, butterflies in the stomach, or blushing. If these symptoms are obvious to your audience as you are speaking, they may function as twirks for you.

Some degree of anxiety about communicating is normal; in fact, there are many legitimate reasons why you might feel anxious. One reason is that there is the expectation, when you are asked or choose to speak, that you will offer something of interest and value to the audience. You also may not be entirely confident that your perspective will be accepted and appreciated by your audience. In addition, a lack of preparation may trigger feelings of anxiety. If you are not as ready as you would like to be for a speaking situation—you have not had adequate preparation time, did not know you would be asked to speak, procrastinated in preparing your presentation, or did not practice your presentation very much—you probably will find yourself experiencing some anxiety.

Even when you are well prepared, you still may experience anxiety because of uncertainties related to your presentation. Perhaps you are planning a presentation with an interactional goal of discovering knowledge and belief. You have prepared fully for the discussion, but it is a mode you do not use very often, and thus it generates anxiety for you. Perhaps your perspective itself is undergoing major shifts, and you feel a natural anxiety about articulating it in its changing form to an audience. Perhaps you are experiencing anxiety because you feel you have nothing to contribute to the interaction. This feeling may be the result of having been silenced in the past, of feeling devalued in a group, or of not having the communication tools to express your perspective adequately. All of these feelings are legitimate and may provoke feelings of anxiety before and during your presentation.

There are other sources of anxiety, however, that are not legitimate and consist of irrational, exaggerated, or needless fear. Most irrational concerns arise because of an *"overconcern for what someone thinks about you."*[30] This kind of anxiety is self-defeating because the worry itself is usually far worse than the actual event. If you experience anxiety of this sort, you are likely to exaggerate the possible outcomes of a speaking situation, and your worrying just increases the likelihood of something unexpected occurring.[31] You may worry, for example, about tripping on the way to the lectern or about being so afraid you won't be able to utter a word. That anything like this will occur is extremely unlikely, but obsessing about it will not keep it from happening.

Whether your anxiety has a legitimate basis or is largely irrational, it can be managed. You may have been given all sorts of advice for dealing with communication anxiety. Not all of it, however, helps create an environment of safety, openness, freedom, and value. You may have been told, for example, to look over the heads of your audience members; to imagine them sitting before you in their underwear; or to say over and over to yourself before you speak, "I'm a better person than they are." All of these techniques generate just the opposite conditions from the ones you are attempting to create. They require you to see yourself as superior to your audience rather than as an equal in an interaction in which everyone's perspective is welcomed and valued. These techniques also assume that you are facing a hostile audience, which is probably not the case.

Managing your communication anxiety appropriately can help in your creation of an environment of safety, openness, freedom, and value. A first step is to deal with the symptoms you tend to experience so that your discomfort with or embarrassment about them does not interfere with your efforts to communicate. If your mouth tends to be dry when you speak, bring water with you to sip throughout your presentation. If your neck turns red when you speak, wear a turtleneck or a scarf that covers it. If shakiness is your body's preferred symptom of speech anxiety, try to engage in some physical activity before your presentation to rid your body of excess energy—take a walk, breathe deeply, or move your head and arms. Once you know that you have addressed your body's symptoms of communication anxiety, you will feel more comfortable and can concentrate on creating the kind of environment you desire.

Communication anxiety is likely to increase if your presentation is not flowing smoothly. Practicing can help avoid that outcome. As you listen to yourself practice, your perspective will become increasingly clear, and you will become more confident about expressing it. Voicing your perspective whenever you get the opportunity is another way to decrease communication anxiety. Whenever you are given the chance to present your ideas, take it. The first several or perhaps the first hundred times you accept the opportunity to share your ideas, you might be uncomfortable and might experience symptoms of anxiety. Gradually, however, they will begin to disappear. You will feel more comfortable with the process of presenting ideas orally, will discover that you have good ideas to contribute, and will find that others appreciate your input into various interactions.

This certainly was the case for us. We were incredibly shy in junior high and high school, so when we had to give a presentation, we wrote every word out on note cards. We turned bright red, our hands and knees shook, and we hated all of those eyes staring at us. Even talking individually with someone we didn't know well was hard for us. But we kept giving presentations, and, eventually, we got pretty good at them. If we can go from our starting point of extreme nervousness to becoming communication majors, teaching communication, writing a book about speaking, and being able to give presentations easily, we are confident you can make progress toward overcoming your speech anxiety, too.

If your stage fright is largely irrational, fueled by exaggerated and needless worry, you can use rational self-talk to address it. Rather than dwelling on and worrying about the things that might go wrong in a presentation, you can minimize or even dispel anxiety by using positive self-talk to focus your attention on all the things that probably will go well. You can put your presentation in perspective. It is only a presentation, and if it does not go perfectly, it is not the end of the world. In fact, no one expects perfection in such a setting; you are a human being conversing with other human beings about something you care about. "Perfection is not my goal with this presentation—an interesting conversation is" might be one statement that becomes part of your positive self-talk. You also might turn your attention to the presentation itself and construct messages to yourself that reinforce the positive features of the presentation—how much you enjoy the opportunity to discuss the subject, how exciting it will be to hear others' perspectives on the same issue, or how delighted you are to have the opportunity to talk to a particular audience. Don't forget, too, that spending your time preparing for your presentation rather than worrying about it will focus your attention where it will do some good.

Just because you have addressed your speech anxiety, however, does not mean you can eradicate it entirely or forever or that it will never be a twirk. Even the most seasoned speakers may experience some symptoms of anxiety in particularly difficult or challenging speaking situations. When you understand why the anxiety is surfacing and remind yourself of what you have going for you in your presentation, how much you have practiced, and how much you want to give expression to your perspective, those anxieties will dissipate and probably disappear.

Language

Twirks of language relate to how something is said and include pronunciation, grammar and usage, jargon, obscenities, and fillers. The conditions of safety, openness, freedom, and value are enhanced when your language matches the language the audience is used to hearing. **Pronunciation** associated with a particular dialect often functions as a twirk. A speaker from the South might have a "drawl," or someone from Boston might add r's to the end of words—*Cub-er* and *Asi-er* instead of *Cuba* and *Asia*. If an audience is unfamiliar with those dialects or expects a standard form of speech, these dialects can become twirks. The way a speaker pronounces a certain word can be a twirk if the pronunciation is different from how audience members say it. Pronouncing a word incorrectly can also be a twirk. A radio station in Albuquerque, where Karen lives, ran an ad for an event sponsored by the library. The individual who was voicing the ad omitted the *r* from the word *library,* and her repeated pronunciation of the word as *libary* became a twirk for Karen. Even dropping the endings of words—*workin'* instead of *working*—or eliding words—*gonna* instead of *going to*—can be twirks for some audiences.

Grammar and usage also function as potential twirks, usually when violations of standard grammar and usage occur. Saying *ain't* instead of *isn't,* using the double negative (*I don't have no money*), or incorrect subject-verb agreement (*Rabbits is cute*) are examples of such violations. For some groups, such grammatical errors interfere with the creation of an environment of safety, openness, freedom, and value.

Jargon might be seen as the opposite of poor grammar in the sense that it involves language that exceeds conversational standards and norms. Jargon is the use of a highly technical vocabulary characteristic of one field or profession. Virtually every discipline has its jargon, but use of such vocabulary with an audience not familiar with it is a twirk. In a presentation about engineering to an audience not acquainted with the field, for example, the use of terms such as *gimbals, ellipse, blow molding, Cartesian coordinates,* and *G-type joint girder* would constitute jargon. *You guys* can be a twirk in professional situations because it is inappropriate in that situation—it is too casual and not gender neutral.

Obscenities or swear words also function as twirks for many audiences. Some audiences are accustomed to hearing such language and have no problem with it, but for others, obscenities are offensive and violate norms for polite and appropriate speech. If you are not sure how an audience will respond to an obscenity, don't use it. For many audiences, obscenities are major detractors from the content of the presentation and affect audience members' attitudes toward you as a speaker. Furthermore, your use of obscenities can keep an audience from feeling safe and valued.

Fillers are words that are inserted between phrases or sentences to avoid silence. Some common fillers are *you know, I mean, uh, um,* and *like.* Because these are natural elements in informal conversation, they are not twirks for most audiences unless they appear so frequently that they become distracting. When this occurs, audience members may start waiting for the next filler to occur instead of listening to the content of the presentation itself. Karen knew a professor who overused the word *actually* as he lectured. One day, a student decided to count each instance of the professor's use of the word *actually* and became so focused on this task that he did not hear when the professor called on him. The professor walked over to his desk, asked what he was doing, and discovered the tally marks. Until that moment, the professor had no idea that he overused *actually,* and he made a concerted effort after that to excise this twirk from his vocabulary.

Linguistic twirks are among the most manageable because, with awareness, you can make changes in your language so that particular aspects of your presentation do not become twirks. You can practice your presentation so that many of your fillers disappear and, with vigilance, you can catch and change grammatical errors. Recording your presentation or asking for feedback from those who hear you practice also can help you become aware of twirks. Language is the vehicle through which your presentation is offered. If you can prevent your language from producing twirks, your audience will be more likely to hear your perspective.

Clothing and Adornment

Your clothing and other forms of adornment can become twirks if they are unacceptable, unusual, or inappropriate for your audience. Major discrepancies in clothing between you and your audience tend to make you and your audience uncomfortable. Speaking in a short-sleeved shirt and khakis when everyone else is wearing a suit is a twirk, just as is presenting in a suit when everyone else is in shorts and T-shirts. For a formal presentation, the norm is that a speaker should be dressed at or slightly above the dress level of the audience; Personal hygiene can become an issue, too, if your deodorant has failed or if you have not taken a shower or washed your hair recently.

Bodily adornment in the form of tattoos and body piercings are ways of expressing identity for many people, but they function as twirks for some audiences. The tattoo on your hand—no matter what the image—may keep some employers from taking you seriously at a job interview regardless of how well you present your ideas. Any tattoo that cannot be covered is a potential twirk, as is an eyebrow ring, tongue stud, nose ring, or pierced lip. Gauged earlobes are considered inappropriate or strange by some audiences and would function as twirks for them.

At times, hair style or hair color can function as a twirk. Hair that is dyed an unusual color—pink, purple, or green, for example—is a twirk if it is all the audience members can see and think about during your presentation. An unusual or dated hairstyle might keep an audience from focusing on what you are presenting as well. Long strands of hair combed over a man's bald spot can be a twirk if audience members focus on the hairstyle instead of on the presentation. Twirks relating to clothing and adornment also can include temporary conditions that affect appearance such as spinach between your front teeth, lipstick on your teeth, a loose hem, spaghetti sauce spilled on a blouse, a tie that has inadvertently flipped over, a collar that is up instead of down, or a fly that is open. If you become aware of temporary quirks while presenting, fix them unobtrusively if you can so that they do not remain twirks for very long.

Conditions related to clothing and appearance that can become twirks usually can be managed with some forethought. Ask the person who asked you to speak for advice about the kind of dress appropriate for the occasion. If your analysis of the speaking situation tells you that adornment such as earrings, piercings, and tattoos will constitute twirks for your audience, remove or cover them for your presentation, if possible. Checking yourself in a mirror immediately before a presentation to make sure there are no temporary problems with your appearance is also a good idea.

Physical Conditions

Physical conditions also can function as distractions for an audience during a presentation. Being in a wheelchair; having a large birthmark on your face; or being hard of hearing, deaf, blind, or cerebral palsied are examples of physical conditions that can function as twirks. Weight (an obese or severely anorexic speaker, for example) may constitute a twirk for some audiences. Speaking in a strong foreign accent also can be perceived as a twirk. Although accents can be changed, adults often have difficulty eliminating accents entirely—and some do not wish to give up this reminder of their native language. If an audience cannot understand you and focuses on that difficulty, your accent has become a twirk.

The best way to manage physical conditions functioning as twirks is to deal with them directly. You may want to explain to the audience near the beginning of your presentation, "I have cerebral palsy," "I am a stutterer," or "I don't hear well," for example. You then can let your audience know how to handle the situation: "Because this may interfere with our communication, please feel free to ask me to repeat or explain whenever necessary. I won't be offended, and I appreciate your patience."[32] By dealing with the twirk directly, you reduce the discomfort of your audience by making the condition something that can be addressed explicitly. As the interaction proceeds, audience members, in all likelihood, will think less and less about it. Instead of spending their time wondering whether to ask if you need help with your wheelchair or whether they can ask you to repeat something they missed because of your accent, you have made the condition something that can be talked about. Audience members then can turn their attention to the presentation itself rather than worrying that something they do or say will offend you or make you uncomfortable.

Your gender constitutes another potential twirk because expectations for speaking can be different for various genders. There was a time when women were not even allowed to speak in public. Not only was speaking considered unladylike for a woman, but it also generally was considered a physical impossibility—women were not believed to have the stamina or temperament required to manage public speaking.[33] Although women now speak in every kind of context, some audiences might begrudge a woman a position of power or influence. Some audiences might perceive the same statement from a man and a woman in different ways. A man who reveals emotion might be seen as sensitive; a woman who does so might be viewed as hysterical or overly emotional. A man who is assertive might be seen as commanding, while a woman who is assertive might be viewed as bitchy. Your gender, then, may function as a twirk for certain audiences, especially if you are speaking on subjects they do not expect to hear about from someone of your gender.

If you are a woman, wearing a revealing, low-cut blouse or a very short skirt may increase an audience's perception of inappropriateness. Karen once worked with a teaching assistant who was particularly attractive and highlighted her figure by wearing extremely short mini skirts and fitted tops. Another professor friend consistently wore jeans and flannel shirts when she taught. Both women had issues with credibility—students did not take them seriously—and thus their dress functioned as twirks for them. Similarly, a transgender woman may find that her voice is a twirk for some audiences because it is lower than what they expect of a woman.

Presentational Aids

Sometimes, twirks result from the misuse of an aspect of delivery that typically would be considered helpful in a presentation. Presentational aids can become twirks when they are of poor quality, are overused, or take too much attention away from the speaker. These conditions were discussed in the earlier section on presentational aids, but they are so important that they deserve discussion again.

If, because of poor quality, an aid does not fulfill its function—to *aid* in the understanding of the content of the presentation—it becomes a twirk. Handwriting on a whiteboard that is illegible or PowerPoint images that not everyone in the audience can see are situations in which presentational aids become twirks. Rather than assisting in the full articulation of your perspective, these aids are likely to irritate your audience members and to take their attention away from the perspective you are offering.

The overuse or excessive use of presentational aids also constitutes a twirk. When an excerpt from a movie consumes the time allotted for your entire presentation, it is functioning as a twirk. Similarly, when you give audience members handouts that duplicate the screens of your PowerPoint presentation, you are overusing aids, and they lose their impact. Even using PowerPoint because "everyone else does" may be too much of a good thing when one speaker after another gives presentations that are very much the same in terms of graphics, layout, color schemes, and outlining formats. As a result, the presentational software not only loses its effectiveness but functions as a twirk.

The delivery of your presentation is more than the means by which your ideas are expressed. It is an additional resource available to you for creating an environment of safety, openness, freedom, and value and for enhancing the articulation of your perspective. Attention to the various components of delivery and how they can become twirks creates a presentation that helps your audience members both understand and remember your presentation.

10

Assessing Choices

You now have made decisions about all aspects of your presentation: focus, frame, forms of elaboration, introduction and conclusion, transitions, and delivery. Your final task before the actual delivery of your presentation is to prepare your speaking plan. We have chosen to discuss the speaking plan here so that you can incorporate information about delivery. The speaking plan summarizes what you plan to do in your presentation. It is an assessment tool you can use to evaluate the decisions you have made about your presentation. As you have been developing your presentation, of course, you have been thinking about all of its components and how they work together. As a result, you might already have conceptualized the key elements of your speaking plan.

One way to think about the speaking plan is that it is a path through your understanding of your ideas and how to present them. It offers a way to think systematically about the components of your presentation and to assess the choices you have made about them. Obviously, there are many presentations you give when you do not have the opportunity to write a speaking plan. If you are able to complete this step, however, it will tell you if what you have planned for your presentation will accomplish your interactional goal and if it will create the desired environment of safety, openness, freedom, and value.

CREATING THE SPEAKING PLAN

Your speaking plan is not a set of speaking notes. Rather, the speaking plan includes the 11 basic components of the process of creating a presentation.

1. **Audience**. Identify your audience.

2. **Setting**. Identify the setting for your presentation.

3. **Interactional goal**. State your interactional goal for the presentation (review chapter 2).

4. **Thesis statement**. Write a thesis statement that captures the perspective on your subject that you plan to develop in the presentation (review chapter 4).

5. **Organizational pattern**. State the organizational pattern you are using to organize your major ideas (review chapter 5).

6. **Major ideas**. State the major ideas you will develop in the presentation. This section is the most extensive part of your speaking plan because it includes the major and supporting ideas of your presentation. Many different formats exist for depicting the major ideas and the relationships among them. One way is to outline them. Translate your major and minor ideas into key words or phrases and arrange them hierarchically in points and subpoints. Your major ideas are major headings, and the elaboration of them—the minor ideas—are subpoints under them in the outline.

   Sometimes, you will find that an outline format cannot capture the vision you have for your presentation because an outline requires that your ideas be structured in a linear, hierarchical way. In such a case, a visual diagram may serve you better as a way to present your major ideas, their elaborations, and the relationships among them. With a visual diagram, you summarize your major ideas with key words and phrases that are connected by lines and arrows to indicate the relationships among them. Both a visual and an outline format are illustrated in the sample speaking plans that follow.

7. **Major forms of elaboration**. List the forms of elaboration you plan to use to develop your major ideas (review chapter 6).

8. **Introduction**. Indicate the type of introduction you plan to use (review chapter 7).

9. **Conclusion**. Indicate the type of conclusion you plan to use (review chapter 7).

10. **Transitions**. Write out the paragraph, sentence(s), or words you plan to use to move from the introduction to the body and from the body to the conclusion of your presentation. You will want to plan other transitions for moving between the main ideas and the forms of elaboration in the body of your presentation, but these do not need to be included in your speaking plan (review chapter 8).

11. **Delivery**. List major strengths and weaknesses you bring to the delivery of your presentation. Strengths are aspects of your deliv-

ery that you believe will facilitate the accomplishment of your goals for the presentation and the creation of the conditions of safety, openness, freedom, and value. For example, you may see as strengths the presentational aid you have prepared, the amount of time you practice your presentations, and your ability to think on your feet to adapt to what is happening in the audience. Weaknesses are aspects of your delivery you want to eliminate or neutralize in your presentation because they make achieving your goals for your presentation more difficult. For example, you may see as weaknesses your tendency to speak too softly, your tendency to say *um* frequently, and your speech anxiety (review chapter 9).

SAMPLE SPEAKING PLANS

Below are seven sample speaking plans. They show different interactional goals, different styles of presenting major ideas, and a variety of organizational patterns and forms of elaboration. If you create speaking plans similar to these before a major presentation, you will have the opportunity to assess your presentation, rethink sections as necessary, and make changes before you actually deliver it.

Speaking Plan for "Who Is a True Friend?"

1. **Audience.** Grade-school students
2. **Setting.** Sunday school class
3. **Interactional goals.** To discover knowledge and belief, to articulate a perspective
4. **Thesis statement.** Let's develop a definition of friendship and see how God can be a friend.
5. **Organizational pattern.** Multiple perspectives
6. **Major ideas:**
   I. Audience members' perspectives on friendship
   II. My definition of friendship
      A. Someone who will respect what I say
      B. Someone who is there for me
   III. What the Bible says about friends
      A. Proverbs 18:24
      B. Proverbs 27:10
   IV. How we can be true friends
      A. Keep secrets
      B. Be trustworthy
   V. God is a trustworthy friend

7. **Major forms of elaboration**. Participation (discussion), comparison and contrast, definition, exaggeration, examples, questions (substantive)

8. **Introduction**. Reference to speaking situation (audience), questions (substantive)

9. **Conclusion**. Summary of basic theme

10. **Transitions**:

 I. **Transition from introduction to body**. These are all excellent ideas about friendship. I hold a similar perspective to yours on friendship.

 II. **Transition from body to conclusion**. At the beginning of my presentation, you shared with me your perspectives on friendship. I hope you can see how God can be a friend in much the same way to you.

11. **Delivery**:

 I. **Strengths**. I know the people in the audience well, so I'll feel comfortable asking them questions and presenting my perspective.

 II. **Weaknesses**. I tend to experience speech anxiety, and my frequent use of *you know* is a problem for me.

This speaking plan was adapted from one developed by Christa Porter at Ohio State University. The presentation for which this speaking plan was developed is included in the presentations at the end of the book.

Speaking Plan for "The Preseason Presentation"

1. **Audience**. Thirty soccer players, ranging in age from 16 to 18 years old

2. **Setting**. First day of school, August 20

3. **Interactional goal**. To build community

4. **Thesis statement**. If we work together, we can build an excellent team this year.

5. **Organizational pattern**. Category

6. **Major ideas**:

 I. We are getting better at all aspects of the game

 A. Practiced hard all summer

 B. Several experienced players

 C. Cohesive team

    II. My expectations for the team

        A. Play with a sense of urgency

           1. Anticipate and play with intensity

           2. Make each other better players

        B. Communicate on the field

           1. Let each other know where you are

           2. Move without the ball

        C. Special responsibilities for the seniors

           1. Step up and take responsibility

           2. Set an example

   III. Team goals for the season

        A. Improve individual scoring

        B. Place in regional tournament

        C. Have fun

7. **Major forms of elaboration.** Explanation, repetition, and restatement

8. **Introduction.** Reference to speaking situation (occasion)

9. **Conclusion.** Summary of main ideas

10. **Transitions:**

    I. **Transition from introduction to body.** We can have a winning season this year if we are willing to develop as a team in three areas: play with a sense of urgency, communicate on the field, and expect our seniors to do a bit extra.

    II. **Transition from body to conclusion.** I have outlined some ambitious goals for the season, but I am confident that we can accomplish them.

11. **Delivery:**

    I. **Strengths.** I feel comfortable giving presentations, and I am happy with how I use gestures and move around in front of an audience.

    II. **Weaknesses.** I have a tendency to go over my time limit, and I get so excited about my ideas that I sometimes forget to pay attention to my audience members and their perspectives.

This speaking plan was adapted from one developed by Wes Zunker at the University of New Mexico.

Speaking Plan for "Violations of the Covenants"

1. **Audience**. Homeowners and representatives from Grubb and Ellis (Grubb and Ellis regulates the homeowner association for my subdivision)

2. **Setting**. A meeting for concerned homeowners to voice concerns to Grubb and Ellis

3. **Interactional goals**. Articulate a perspective, seek adherence, build community

4. **Thesis statement**. In my opinion, unintended and uncorrected violations of the covenants allow for the deterioration of the subdivision, and we should all work to see that these violations are corrected.

5. **Organizational pattern**. Metaphor

6. **Major ideas:**

   I.   Broken windows as metaphor for decline in neighborhood

   II. Explanation of broken-windows theory

   III. Examples of broken-windows theory

   IV. Violations of covenants in neighborhood as "broken windows"

7. **Major forms of elaboration**. Figure of speech (metaphor), sensory images, explanation, participation (discussion)

8. **Introduction**. Reference to speaking situation (audience)

9. **Conclusion**. Call to action

10. **Transitions**.

    I. **Transition from introduction to body.** Unintended and uncorrected violations of the covenants allow for the deterioration of the subdivision, as the broken-window theory of community development suggests.

    II. **Transition from body to conclusion.** The broken-window theory suggests that broken windows are a metaphor for the decline of neighborhoods. So, too, the violations of the covenants of our community, if left unchecked, can lead to the decline of our community.

11. **Delivery:**

    I. **Strengths**. I have a style of delivery that many people see as warm and friendly.

    II. **Weaknesses**. My hair color may distract the audience, and I tend to talk too fast.

This speaking plan was adapted from one developed by Joanne Villa at the University of New Mexico.

Speaking Plan for "First Day of Class"

1. **Audience**. College students in an Anthropology 101 class
2. **Setting**. The first day of the semester
3. **Interactional goal**. Assert individuality, seek adherence
4. **Thesis statement**. I want to communicate my goals, assignments, and policies for Anthropology 101.
5. **Organizational pattern**. Web
6. **Major ideas**.

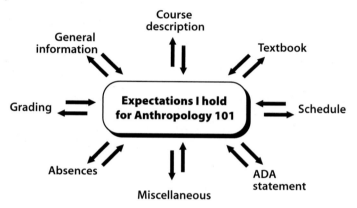

7. **Major forms of elaboration**. Definition, example, explanation, humor, presentational aids, credentials
8. **Introduction**. Questions (substantive), reference to speaking situation (audience, occasion)
9. **Conclusion**. Summary of main ideas
10. **Transitions**:
    I. **Transition from introduction to body**. I'd like to go over the syllabus now to see if you have any questions about the course and about my expectations for you.
    II. **Transition from body to conclusion**. These are my plans and expectations for the course.
11. **Delivery**:
    I. **Strengths**. I am able to speak conversationally while giving presentations, and I move around the room to make my presentation lively.
    II. **Weaknesses**. The fact that I'll be going over a syllabus may keep me too tied to this handout, diminishing movement and eye contact.

This speaking plan was adapted from one developed by Madalena Salazar at the University of New Mexico.

Speaking Plan for "Creating an Educational Foundation"

1. **Audience.** Students at Crownpoint High School
2. **Setting.** Student assembly in large auditorium
3. **Interactional goal.** To articulate a perspective
4. **Thesis statement.** It is important to create a firm educational foundation in preparation for college.
5. **Organizational pattern.** Problem-solution
6. **Major ideas:**
    I. **Problem:** Native Americans sometimes have difficulty in college
        A. Different values
        B. Lack of adequate preparation
        C. Lack of role models for success in college
    II. My perspective on education
        A. Education has always been important to me
            1. To set a good example for my younger sister and older brother
            2. To prove to my parents that I could do it
            3. To get a good job
    III. **Solution:** It's important to get a good education
        A. Take pride in who you are
        B. Don't let school get in the way of your education
        C. Approach each situation with a positive attitude
        D. Do more than you are expected to do with any assignment you are given or any task you face
7. **Major forms of elaboration.** Examples, explanation, narratives
8. **Introduction.** Reference to speaking situation (self)
9. **Conclusion.** Call to action
10. **Transitions:**
    I. **Transition from introduction to body.** I once held the same view of education that most of you do. I've since developed a new perspective and would like to suggest that it's important to create a firm educational foundation in preparation for college.
    II. **Transition from body to conclusion.** I did the best I could when I was in high school to make good use of what my teachers had to offer, but I know now there were many other things I could have done. Taking pride in who you are, refusing to let school get in the way of your education, approaching each situation with a positive attitude, and doing more

than expected at any task are ways that anyone can create a firm educational foundation for college.

11. **Delivery:**

 I. **Strengths.** I practice my presentations a lot so they flow easily.

 II. **Weaknesses.** I don't have much vocal variation.

This speaking plan was adapted from one developed by Tracy J. Tsosie at the University of New Mexico.

Speaking Plan for "Medical School Interview"

1. **Audience.** An interviewer at an interview for medical school asks, "What influenced you to want to become a doctor?"

2. **Setting.** Office/small meeting room at medical school

3. **Interactional goal.** Assert individuality, seek adherence

4. **Thesis statement.** I want to share how my life experiences have led me to want to become a pediatrician.

5. **Organizational pattern.** Narrative progression

6. **Major ideas:**

 I. Babysitting

 A. Story about babysitting sick nephew

 II. Past volunteer work

 A. Story about work at Camp Fire day camp

 B. Story about volunteering at hospital

 III. Summer job

 A. Story about working as a life guard at a swimming pool

 IV. Religious experience

 A. Story about experience at hospital chapel

 V. Education

 A. Story about fifth-grade science project

 B. Story about internship in college

 VI. Current volunteer work

 A. Story about work with Doctors Without Borders

7. **Major forms of elaboration.** Stories, questions (substantive)

8. **Introduction.** Reference to speaking situation (occasion)

9. **Conclusion.** Summary of main ideas

10. **Transitions:**

 I. **Transition from introduction to body.** What I hope to convey to you in the short time I have here is how my life experiences have led me to want to become a pediatrician.

   II. **Transition from body to conclusion**. I've told you a number
       of stories of various experiences I've had that show how my
       interest in becoming a pediatrician developed.

11. **Delivery**:
    I. **Strengths**. I know my stories well and have told them many
       times, so I should be able to tell them in a way that suggests
       my passion and excitement for my topic.
    II. **Weaknesses**. I have a tendency to keep going once I start, so
        I need to watch the time and pay attention to the response
        I'm getting from the interviewer as I tell the stories.

This speaking plan was adapted from one developed by Cuoghi Edens at
the University of New Mexico.

Speaking Plan for "Increased Funding for the Colorado Council on the Arts"

1. **Audience**. Representatives in the Colorado legislature
2. **Setting**. Hearing room in state capital
3. **Interactional goal**. To articulate a perspective, to seek adherence
4. **Thesis statement**. The legislature should increase its appropriation to the Colorado Council on the Arts.
5. **Organizational pattern**. Circle
6. **Major ideas**.

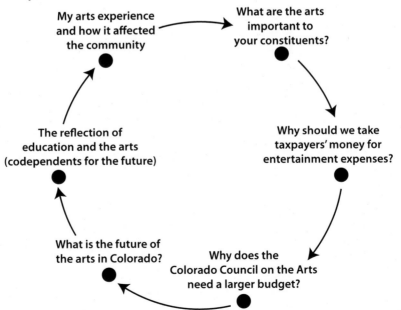

7. **Major forms of elaboration**. Explanation, examples, stories, presentational aids

8. **Introduction**. Narrative

9. **Conclusion**. Call to action

10. **Transitions**:

   I. **Transition from introduction to body**. Why am I suggesting that the budget of the Colorado Council on the Arts be increased? Because of the importance of the arts for your constituencies.

   II. **Transition from body to conclusion**. I've suggested many reasons why the arts are important in our communities. That's why I'm asking for your support for an increase in the legislative appropriation to the Colorado Council on the Arts.

11. **Delivery**:

   I. **Strengths**. Visual aid provides a clear summary of the budget, so the audience will be able to understand my perspective easily, and I practice my presentations a lot.

   II. **Weaknesses**. I will experience speech anxiety because this is a very important presentation, and I've never testified before the legislature before. My hands tend to shake and my face turns red when I experience stage fright.

This speaking plan was adapted from one developed by Jason Renak at the University of Colorado Denver.

ASSESSING YOUR SPEAKING PLAN

Your speaking plan allows you to assess the presentation you have developed and to decide whether your plans for the presentation match up with the mental vision you have for it. It also allows you to do a final check of whether the options you have selected facilitate or impede the creation of an environment in which transformation may occur—whether they contribute to the creation of safety, openness, freedom, and value in the interaction. The following questions will help you determine if the various decisions you have made about your presentation create or inhibit possibilities for transformation. If a check of your speaking plan reveals any problems, this is the time to revise it. Do not be afraid to change or abandon parts of your presentation if you discover that some of the decisions you have made do not contribute to the accomplishment of your goals for the interaction.

Audience. How carefully have you considered the characteristics of your audience members, their interest in this interaction, and their willingness to be changed as a result of it? How comfortable are you with your audience?

Setting. Is there anything special about your setting that you need to keep in mind as you plan your presentation? What have you done to minimize distracting environmental factors that might inhibit or negate your efforts at establishing the conditions of safety, openness, freedom, and value?

Interactional goal. Does your interactional goal promote the creation of conditions that maximize possibilities for transformation? Is your selected interactional goal one that can be accomplished in the amount of time you have?

Thesis statement. Is your thesis statement clear and effectively placed within the presentation? Do you suggest, in your presentation, that you are willing to follow the interaction wherever it goes and to be transformed in the process? In communicating your thesis statement, do you suggest that you value the perspectives of audience members, no matter how different they may be from yours?

Organizational pattern. Does your organizational pattern help make evident your interactional goal? Do you provide sufficient unity and coherence in your presentation so your audience members can follow you without difficulty and understand your perspective easily?

Major ideas. Do your major ideas communicate the essence of your perspective so that your audience members can understand it? Have you identified clear and appropriate sub-points under your main ideas?

Forms of elaboration. Do your forms of elaboration provide sufficient development of your ideas so your audience members are able to understand your perspective? Are the feelings evoked through your choice of forms of elaboration ones that facilitate or impede the possibility of transformation? Do your forms of elaboration silence other participants because they are presented, for example, in technical jargon? Do you use sufficient variety in terms of your forms of elaboration in order to maintain the interest of audience members?

Introduction. Does your introduction function to orient your audience to your topic? Does your introduction begin to establish the conditions of safety, openness, freedom, and value?

Conclusion. Does your conclusion function to reemphasize your main idea? Does your conclusion convey what you would like to have happen next in the interaction?

Transitions. Do the transitions you have planned move you from the introduction to the body and from the body to the conclusion so that audience members can follow the progression of your ideas? Are your transitions—word, sentence, or paragraph—appropriate for the length of your presentation?

Delivery. How do you plan to use the strengths you have identified about your delivery to facilitate your goals for your presentation? How will the weaknesses you have identified about your delivery negatively impact your presentation? What can you do to ensure that you minimize them as much as possible?

You now have the basic information you need to create and deliver a presentation that invites consideration of diverse perspectives, facilitates an equal interaction between speaker and audience, and encourages transformation. We don't expect you to remember everything we've discussed here—how to develop an appropriate interactional goal, an organizational pattern, main points, transitions, an introduction and conclusion, and a style of delivery that facilitates a transformative environment. But we hope you will use this book as a handy resource when you need to give presentations—at school, in the workplace, and in your personal life. If you thoughtfully engage the various elements discussed here, the possibility increases that you will have a successful speaking experience—one in which you not only feel comfortable as the presenter but one that enables everyone involved to better understand and appreciate one another as a result of the interaction. Here's to a lifetime of creative, enjoyable, and rewarding presentations as you make your way through our wonderfully diverse world!

Sample Presentations

Asserting Individuality

Retailing Clothing and Cosmetics:
Response to an Interview Question

Liz Stroben
Student, Ohio State University

In this presentation, Liz Stroben is responding to a question asked during an interview for a position with a retail firm that sells clothing and cosmetics. The question is: "What inspired you to pursue a career in women's fashion and cosmetics?" Used with permission of Liz Stroben.

When I think back over my life and my experience, three specific times in my life come to mind that have emphasized my interest in a career in retail. First, when I was about five years old, my mom took me to an antique shop owned by a friend of hers. As you know, antique stores are often small and have lots of objects in them—lots of glass, lots of plates, lots of things that are breakable. As you can imagine, my mom was watching me closely so I didn't run around too much. But I was mesmerized by one table, and as my mom and her friend were talking, they realized that I had started to arrange the different items on the table. They didn't say anything to me because I was being very careful in moving the things around and doing so very slowly. When I was done, they asked me, "Liz, why did you rearrange that table?" And I said, "Well, I like it this way." My mom's friend looked at it and said, "I like it, too—but I can't believe a five-year-old is merchandising my antique store." She led me around that day to different tables, and I got to arrange them as well. From the age of five through high school, then, I went twice a month to her store and did all of her displays as well as some designs for her customers who wanted ideas for how to arrange their furniture and antiques. This experience really helped me later on as I moved into my official retailing career, where I did floor plans and rearranged stores to help customers find things more easily and to help sales. That was my start in the retailing business.

Around the age of 12 or 13—the age when a lot of young women get into clothing and make-up—my friends and I were no different. Every Friday, we'd go to a different person's house, and we'd do what we called *fashion show*. We'd all bring our suitcases with a bunch of clothes, and we'd mix and match them and play fashion show. I was the person who would create the different outfits for everybody. So, again, I learned how to put things together—colors and textures—and I also learned something that really helped me later. I learned that I really like working with people, and I like helping clients choose things for themselves. That's what helped me later on when I worked in various stores. I really enjoy customer contact and the positive feedback from the people I've helped. This experience, then, pretty much solidified the fact that I was going to stay in retailing.

The most recent experience—and probably the most important experience that confirmed my interest in fashion retailing—was my work with Calvin Klein. This was an official working position. It wasn't playtime or me at the age of five. And what I learned in this position was that you really can combine clothing and cosmetics in a single business because, as you know, they have a couture line, a sportswear line, and a cosmetics and fragrance line. At Calvin Klein, I also learned that clothing is not just an outer shell. When you see someone, you think, "Oh, they have a sweater on," or "Oh, they have a T-shirt on." But clothing and cosmetics are not just a superficial way of expressing your personality. They are really an expression of you; they are not just something superficial. Most women and most men don't do clothing for someone else—they do it for themselves—as a way to express their personalities.

Obviously, my most recent experience has been with you as a summer intern, and this work has had the most impact on my career thus far. It has been an incredible learning experience because it has been my first time working in a corporate setting instead of in the store setting with clients. The personnel have been incredible; they are really, really supportive; they've helped me any time I've asked; and they answered any questions I had, no matter how trivial; and they made me feel important. Your company image is very much in keeping with the image that I have for the kind of place in which I'd like to work. Not only do you have a clothing line, but you have also added a new division—a cosmetics and body-care line.

One of the questions you asked me earlier and that I'd like to incorporate into this answer as well is, "Would I be the right person for this job?" I believe that I've explained how, from a very early age, I've had the inclination and the desire to design, to arrange things, and to sell things. These have been very important to me, and I'd like to keep doing them as part of your company.

Exhibiting With Pride

Janet K. Hughes
Artist

This presentation was given at the University of Missouri, Columbia, on March 5, 1993, as part of a panel discussion of artists whose work had been selected for inclusion in the Missouri Visual Artists' Biennial. Used with permission of Janet K. Hughes.

She's an exhibitionist
She exhibits with pride
She exhibits her work in the Missouri Visual Artists' Biennial.

She collected her thoughts
    dust
    and her award.

She means what she says
She means well
She now has the means to continue and expand her work.

For her it was a time of renewal
She renewed her spirit
    an old acquaintance
    and her contract at Indiana State University.

She moved from private to public
and enjoyed the exposure.
The exposure was wide.
She exposed herself.
She was well read.

She became widely read.
She painted the town
    the picture
    and her lips.
Her lips were read.
Her lips were red.

She moved from the margin
Into the center
And preferred the view.

I Am a Man, a Black Man, an American

Clarence Thomas
Justice, US Supreme Court

This presentation was given in Memphis, Tennessee, on July 29, 1998, at the annual meeting of the National Bar Association. Thanks to TeachingAmericanHistory.org for including Thomas's speech on its website.

Thirty years ago, we all focused intently on this city as the trauma of Dr. King's death first exploded, then sank into our lives. For so many of us who were trying hard to do what we thought was required of us in the process of integrating this society, the rush of hopelessness and isolation was immediate and overwhelming. It seemed that the whole world had gone mad. I am certain that each of us has his or her memories of that terrible day in 1968. For me it was the final straw in the struggle to retain my vocation to become a Catholic priest. Suddenly, this cataclysmic event ripped me from the moorings of my grandparents, my youth and my faith, and catapulted me headlong into the abyss that Richard Wright seemed to describe years earlier.

It was this event that shattered my faith in my religion and my country. I had spent the mid-'60s as a successful student in a virtually white environment. I had learned Latin, physics and chemistry. I had accepted the loneliness that came with being "the integrator," the first and the only. But this event, this trauma I could not take, especially when one of my fellow seminarians, not knowing that I was standing behind him, declared that he hoped the S.O.B died. This was a man of God, mortally stricken by an assassin's bullet, and one preparing for the priesthood had wished evil upon him.

The life I had dreamed of so often during those hot summers on the farm in Georgia or during what seemed like endless hours on the oil truck with my grandfather, expired as Dr. King expired. As so many of you do, I still know exactly where I was when I heard the news. It was a low moment in our nation's history and a demarcation between hope and hopelessness for many of us.

But three decades have evaporated in our lives, too quickly and without sufficient residual evidence of their importance. But much has changed since then. The hope that there would be expeditious resolutions to our myriad problems has long since evaporated with those years. Many who debated and hoped then, now do neither. There now seems to be a broad acceptance of the racial divide as a permanent state. While we once celebrated those things that we had in common with our fellow citizens who did not share our race, so many now are triumphal about our differences, finding little, if anything, in common. Indeed, some go so far as to all but define each of us by our race and establish the range of our thinking and our opinions, if not our deeds by our color.

I, for one, see this in much the same way I saw our denial of rights—as nothing short of a denial of our humanity. Not one of us has the "gospel," nor are our opinions based upon some revealed precepts to be taken as faith. As thinking, rational individuals, not one of us can claim infallibility, even from the overwhelming advantage of hindsight and Monday-morning quarterbacking.

This makes it all the more important that our fallible ideas be examined as all ideas are in the realm of reason, not as some doctrinal or racial heresy. None of us—none of us—have been appointed by God or appointed God. And if any of us has, then my question is why hasn't he or she solved all these problems?

I make no apologies for this view now, nor do I intend to do so in the future. I have now been on the Court for seven terms. For the most part, it has been much like other endeavors in life. It has its challenges and requires much of the individual to master the workings of the institution. We all know that. It is, I must say, quite different from what I might have anticipated if I had the opportunity to do so.

Unlike the unfortunate practice or custom in Washington and in much of the country, the Court is a model of civility. It's a wonderful place. Though there have been many contentious issues to come before the Court during these initial years of my tenure, I have yet to hear the first unkind words exchanged among my colleagues. And quite frankly, I think that such civility is the sine qua non of conducting the affairs of the Court and the business of the country.

As such, I think that it would be in derogation of our respective oaths and our institutional obligations to our country to engage in uncivil behavior. It would also be demeaning to any of us who engages in such conduct. Having worn the robe, we have a lifetime obligation to conduct ourselves as having deserved to wear the robe in the first instance.

One of the interesting surprises is the virtual isolation, even within the Court. It is quite rare that the members of the Court see each other during those periods when we're not sitting or when we're not in conference. And the most regular contact beyond those two formal events are the lunches we have on conference and Court days.

With respect to my following, or, more accurately, being led by other members of the Court, that is silly, but expected since I couldn't possibly think for myself. And what else could possibly be the explanation when I fail to follow the jurisprudential, ideological and intellectual, if not anti-intellectual, prescription assigned to blacks. Since thinking beyond this prescription is presumptively beyond my abilities, obviously someone must be putting these strange ideas into my mind and my opinions. Though being underestimated has its advantages, the stench of racial inferiority still confounds my olfactory nerves.

As Ralph Ellison wrote more than 35 years ago, "Why is it so often true that when critics confront the American as Negro, they suddenly drop their advance critical armament and revert with an air of confident superiority to quite primitive modes of analysis?" Those matters accomplished by whites are routinely subjected to sophisticated modes of analysis. But when the selfsame matters are accomplished by blacks, the opaque racial prism of analysis precludes such sophistication, and all is seen in black and white. And some who would not venture onto the more sophisticated analytical turf are quite content to play in the minor leagues of primitive harping.

The more things change, the more they remain the same. Of course there is much criticism of the Court by this group or that, depending on the Court's decisions in various highly publicized cases. Some of the criticism is profoundly uninformed and unhelpful. And all too often, uncivil second-guessing is not encumbered by the constraints of facts, logic or reasoned analysis.

On the other hand, the constructive and often scholarly criticism is almost always helpful in thinking about or rethinking decisions. It is my view that constructive criticism goes with the turf, especially when the stakes are so high and the cases arouse passions and emotions. And, in a free society, [where it is found] the precious freedom of speech and the strength of ideas, we at the Court could not possibly claim exemption from such criticism. Moreover, we are not infallible, just final.

As I have noted, I find a thoughtful, analytical criticism most helpful. I do not think any judge can address a vast array of cases and issues without testing and re-testing his or her reasoning and opinions in the crucible of debate. However, since we are quite limited in public debate about matters that may come before the Court, such debate must, for the most part, occur intramurally, thus placing a premium on outside scholarship.

Unfortunately, from time to time, the criticism of the Court goes beyond the bounds of civil debate and discourse. Today it seems quite acceptable to attack the Court and other institutions when one disagrees with an opinion or policy.

I can still remember traveling along Highway 17 in south Georgia, the Coastal Highway, during the '50s and '60s and seeing the "Impeach Earl Warren" signs. Clearly, heated reactions to the Court or to its members are not unusual. Certainly, Justice Blackmun was attacked repeatedly because many disagreed, as I have, with the opinion he offered on behalf of the Court in Roe vs. Wade. Though I have joined opinions disagreeing with Justice Blackmun, I could not imagine ever being discourteous to him merely because we disagreed.

I have found during my almost 20 years in Washington that the tendency to personalize differences has grown to be an accepted way of doing business. One need not do the hard work of dissecting an argument. One need only attack and thus discredit the person making the argument. Though the matter being debated is not effectively resolved, the debate is reduced to unilateral pronouncements and glib but quotable clichés.

I, for one, have been singled out for particularly bilious and venomous assaults. These criticisms, as near as I can tell, and I admit that it is rare that I take notice of this calumny, have little to do with any particular opinion, though each opinion does provide one more occasion to criticize. Rather, the principal problem seems to be a deeper antecedent offense. I have no right to think the way I do because I'm black.

Though the ideas and opinions themselves are not necessarily illegitimate if held by non-black individuals, they, and the person enunciating them, are illegitimate if that person happens to be black. Thus, there's a subset of criticism that must of necessity be reserved for me, even if every non-black member of the Court agrees with the idea or the opinion. You see, they are exempt from this kind of criticism, precisely because they are not black. As noted earlier, they are more often than not subjected to the whites-only sophisticated analysis.

I will not catalogue my opinions to which there have been objections since they are a matter of public record. But I must note in passing that I can't help but wonder if some of my critics can read.

One opinion that is trotted out for propaganda, for the propaganda parade, is my dissent in Hudson vs. McMillian. The conclusion reached by the long arms of the critics is that I supported the beating of prisoners in that case. Well, one must either be illiterate or fraught with malice to reach that conclusion.

Though one can disagree with my dissent, and certainly the majority of the Court disagreed, no honest reading can reach such a conclusion. Indeed, we took the case to decide the quite narrow issue, whether a prisoner's rights were violated under the "cruel and unusual punishment" clause of the Eighth Amendment as a result of a single incident of force by the prison guards which did not cause a significant injury.

In the first section of my dissent, I stated the following. "In my view, a use of force that causes only insignificant harm to a prisoner may be immoral; it may be tortuous; it may be criminal, and it may even be remediable under other provisions of the Federal Constitution. But it is not cruel and unusual punishment."

Obviously, beating prisoners is bad. But we did not take the case to answer this larger moral question or a larger legal question of remedies under other statutes or provisions of the Constitution. How one can extrapolate these larger conclusions from the narrow question before the Court is beyond me, unless, of course, there's a special segregated mode of analysis.

It should be obvious that the criticism of this opinion serves not to present counter-arguments, but to discredit and attack me because I've deviated from the prescribed path. In his intriguing and thoughtful essay on "My Race Problem and Ours," Harvard law professor Randall Kennedy, a self-described social Democrat, correctly observes that "if racial loyalty is deemed essentially and morally virtuous, then a black person's adoption of positions that are deemed racially disloyal will be seen by racial loyalists as a supremely threatening sin, one warranting the harsh punishments that have historically been visited upon alleged traitors." Perhaps this is the defensive solidarity to which Richard Wright refers. If so, it is a reaction I understand, but resolutely decline to follow.

In the final weeks of my seminary days, shortly after Dr. King's death, I found myself becoming consumed by feelings of animosity and anger. I was disenchanted with my church and my country. I was tired of being in the minority, and I was tired of turning the other cheek. I, along with many blacks, found ways to protest and try to change the treatment we received in this country. Perhaps my passion for Richard Wright novels was affecting me. Perhaps it was listening too intently to Nina Simone. Perhaps, like Bigger Thomas, I was being consumed by the circumstances in which I found myself, circumstances that I saw as responding only to race.

My feelings were reaffirmed during the summer of 1968 as a result of the lingering stench of racism in Savannah and the assassination of Bobby Kennedy. No matter what the reasons were, I closed out the '60s as one angry young man waiting on the revolution that I was certain would soon come. I saw no way out. I, like many others, felt the deep chronic agony of anomie and alienation. All seemed to be defined by race. We became a reaction to the "man," his ominous reflection.

The intensity of my feelings was reinforced by other events of the late '60s, the riots, the marches, the sense that something had to be done, done quickly to resolve the issue of race. In college there was an air of excitement, apprehension and anger. We started the Black Students Union. We protested. We worked in the Free Breakfast Program. We would walk out of school in the winter of 1969 in protest.

But the questioning for me started in the spring of 1970 after an unauthorized demonstration in Cambridge, Massachusetts, to "free the political prisoners." Why was I doing this rather than using my intellect? Perhaps I was empowered by the anger and relieved that I could now strike back at the faceless oppressor. But why was I conceding my intellect and rather fighting much like a brute? This I could not answer, except to say that I was tired of being restrained.

> I am a man,
> A black man,
> An American.

Somehow I knew that unless I contained the anger within me I would suffer the fates of Bigger Thomas and Cross Damon. It was intoxicating to act upon one's rage, to wear it on one's shoulder, to be defined by it. Yet, ultimately, it was destructive, and I knew it.

So in the spring of 1970, in a nihilistic fog, I prayed that I'd be relieved of the anger and the animosity that ate at my soul. I did not want to hate any more, and I had to stop before it totally consumed me. I had to make a fundamental choice. Do I believe in the principles of this country or not? After such angst, I concluded that I did. But the battle between passion and reason would continue, although abated, still intense.

Ironically, many of the people who are critics today were among those we called half-steppers, who had [been] co-opted by "the man" because they were part of the system that oppressed us. When the revolution came, all of the so-called Negroes needed to be dealt with. It is interesting to remember that someone gave me a copy of Professor Thomas Sowell's book, *Education, Myths and Tragedies,* in which he predicted much of what has happened to blacks and education. I threw it in the trash, unread, declaring that he was not a black man since no black could take the positions that he had taken, whatever they were, since I had only heard his views were not those of a black man.

I was also upset to hear of a black conservative in Virginia named Jay Parker. How could a black man call himself a conservative? In a twist of fate, they both are dear friends today, and the youthful wrath I visited upon them is now being visited upon me, though without the youth.

What goes around does indeed come around.

The summer of 1971 was perhaps one of the most difficult of my life. It was clear to me that the road to destruction was paved with anger, resentment and rage. But where were we to go? I would often spend hours in our small efficiency apartment in New Haven pondering this question and listening to Marvin Gaye's then new album, "What's Going On?"

To say the least, it was a depressing summer. What were we to do? What's going on?

As I think back on those years, I find it interesting that many people seemed to have trouble with their identities as black men. Having had to accept my blackness in the cauldron of ridicule from some of my black schoolmates under segregation, then immediately thereafter remain secure in that identity during my years at an all-white seminary, I had few racial identity problems. I knew who I was and needed no gimmicks to affirm my identity. Nor, might I add, do I need anyone telling me who I am today. This is especially true of the psycho-silliness about forgetting my roots or self-hatred.

If anything, this shows that some people have too much time on their hands. There's a rush today to prescribe who is black, to prescribe what [are] our differences, or to ignore what our differences are. Of course, those of us who came from the rural South were different from the blacks who came from the large northern cities, such as Philadelphia and New York. We were all black. But that similarity did not mask the richness of our differences. Indeed, one of the advantages of growing up in a black neighborhood was that we were richly blessed with the ability to see the individuality of each black person with all its fullness and complexity. We saw those differences at school, at home, at church, and definitely at the barbershop on Saturday morning.

Intra-racially, we consistently recognized our differences. It is quite counter-factual to suggest that such differences have not existed throughout our history. Indeed, when I was on the other side of the ideological divide, arguing strenuously with my grandfather that the revolution was imminent and that we all had to stick together as black people, he was quick to remind me that he had lived much longer than I had, and during far more difficult times, and that, in any case, it took all kinds to make a world.

I agree with Ralph Ellison when he asked, perhaps rhetorically, why is it that so many of those who would tell us the meaning of Negro, of Negro life, never bothered to learn how varied it really is. That is particularly true of many whites who have elevated condescension to an art form by advancing a monolithic view of blacks in much the same way that the mythic, disgusting image of the lazy, dumb black was advanced by open, rather than disguised, bigots.

Today, of course, it is customary to collapse, if not overwrite, our individual characteristics into new, but now acceptable stereotypes. It no longer matters whether one is from urban New York City or rural Georgia. It doesn't matter whether we came from a highly educated family or a barely literate one. It does not matter if you are a Roman Catholic or a Southern Baptist. All of these differences are canceled by race, and a revised set of acceptable stereotypes has been put in place.

Long gone is the time when we opposed the notion that we all looked alike and talked alike. Somehow we have come to exalt the new black stereotype above all and to demand conformity to that norm. It is this notion—that our race defines us—that Ralph Ellison so eloquently rebuts in his essay, "The World and the Jug." He sees the lives of black people as more than a burden, but also a discipline, just as any human life which has endured so long is a discipline, teaching its own insights into the human condition, its own strategies of survival. There's a fullness and even a richness here. And here despite the realities of politics, perhaps, but nevertheless here and real because it is human life.

Despite some of the nonsense that has been said about me by those who should know better, and so much nonsense, or some of which subtracts from the sum total of human knowledge, despite this all, I am a man, a black man, an American. And my history is not unlike that of many blacks from the deep South. And in many ways it is not that much different from that of many other Americans.

It goes without saying that I understand the comforts and security of racial solidarity, defensive or otherwise. Only those who have not been set upon by hatred and repelled by rejection fail to understand its attraction. As I have suggested, I have been there. The inverse relationship between the bold promises and the effectiveness of the proposed solutions, the frustrations with the so-called system, the subtle and not-so-subtle bigotry and animus towards members of my race made radicals and nationalists of many of us. Yes, I understand the reasons why this is attractive. But it is precisely this—in its historic form, not its present-day diluted form—that I have rejected.

My question was whether as an individual I truly believed that I was the equal of individuals who were white. This I had answered with a resounding "yes" in 1964 during my sophomore year in the seminary. And that answer continues to be yes. Accordingly, my words and my deeds are consistent with this answer.

Any effort, policy or program that has as a prerequisite the acceptance of the notion that blacks are inferior is a non-starter with me. I do not believe that kneeling is a position of strength. Nor do I believe that begging is an effective tactic. I am confident that the individual approach, not the group approach, is the better, more acceptable, more supportable and less dangerous one. This approach is also consistent with the underlying principles of this country and the guarantees of freedom through government by consent. I, like Frederick Douglass, believe that whites and blacks can live together and be blended into a common nationality.

Do I believe that my views or opinions are perfect or infallible? No, I do not. But in admitting that I have no claim to perfection or infallibility, I am also asserting that competing or differing views similarly have no such claim. And they should not be accorded a status of infallibility or any status that suggests otherwise.

With differing, but equally fallible views, I think it is best that they be aired and sorted out in an environment of civility, consistent with the institutions in which we are involved—in this case, the judicial system.

It pains me deeply, or more deeply than any of you can imagine, to be perceived by so many members of my race as doing them harm. All the sacrifice, all the long hours of preparation were to help, not to hurt. But what hurts more, much more, is the amount of time and attention spent on manufactured controversies and media sideshows when so many problems cry out for constructive attention.

I have come here today not in anger or to anger, though my mere presence has been sufficient, obviously, to anger some. Nor have I come to defend my views, but rather to assert my right to think for myself, to refuse to have my ideas assigned to me as though I was an intellectual slave because I'm black. I come to state that I'm a man, free to think for myself and do as I please. I've come to assert that I am a judge and I will not be consigned the unquestioned opinions of others.

But even more than that, I have come to say that isn't it time to move on? Isn't it time to realize that being angry with me solves no problems?

Isn't it time to acknowledge that the problem of race has defied simple solutions and that not one of us, not a single one of us can lay claim to the solution?

Isn't it time that we respect ourselves and each other as we have demanded respect from others?

Isn't it time to ignore those whose sole occupation is sowing seeds of discord and animus? That is self-hatred.

Isn't it time to continue diligently to search for lasting solutions?

I believe that the time has come today.

God bless each of you, and may God keep you.

Acceptance Speech:
Prince of Asturias Award for Literature

Leonard Cohen
Poet and Musician

This presentation was given in Oviedo, Spain, on October 21, 2011, when Leonard Cohen accepted the Prince of Asturias Award for Literature. Thanks to the Fundación Princesa de Asturias for including Cohen's speech on its website.

It is a great honor to stand here before you tonight. Perhaps, like the great maestro, Riccardo Muti, I'm not used to standing in front of an audience without an orchestra behind me, but I will do my best as a solo artist tonight.

I stayed up all night last night wondering what I might say to this assembly. After I had eaten all the chocolate bars and peanuts from the minibar, I scribbled a few words. I don't think I have to refer to them. Obviously, I'm deeply touched to be recognized by the Foundation. But I have come here tonight to express another dimension of gratitude; I think I can do it in three or four minutes and I will try.

When I was packing in Los Angeles, I had a sense of unease because I've always felt some ambiguity about an award for poetry. Poetry comes from a place that no one commands, that no one conquers. So I feel somewhat like a charlatan to accept an award for an activity which I do not command. In other words, if I knew where the good songs came from I would go there more often.

I was compelled in the midst of that ordeal of packing to go and open my guitar.

I have a Conde guitar, which was made in Spain in the great workshop at Number 7 Gravina Street. I pick[ed] up an instrument I acquired over 40 years ago. I took it out of the case, I lifted it, and it seemed to be filled with helium it was so light. And I brought it to my face and I put my face close to the beautifully designed rosette, and I inhaled the fragrance of the living wood. You know that wood never dies. I inhaled the fragrance of the cedar as fresh as the first day that I acquired the guitar. And a voice seemed to say to me, "You are an old man, and you have not said thank you, you have not brought your gratitude back to the soil from which this fragrance arose." And so I come here tonight to thank the soil and the soul of this land that has given me so much. Because I know that just as an identity card is not a man, a credit rating is not a country.

Now, you know of my deep association and confraternity with the poet Federico García Lorca. I could say that when I was a young man, an adolescent, and I hungered for a voice, I studied the English poets and I knew their work well, and I copied their styles, but I could not find a voice. It was only when I read, even in translation, the works of Lorca that I understood that there was a voice. It is not that I copied his voice; I would not dare. But he gave me permission to find a voice, to locate a voice, that is to locate a self, a self that is not fixed, a self that struggles for its own existence. As I grew older, I understood that instructions came with this voice. What were these instructions? The instructions were never to lament casually. And if one is to express the great inevitable defeat that awaits us all, it must be done within the strict confines of dignity and beauty.

And so I had a voice, but I did not have an instrument. I did not have a song.

And now I'm going to tell you very briefly a story of how I got my song.

Because I was an indifferent guitar player, I managed a few chords. I only knew a few of them. I sat around with my college friends, drinking and singing the folk songs and the popular songs of the day, but I never in a thousand years thought of myself as a musician or as a singer.

One day in the early sixties, I was visiting my mother's house in Montreal. Her house is beside a park and in the park was a tennis court where many people come to watch the beautiful young tennis players enjoy their sport. I wandered back to this park, which I'd known since my childhood, and there was a young man playing a guitar. He was playing a flamenco guitar, and he was surrounded by two or three girls and boys who were listening to him. I loved the way he played. There was something about the way he played that captured me. It was the way that I wanted to play and knew that I would never be able to play.

And, I sat there with the other listeners for a few moments and when there was a silence, an appropriate silence, I asked him if he would give me guitar lessons. He was a young man from Spain, and we could only communicate in my broken French and his broken French. He didn't speak English. And he agreed to give me guitar lessons. I pointed to my mother's house, which you could see from the tennis court, and we made an appointment and settled a price.

He came to my mother's house the next day and he said, "Let me hear you play something." I tried to play something, and he said, "You don't know how to play, do you?"

I said, "No, I don't know how to play." He said, "First of all, let me tune your guitar. It's all out of tune." So he took the guitar, and he tuned it. He said, "It's not a bad guitar." It wasn't the Conde, but it wasn't a bad guitar. So, he handed it back to me. He said, "Now play." I couldn't play any better.

He said "Let me show you some chords." And he took the guitar, and he produced a sound from that guitar I had never heard. And he played a sequence of chords with a tremolo, and he said, "Now you do it." I said, "It's out of the question. I can't possibly do it." He said, "Let me put your fingers on the frets," and he put my fingers on the frets. And he said, "Now, now play." It was a mess. He said, "I'll come back tomorrow."

He came back tomorrow, he put my hands on the guitar, he placed it on my lap in the way that was appropriate, and I began again with those six chords—a six-chord progression that many, many flamenco songs are based on. I was a little better that day. The third day—improved, somewhat improved. But I knew the chords now. And, I knew that although I couldn't coordinate my fingers with my thumb to produce the correct tremolo pattern, I knew the chords; I knew them very, very well by this point.

The next day, he didn't come. He didn't come. I had the number of his, of his boarding house in Montreal. I phoned to find out why he had missed the appointment, and they told me that he had taken his life. That he committed suicide.

I knew nothing about the man. I did not know what part of Spain he came from. I did not know why he came to Montreal. I did not know why he stayed there. I did not know why he appeared there at that tennis court. I did not know why he took his life. I was deeply saddened, of course.

But now I disclose something that I've never spoken in public. It was those six chords, it was that guitar pattern that has been the basis of all my songs and all my music. So, now you will begin to understand the dimensions of the gratitude I have for this country.

Everything that you have found favorable in my work comes from this place. Everything, everything that you have found favorable in my songs and my poetry are inspired by this soil.

So, I thank you so much for the warm hospitality that you have shown my work because it is really yours, and you have allowed me to affix my signature to the bottom of the page.

Thank you so much, ladies and gentlemen.

Self-Introduction

Nancy Milton
Author, Coach, and Motivational Speaker

At meetings, individuals are often asked to go around the room and introduce themselves. Nancy Milton developed this self-introduction to avoid the typical introduction most people give on such occasions— name, occupation, number of children, and interests. She posted this sample introduction on January 30, 2012, on YouTube. She describes the process by which she arrived at this introduction in more detail in her book, The Happy Place *(Bloomington, IN: iUniverse, 2013), chapter 1. Used with permission of Nancy Milton.*

I love ice cream so much it scares me. Fresh air is fresh perspective for me. If I start my day with a jog, it's a brand-new day. And if I end it with a walk, I'm set, and I have a great night's sleep. Vulnerability is really important to me and taking risks in life. If it doesn't scare me, it's not worth doing. I'm Nancy Milton.

Articulating a Perspective

City Planning as a Career

Andrea Armstrong
Student, Ohio State University

In this presentation, Andrea Armstrong assumed the role of a city planner, speaking to first-grade students on career day. Used with permission of Andrea Armstrong.

Hi, I'm Ms. Armstrong, and I'm a city planner for the city of Columbus. I'd like to ask you a couple questions. Do any of you have a favorite city?
Student: Columbus.
Columbus? Anybody else?
Student: Chicago.
Chicago? Yes?
Student: Las Vegas.
What do you all like about Columbus, since that's where we're living right now?
Student: The zoo.
Student: I like the playgrounds.
The playgrounds? Anything else?
Student: It doesn't take long to get anywhere.
Student: The fair.
The fair—the state fair. You like going to the fair? I like going to the fair, too. OK, those are some of the things you like about Columbus, but a long time ago, cities weren't such nice places to be. There were a lot of factories, there was a lot of smoke, cities were crowded, and there weren't very many parks. Kids actually used to have to play in cemeteries because there weren't parks in their neighborhoods to play in—that was the only green space they could find. That was before planning. What planners try to do is to make places nicer for people. They make cities places where people want to live and want to be.

Planners try to make cities better in a lot of different ways. For instance, they try to decide where schools should be. They try to make sure that there are enough parks and playgrounds in neighborhoods for families and friends to play in. They have to make sure there are police and fire services for everyone in the city. They need to make sure that there are enough water lines and sewer lines. They have to make sure that buildings are built correctly.

City planners have to know a lot about a lot of things. They have to know about law because they have to know laws that affect where and how things can be built. City planners also have to be good public speakers because they have to explain ideas and plans to people. They need to be architects and engineers—they need to know how things are built and how they can be built. They need to be computer users; they use computers to figure things out. They need to be demographers—they need to know how to use numbers and statistics and to figure out how many people are in cities.

City planners also need to be mapmakers. I've brought along a few of the maps I use at work every day. These are the kinds of maps that planners use and make. The first map is an annexation map. Annexation is how a city grows—how it gets more land. The purple area in this map shows Columbus in 1900; that's all the bigger Columbus was in 1900. If any of you have a grandmother who is 93 years old, that's how big Columbus was when she was born. Today, Columbus is as big as all the areas that are colored on this map. Planners need to know this, and they need to be able to provide services in all these areas. They need to make sure that there are police, fire, water, and roads and everything for all this area.

Your school is in this area, near the river. City planners need to know where the flood plain is for the river. We have something called 100- and 500-year floods. That means that we have a 1-in-100 chance to get a flood or a 1-in-500 chance to get a flood, which means the river will go outside of its banks. We need to know this so we don't build in those flood plains—people lose their houses and belongings if they do. Ohio State University's campus is located right here. It is in part of the flood plain, so part of this land may flood. We need to know that ahead of time.

This map shows flight contours for the airport, which is west of town—Port Columbus Airport. Every line on here is how loud the noise is from the air traffic in the air. We need to know this because nobody wants to live within these noise contours because it's loud, it hurts our ears, it's not good for our health. We need to make sure we don't build in those areas—it's not good for us.

Finally, we need to know where fire stations are located in our city. We need to make sure that if your house catches on fire, there's a fire station nearby that will be able to put the fire out. All the red circles are Columbus fire stations.

There are planning issues going on now that you might have heard about in the news or from your parents. The Tuttle Crossing area is a planning issue in Columbus. This is a mall that's being developed on the north side of town. It involves city planners who are trying to do all the things necessary to make sure the mall is a nice place.

So, planners do a lot of different things in their jobs. They have to know a lot of different things. Planning is a good profession for people who are curious. So, if you're a curious person and like to do a lot of different things, planning might be a profession for you someday.

A More Perfect Union

Barack Obama
US Presidential Candidate

This presentation was given at the National Constitution Center in Philadelphia, Pennsylvania, on March 18, 2008, during Barack Obama's presidential campaign. Thanks to Obamaspeeches.com for including Obama's speech on its website.

"We the people, in order to form a more perfect union."

Two-hundred-and-twenty-one years ago, in a hall that still stands across the street, a group of men gathered and, with these simple words, launched America's improbable experiment in democracy. Farmers and scholars, statesmen and patriots who had traveled across the ocean to escape tyranny and persecution finally made real their Declaration of Independence at a Philadelphia convention that lasted through the spring of 1787.

The document they produced was eventually signed but ultimately unfinished. It was stained by this nation's original sin of slavery, a question that divided the colonies and brought the convention to a stalemate until the founders chose to allow the slave trade to continue for at least twenty more years, and to leave any final resolution to future generations.

Of course, the answer to the slavery question was already embedded within our Constitution—a Constitution that had at its very core the ideal of equal citizenship under the law; a Constitution that promised its people liberty, and justice, and a union that could be and should be perfected over time.

And yet words on a parchment would not be enough to deliver slaves from bondage, or provide men and women of every color and creed their full rights and obligations as citizens of the United States. What would be needed were Americans in successive generations who were willing to do their part—through protests and struggle, on the streets and in the courts, through a civil war and civil disobedience and always at great risk—to narrow that gap between the promise of our ideals and the reality of their time.

This was one of the tasks we set forth at the beginning of this campaign—to continue the long march of those who came before us, a march for a more just, more equal, more free, more caring, and more prosperous America. I chose to run for the presidency at this moment in history because I believe deeply that we cannot solve the challenges of our time unless we solve them together—unless we perfect our union by understanding that we may have different stories, but we hold common hopes; that we may not look the same and may not have come from the same place, but we all want to move in the same direction—towards a better future for our children and our grandchildren.

And this belief comes from my unyielding faith in the decency and generosity of the American people. But it also comes from my own American story.

I am the son of a black man from Kenya and a white woman from Kansas. I was raised with the help of a white grandfather who survived a Depression to serve in Patton's Army during World War II and a white grandmother who worked on a bomber assembly line at Fort Leavenworth while he was overseas. I've gone to some of the best schools in America and lived in one of the world's poorest nations. I am married to a black American who carries within her the blood of slaves and slave owners—an inheritance we pass on to our two precious daughters. I have brothers, sisters, nieces, nephews, uncles and cousins, of every race and every hue, scattered across three continents, and for as long as I live, I will never forget that in no other country on Earth is my story even possible.

It's a story that hasn't made me the most conventional candidate. But it is a story that has seared into my genetic makeup the idea that this nation is more than the sum of its parts—that out of many, we are truly one.

Throughout the first year of this campaign, against all predictions to the contrary, we saw how hungry the American people were for this message of unity. Despite the temptation to view my candidacy through a purely racial lens, we won commanding victories in states with some of the whitest populations in the country. In South Carolina, where the Confederate flag still flies, we built a powerful coalition of African Americans and white Americans.

This is not to say that race has not been an issue in this campaign. At various stages in the campaign, some commentators have deemed me either "too black" or "not black enough." We saw racial tensions bubble to the surface during the week before the South Carolina primary. The press has scoured every exit poll for the latest evidence of racial polarization, not just in terms of white and black but black and brown as well.

And yet, it's only been in the last couple of weeks that the discussion of race in this campaign has taken a particularly divisive turn.

On one end of the spectrum, we've heard the implication that my candidacy is somehow an exercise in affirmative action; that it's based solely on the desire of wide-eyed liberals to purchase racial reconciliation on the cheap. On the other end, we've heard my former pastor, Reverend Jeremiah Wright, use incendiary language to express views that have the potential not only to widen the racial divide, but views that denigrate both the greatness and the goodness of our nation; that rightly offend white and black alike.

I have already condemned, in unequivocal terms, the statements of Reverend Wright that have caused such controversy. For some, nagging questions remain: Did I know him to be an occasionally fierce critic of American domestic and foreign policy? Of course. Did I ever hear him make remarks that could be considered controversial while I sat in church? Yes. Did I strongly disagree with many of his political views? Absolutely—just as I'm sure many of you have heard remarks from your pastors, priests, or rabbis with which you strongly disagreed.

But the remarks that have caused this recent firestorm weren't simply controversial. They weren't simply a religious leader's efforts to speak out against perceived injustice. Instead, they expressed a profoundly distorted view of this country—a view that sees white racism as endemic, and that elevates what is wrong with America above all that we know is right with America; a view that sees the conflicts in the Middle East as rooted primarily in the actions of stalwart allies like Israel, instead of emanating from the perverse and hateful ideologies of radical Islam.

As such, Reverend Wright's comments were not only wrong but divisive, divisive at a time when we need unity; racially charged at a time when we need to come together to solve a set of monumental problems—two wars, a terrorist threat, a falling economy, a chronic health care crisis, and potentially devastating climate change; problems that are neither black or white or Latino or Asian but rather problems that confront us all.

Given my background, my politics, and my professed values and ideals, there will no doubt be those for whom my statements of condemnation are not enough. Why associate myself with Reverend Wright in the first place, they may ask? Why not join another church? And I confess that if all that I knew of Reverend Wright were the snippets of those sermons that have run in an endless loop on the television sets and YouTube, if Trinity United Church of Christ conformed to the caricatures being peddled by some commentators, there is no doubt that I would react in much the same way.

But the truth is, that isn't all that I know of the man. The man I met more than 20 years ago is a man who helped introduce me to my Christian faith, a man who spoke to me about our obligations to love one another; to care for the sick and lift up the poor. He is a man who served his country as a U.S. Marine; who has studied and lectured at some of the finest universities and seminaries in the country, and who over 30 years led a church that serves the community by doing God's work here on Earth—by housing the homeless, ministering to the needy, providing day-care services and scholarships and prison ministries, and reaching out to those suffering from HIV/AIDS.

In my first book, *Dreams from My Father*, I described the experience of my first service at Trinity:

> "People began to shout, to rise from their seats and clap and cry out, a forceful wind carrying the reverend's voice up to the rafters. . . . And in that single note—hope—I heard something else; at the foot of that cross, inside the thousands of churches across the city, I imagined the stories of ordinary black people merging with the stories of David and Goliath, Moses and Pharaoh, the Christians in the lion's

den, Ezekiel's field of dry bones. Those stories—of survival and free-dom, and hope—became our story, my story; the blood that had spilled was our blood; the tears our tears; until this black church, on this bright day, seemed once more a vessel carrying the story of a people into future generations and into a larger world. Our trials and triumphs became at once unique and universal, black and more than black; in chronicling our journey, the stories and songs gave us a means to reclaim memories that we didn't need to feel shame about . . . memories that all people might study and cherish—and with which we could start to rebuild."

That has been my experience at Trinity. Like other predominantly black churches across the country, Trinity embodies the black community in its entirety—the doctor and the welfare mom, the model student and the former gang-banger. Like other black churches, Trinity's services are full of raucous laughter and sometimes bawdy humor. They are full of dancing, clapping, screaming and shouting that may seem jarring to the untrained ear. The church contains in full the kindness and cruelty, the fierce intelligence and the shocking ignorance, the struggles and suc-cesses, the love and yes, the bitterness and bias that make up the black experience in America.

And this helps explain, perhaps, my relationship with Reverend Wright. As imperfect as he may be, he has been like family to me. He strengthened my faith, officiated my wedding, and baptized my children. Not once in my conversations with him have I heard him talk about any ethnic group in derogatory terms, or treat whites with whom he inter-acted with anything but courtesy and respect. He contains within him the contradictions—the good and the bad—of the community that he has served diligently for so many years.

I can no more disown him than I can disown the black community. I can no more disown him than I can my white grandmother—a woman who helped raise me, a woman who sacrificed again and again for me, a woman who loves me as much as she loves anything in this world, but a woman who once confessed her fear of black men who passed her by on the street and who on more than one occasion has uttered racial or eth-nic stereotypes that made me cringe.

These people are part of me. And they are part of America, this coun-try that I love.

Some will see this as an attempt to justify or excuse comments that are simply inexcusable. I can assure you it is not. I suppose the politically safe thing to do would be to move on from this episode and just hope that it fades into the woodwork. We can dismiss Reverend Wright as a crank or a demagogue, just as some have dismissed Geraldine Ferraro in the aftermath of her recent statements as harboring some deep-seated bias.

But race is an issue that I believe this nation cannot afford to ignore right now. We would be making the same mistake that Reverend Wright made in his offending sermons about America—to simplify and stereo-type and amplify the negative to the point that it distorts reality.

The fact is that the comments that have been made and the issues that have surfaced over the last few weeks reflect the complexities of race in this country that we've never really worked through--a part of our union that we have yet to perfect. And if we walk away now, if we simply retreat into our respective corners, we will never be able to come together and solve challenges like health care, or education, or the need to find good jobs for every American.

Understanding this reality requires a reminder of how we arrived at this point. As William Faulkner once wrote, "The past isn't dead and bur-ied. In fact, it isn't even past." We do not need to recite here the history of racial injustice in this country. But we do need to remind ourselves that so many of the disparities that exist in the African-American community today can be directly traced to inequalities passed on from an earlier gen-eration that suffered under the brutal legacy of slavery and Jim Crow.

Segregated schools were, and are, inferior schools; we still haven't fixed them fifty years after Brown vs. Board of Education, and the inferior education they provided, then and now, helps explain the pervasive achievement gap between today's black and white students.

Legalized discrimination—where blacks were prevented, often through violence, from owning property, or loans were not granted to African-American business owners, or black homeowners could not access FHA mortgages, or blacks were excluded from unions, or the police force, or fire departments—meant that black families could not amass any meaningful wealth to bequeath to future generations. That history helps explain the wealth and income gap between black and white, and the concentrated pockets of poverty that persist in so many of today's urban and rural communities.

A lack of economic opportunity among black men, and the shame and frustration that came from not being able to provide for one's family, con-tributed to the erosion of black families—a problem that welfare policies for many years may have worsened. And the lack of basic services in so many urban black neighborhoods—parks for kids to play in, police walking the beat, regular garbage pick-up, and building code enforcement—all helped create a cycle of violence, blight and neglect that continues to haunt us.

This is the reality in which Reverend Wright and other African Amer-icans of his generation grew up. They came of age in the late fifties and early sixties, a time when segregation was still the law of the land and opportunity was systematically constricted. What's remarkable is not how many failed in the face of discrimination, but rather how many men and women overcame the odds, how many were able to make a way out of no way for those like me who would come after them.

But for all those who scratched and clawed their way to get a piece of the American Dream, there were many who didn't make it—those who were ultimately defeated, in one way or another, by discrimination. That legacy of defeat was passed on to future generations—those young men and increasingly young women who we see standing on street corners or languishing in our prisons, without hope or prospects for the future. Even for those blacks who did make it, questions of race, and racism, continue to define their worldview in fundamental ways. For the men and women of Reverend Wright's generation, the memories of humiliation and doubt and fear have not gone away; nor has the anger and the bitterness of those years. That anger may not get expressed in public, in front of white co-workers or white friends. But it does find voice in the barbershop or the beauty shop or around the kitchen table. At times, that anger is exploited by politicians to gin up votes along racial lines or to make up for a politician's own failings.

And occasionally it finds voice in the church on Sunday morning, in the pulpit, and in the pews. The fact that so many people are surprised to hear that anger in some of Reverend Wright's sermons simply reminds us of the old truism that the most segregated hour of American life occurs on Sunday morning. That anger is not always productive; indeed, all too often it distracts attention from solving real problems; it keeps us from squarely facing our own complicity in our own condition, and prevents the African-American community from forging the alliances it needs to bring about real change. But the anger is real; it is powerful; and to simply wish it away, to condemn it without understanding its roots, only serves to widen the chasm of misunderstanding that exists between the races.

In fact, a similar anger exists within segments of the white community. Most working- and middle-class white Americans don't feel that they have been particularly privileged by their race. Their experience is the immigrant experience—as far as they're concerned, no one handed them anything, they've built it from scratch. They've worked hard all their lives, many times only to see their jobs shipped overseas or their pensions dumped after a lifetime of labor. They are anxious about their futures, and they feel their dreams slipping away; in an era of stagnant wages and global competition, opportunity comes to be seen as a zero sum game, in which your dreams come at my expense. So when they are told to bus their children to a school across town; when they hear that an African American is getting an advantage in landing a good job or a spot in a good college because of an injustice that they themselves never committed; when they're told that their fears about crime in urban neighborhoods are somehow prejudiced, resentment builds over time.

Like the anger within the black community, these resentments aren't always expressed in polite company. But they have helped shape the political landscape for at least a generation. Anger over welfare and affirmative action helped forge the Reagan coalition. Politicians routinely exploited fears of crime for their own electoral ends. Talk show hosts and conservative commentators built entire careers unmasking bogus claims of racism while dismissing legitimate discussions of racial injustice and inequality as mere political correctness or reverse racism.

Just as black anger often proved counterproductive, so have these white resentments distracted attention from the real culprits of the middle class squeeze—a corporate culture rife with inside dealing, questionable accounting practices, and short-term greed; a Washington dominated by lobbyists and special interests; economic policies that favor the few over the many. And yet, to wish away the resentments of white Americans, to label them as *misguided* or even *racist* without recognizing they are grounded in legitimate concerns—this too widens the racial divide, and blocks the path to understanding.

This is where we are right now. It's a racial stalemate we've been stuck in for years. And contrary to the claims of some of my critics, black and white, I have never been so naïve as to believe that we can get beyond our racial divisions in a single election cycle, or with a single candidacy—particularly a candidacy as imperfect as my own.

But I have asserted a firm conviction—a conviction rooted in my faith in God and my faith in the American people—that working together we can move beyond some of our old racial wounds, and that in fact we have no choice if we are to continue on the path of a more perfect union.

For the African-American community, that path means embracing the burdens of our past without becoming victims of our past. It means continuing to insist on a full measure of justice in every aspect of American life. But it also means binding our particular grievances—for better health care, and better schools, and better jobs—to the larger aspirations of all Americans—the white woman struggling to break the glass ceiling, the white man who's been laid off, the immigrant trying to feed his family. And it means taking full responsibility for our own lives—by demanding more from our fathers, and spending more time with our children, and reading to them, and teaching them that while they may face challenges and discrimination in their own lives, they must never succumb to despair or cynicism; they must always believe that they can write their own destiny.

Ironically, this quintessentially American—and, yes, conservative—notion of self-help found frequent expression in Reverend Wright's sermons. But what my former pastor too often failed to understand is that embarking on a program of self-help also requires a belief that society can change.

The profound mistake of Reverend Wright's sermons is not that he spoke about racism in our society. It's that he spoke as if our society was static; as if no progress had been made; as if this country—a country that has made it possible for one of his own members to run for the highest office in the land and build a coalition of white and black, Latino, Asian, rich, poor, young and old—is still irrevocably bound to a tragic past. But what we know—what we have seen—is that America can change. That is the true genius of this nation. What we have already achieved gives us hope—the audacity to hope—for what we can and must achieve tomorrow.

In the white community, the path to a more perfect union means acknowledging that what ails the African-American community does not just exist in the minds of black people; that the legacy of discrimination—and current incidents of discrimination, while less overt than in the past—these things are real and must be addressed. Not just with words, but with deeds—by investing in our schools and our communities; by enforcing our civil rights laws and ensuring fairness in our criminal justice system; by providing this generation with ladders of opportunity that were unavailable for previous generations. It requires all Americans to realize that your dreams do not have to come at the expense of my dreams; that investing in the health, welfare, and education of black and brown and white children will ultimately help all of America prosper.

In the end, then, what is called for is nothing more, and nothing less, than what all the world's great religions demand—that we do unto others as we would have them do unto us. Let us be our brother's keeper, Scripture tells us. Let us be our sister's keeper. Let us find that common stake we all have in one another, and let our politics reflect that spirit as well.

For we have a choice in this country. We can accept a politics that breeds division, and conflict, and cynicism. We can tackle race only as spectacle—as we did in the OJ trial—or in the wake of tragedy, as we did in the aftermath of Katrina, or as fodder for the nightly news. We can play Reverend Wright's sermons on every channel, every day and talk about them from now until the election, and make the only question in this campaign whether or not the American people think that I somehow believe or sympathize with his most offensive words. We can pounce on some gaffe by a Hillary supporter as evidence that she's playing the race card, or we can speculate on whether white men will all flock to John McCain in the general election regardless of his policies.

We can do that.

But if we do, I can tell you that in the next election, we'll be talking about some other distraction and then another one and then another one. And nothing will change.

That is one option. Or, at this moment, in this election, we can come together and say, "Not this time." This time we want to talk about the crumbling schools that are stealing the future of black children and white children and Asian children and Hispanic children and Native American children. This time we want to reject the cynicism that tells us that these kids can't learn; that those kids who don't look like us are somebody else's problem. The children of America are not those kids, they are our kids, and we will not let them fall behind in a 21st century economy. Not this time.

This time we want to talk about how the lines in the Emergency Room are filled with whites and blacks and Hispanics who do not have health care; who don't have the power on their own to overcome the special interests in Washington, but who can take them on if we do it together.

This time we want to talk about the shuttered mills that once provided a decent life for men and women of every race, and the homes for sale that once belonged to Americans from every religion, every region, every walk of life. This time we want to talk about the fact that the real problem is not that someone who doesn't look like you might take your job; it's that the corporation you work for will ship it overseas for nothing more than a profit.

This time we want to talk about the men and women of every color and creed who serve together, and fight together, and bleed together under the same proud flag. We want to talk about how to bring them home from a war that never should've been authorized and never should've been waged, and we want to talk about how we'll show our patriotism by caring for them, and their families, and giving them the benefits that they have earned.

I would not be running for president if I didn't believe with all my heart that this is what the vast majority of Americans want for this country. This union may never be perfect, but generation after generation has shown that it can always be perfected. And today, whenever I find myself feeling doubtful or cynical about this possibility, what gives me the most hope is the next generation—the young people whose attitudes and beliefs and openness to change have already made history in this election.

There is one story in particular that I'd like to leave you with today— a story I told when I had the great honor of speaking on Dr. King's birthday at his home church, Ebenezer Baptist, in Atlanta.

There is a young, twenty-three-year-old woman, a white woman named *Ashley Baia*, who organized for our campaign in Florence, South Carolina. She'd been working to organize a mostly African-American community since the beginning of this campaign, and one day she was at a roundtable discussion where everyone went around telling their story and why they were there.

And Ashley said that when she was nine years old, her mother got cancer. And because she had to miss days of work, she was let go and lost her health care. They had to file for bankruptcy, and that's when Ashley decided that she had to do something to help her mom.

She knew that food was one of their most expensive costs, and so Ashley convinced her mother that what she really liked and really wanted to eat more than anything else was mustard and relish sandwiches because that was the cheapest way to eat.

She did this for a year until her mom got better, and she told everyone at the roundtable that the reason she had joined our campaign was so that she could help the millions of other children in the country who want and need to help their parents too.

Now Ashley might have made a different choice. Perhaps somebody told her along the way that the source of her mother's problems were blacks who were on welfare and too lazy to work, or Hispanics who were coming into the country illegally. But she didn't. She sought out allies in her fight against injustice.

Anyway, Ashley finishes her story and then goes around the room and asks everyone else why they're supporting the campaign. They all have different stories and different reasons. Many bring up a specific issue. And finally they come to this elderly black man who's been sitting there quietly the entire time. And Ashley asks him why he's there. And he does not bring up a specific issue. He does not say health care or the economy. He does not say education or the war. He does not say that he was there because of Barack Obama. He simply says to everyone in the room, "I am here because of Ashley."

"I'm here because of Ashley." By itself, that single moment of recognition between that young white girl and that old black man is not enough. It is not enough to give health care to the sick, or jobs to the jobless, or education to our children.

But it is where we start. It is where our union grows stronger. And as so many generations have come to realize over the course of the two-hundred and twenty-one years since a band of patriots signed that document right here in Philadelphia, that is where the perfection begins.

A Statement for Voices Unheard:
A Challenge to the National Book Awards

Adrienne Rich, Audre Lorde, and Alice Walker
Writers

At the National Book Award ceremony in New York City, on April 18, 1974, Adrienne Rich read the following statement, prepared by Audre Lorde, Alice Walker, and Rich—all of whom had been nominated for the poetry award. They agreed that whoever was chosen to receive the award from among the three would read the statement. Reprinted with permission of Ms.

We, Audre Lorde, Adrienne Rich, and Alice Walker, together accept this award in the name of all the women whose voices have gone and still go unheard in a patriarchal world, and in the name of those who, like us, have been tolerated as token women in this culture, often at great cost and in great pain. We believe that we can enrich ourselves more in supporting and giving to each other than by competing against each other; and that poetry—if it is poetry—exists in a realm beyond ranking and comparison. We symbolically join together here in refusing the terms of patriarchal competition and declaring that we will share this prize among us, to be used as best we can for women.

We appreciate the good faith of the judges for this award, but none of us could accept this money for herself, nor could she let go unquestioned the terms on which poets are given or denied honor and livelihood in this world, especially when they are women. We dedicate this occasion to the struggle for self-determination of all women, of every color, identification, or derived class: the poet, the housewife, the lesbian, the mathematician, the mother, the dishwasher, the pregnant teenager, the teacher, the grandmother, the prostitute, the philosopher, the waitress, the women who will understand what we are doing here and those who will not understand yet, the silent women whose voices have been denied us, the articulate women who have given us strength to do our work.

Guerilla Gardening

Karen A. Foss
Regents' Professor Emeritus, Communication & Journalism,
University of New Mexico

This presentation was given in Albuquerque, New Mexico, in February 2011, at the grand opening of a garden shop called Urban Store. It was one of several talks and demonstrations related to gardening given as part of the store's opening. Used with permission of Karen A. Foss.

When you think of urban adventure, what comes to mind? Maybe travel and exploring the great cities of the world—Paris, Rome, or Amsterdam. Maybe it means exploring a part of a city you live in but never have taken the time to get to know before. Maybe urban adventure just means visiting the bars on Central Avenue on a Friday night. Today, I'm going to share with you another kind of urban adventure—guerilla gardening—in which you don't just explore your city but actively engage it, beautify it, and have fun at the same time.

We're all familiar with guerrilla warfare: irregular fighting forces that go in, get the job done, and get out. It's warfare by stealth. Guerilla gardening is gardening by stealth. You garden neglected public spaces, without permission, usually in the middle of the night. You get in, do the job, and get out. Projects can range from starting gardens in abandoned lots, grafting fruit trees onto ornamental trees to create food for the homeless, planting primroses in potholes in city streets, weeding, and picking up trash. Some guerilla gardeners have even jackhammered up sections of parking lots to plant trees.

Johnny Appleseed, whose real name was *John Chapman*, was probably one of the first guerilla gardeners. He moved into the frontier, planting apples for cider—usually on land by rivers—land he didn't own. He would then sell the orchards to new settlers moving in, and he himself would move on to plant more orchards. Richard Reynolds, a contemporary guerilla gardener in London, is famous for planting sunflowers in vacant lots all around the Parliament building. There are guerrilla gardening groups all over the world. They materialize in response to a text that asks them to meet at a certain place and time, ready for a gardening adventure.

I became a guerrilla gardener by chance more than by design. I moved into a house downtown, which as some of you may know, is characterized by what I like to call *mixed aesthetics*. Some people keep their houses and yards up nicely, and some don't. One of those who didn't was my neighbor—there were weeds several feet tall in her front yard, and I had to look at them every day. One day, I had an epiphany. I realized that I could weed that yard because while that was not my house, it was my neighborhood, my city, and my world. So about 5:00 a.m. one morning, I headed over and started weeding. Since then, I've weeded yards, trimmed bushes, picked up trash, raked leaves—I'll do what I can to try to help my neighborhood look better.

So what's required if you want to be a guerilla gardener? I've developed an acronym, RATTY, to help you remember the five things you need to be a successful guerilla gardener. It also is a reminder of what a space can look like before the guerilla gardener swoops in—ratty! So what does RATTY stand for?

- **R = Redefine.** You need to redefine your role as a citizen in relation to public and private spaces. When I had my epiphany about dealing with my neighbor's weeds, I had to get comfortable walking into someone's yard and doing what I thought needed to be done. Rather than thinking about my neighborhood as consisting of houses and yards, privately owned by different people, I needed to think more broadly—that these were spaces that essentially "belonged" to all of us in the neighborhood, and we could all help out with them.

- **A = Attitude.** You need a particular attitude to be a good guerrilla gardener. You need a sense of mischief and a whole lot of boldness. Because not only are you essentially trespassing onto other people's property, but you can be arrested as a guerilla gardener—for excavating on public land without a permit, breach of peace, willful damage to property, and disruption of traffic, to name a few.

- **T = Tools.** Certain tools are required for guerilla gardening as well. Most important is a hand trowel, clippers, and some kind of tub or container for carrying your tools and to collect the weeds, trimmings, or trash that you collect. A flashlight is also crucial since you're usually working late at night or in the early morning, and when you put your trowel down, sometimes you can't find it in the dark. And then I had another epiphany, because sometimes it really is too dark at night to see what it is you want to do. If you wear a safety vest and hard hat, you can guerilla garden in broad daylight [here Karen removed her jacket to reveal a safety vest underneath; she also picked up a hard hat from her tub of tools and put it on.] People see what they expect to see, and if you are dressed appropriately, they think you are a city worker tackling some city-approved project.

- **T = Task.** You also need a task, a project, or a mission. What needs to be done in your neighborhood? What do you like to do? Redo landscape that isn't working? Plant some trees? Weed? Plant a garden? The sky's the limit.

- **Y = Yikes.** The last tool you need is what I call *yikes*. It's something to say, a line to use if someone stops you and asks what you're doing. It's that "yikes" moment when you know you're going to have to account for what you're doing, and you say to yourself, "Yikes! What am I doing out here?" So that's when your pre-planned line comes in handy. Mine is: "I'm part of a volunteer group working to improve our neighborhood. Won't you join me?"

I hope I've given you a sense of what guerilla gardening is all about. It is a fun way to have a different kind of urban adventure and, in the process, you're making your neighborhood a better place in which to live. So, "I'm part of a volunteer group working to improve our neighborhood." And maybe the next time a text goes out to meet at midnight for a round of guerilla gardening, I'll see you there!

Building Community

A Flair for Fashion:
A Welcome to New Employees

Erika Fair
Student, Ohio State University

In this presentation, Erika Fair assumed the role of the owner of Erika Fair's Fashion Fair International, welcoming new employees to her company. Used with permission of Erika Fair.

Welcome to Erika Fair's Fashion Fair International. I would personally like to express my congratulations and wishes for good luck to each of you. As you know, you were hired because of your flair for fashion and your sense of individuality. This company is built on employees like you.

As each of you knows, my company has a very individual style. Our clothes express the feminine side of a woman. These clothes are playful yet sophisticated, exciting yet subtle, durable yet delicate. Our clothes say, "I'm a professional, a mother, a wife, and even an athlete." Our clothes are versatile. For example, with this belt and these earrings, this outfit says, "Let's go to work, let's give a speech, or even let's have a romantic dinner." Get rid of the belt, throw on a pair of flats, and it says, "I'm ready for a day of shopping or just a day of relaxation."

This is where you come in. You know our reputation, you know what our clothes say and how to wear them. All you have to do is help build this reputation. As buyers, you are skilled enough to know what Erika Fair says and what it doesn't. I expect each of you to assert your individuality when faced with a buying decision but at the same time to be mindful of the company's look.

Look around you—these are your team members. You need to know each other. You need to be able to work with each other as a family unit, to be able to trust one another's judgments, and, at the same time, to be able to accept one another's downfalls.

You are at the top of the line, and I already cherish each of you as a part of the family. If you ever have a problem, feel free to contact me, even at home, if necessary. Think of these headquarters as your home away from home and me as your mom away from mom. I'm here not as a disciplinarian but as an advisor, friend, and confidante.

You were hired because you are the best at what you do, and you all are here because you know that Erika Fair Fashions is the best: The best working with and for the best—what more can we ask for?

Again, I would like to express my sincere congratulations and wishes of good luck to each of you, and I hope that your experience here at Erika Fair Fashions International is rewarding and exciting for you.

Knock, Knock

Daniel Beaty
Actor, Writer, Singer, and Activist

This presentation is from the play, Emergency, *written by Daniel Beaty (2008). A video of the presentation is available on YouTube. Used with permission of Daniel Beaty, www.DanielBeaty.com.*

As a boy, I shared a game with my father.
Played it every morning 'til I was 3.
He would knock knock on my door,
and I'd pretend to be asleep
'til he got right next to the bed.
Then I would get up and jump into his arms.
"Good morning, Papa."
And my papa, he would tell me that he loved me.
We shared a game.
Knock Knock

Until that day when the knock never came,
and my momma takes me on a ride past cornfields
on this never-ending highway 'til we reach a place of high
rusty gates.
A confused little boy,
I entered the building carried in my mama's arms.
Knock Knock

We reach a room of windows and brown faces.
Behind one of the windows sits my father.
I jump out of my mama's arms
and run joyously towards my papa
only to be confronted by this window.
I knock knock, trying to break through the glass,
trying to get to my father.
I knock knock as my mama pulls me away
before my papa even says a word.

And for years, he has never said a word
And so 25 years later, I write these words
for the little boy in me who still awaits his papa's knock.

Papa, come home 'cause I miss you.
I miss you waking me up in the morning and telling me you love me.
Papa, come home 'cause there's things I don't know,

and I thought maybe you could teach me:
How to shave;
how to dribble a ball;
how to talk to a lady;
how to walk like a man.
Papa, come home because I decided a while back
I wanted to be just like you,
but I'm forgetting who you are.

And 25 years later, a little boy cries,
and so I write these words and try to heal
and try to father myself,
and I dream up a father who says the words my father did not.

Dear Son,
I'm sorry I never came home.
For every lesson I failed to teach, hear these words:
Shave in one direction in strong deliberate strokes to avoid irritation.

Dribble the page with the brilliance of your ballpoint pen.
Walk like a god, and your goddess will come to you.
No longer will I be there to knock on your door,
So you must learn to knock for yourself.
Knock knock down doors of racism and poverty that I could not.
Knock knock down doors of opportunity
for the lost brilliance of the black men who crowd these cells.
Knock knock with diligence for the sake of your children.
Knock knock for me for, as long as you are free,
these prison gates cannot contain my spirit.
The best of me still lives in you.
Knock knock with the knowledge that you are my son, but you are not
my choices.
Yes, we are our fathers' sons and daughters,
But we are not their choices.
For despite their absences, we are still here.
Still alive, still breathing
With the power to change this world,
One little boy and girl at a time.
Knock knock
Who's there?
We are.

Poverty, Money—and Love

Jessica Jackley
**Co-Founder and Former Chief Marketing Officer of Kiva Microfunds,
Founder and Chief Executive Officer of ProFounder**

*This presentation was filmed at TEDGlobal in Oxford, UK, in July
2010. A video of the presentation can be viewed on YouTube. Used
with permission of Jessica Jackley.*

The stories we tell about each other matter very much. The stories
we tell ourselves about our own lives matter. And, most of all, I think the
way that we participate in each other's stories is of deep importance.

I was six years old when I first heard stories about the poor. Now, I
didn't hear those stories from the poor themselves, I heard them from
my Sunday school teacher and Jesus, via my Sunday school teacher. I
remember learning that people who were poor needed something material—food, clothing, shelter—that they didn't have. And I also was
taught, coupled with that, that it was my job—this classroom full of five-
and six-year-old children—it was our job, apparently, to help. This is
what Jesus asked of us. And then he said, "What you do for the least of
these, you do for me." Now, I was pretty psyched. I was very eager to be
useful in the world. I think we all have that feeling. Also, it was interesting that God needed help. That was news to me, and it felt like it was a
very important thing to get to participate in.

But I also learned very soon thereafter that Jesus also said, and I'm
paraphrasing, "the poor would always be with us." This frustrated and
confused me. I felt like I had been just given a homework assignment
that I had to do—and I was excited to do—but no matter what I would
do, I would fail. So I felt confused, a little bit frustrated, and angry, like
maybe I'd misunderstood something here. And I felt overwhelmed. For
the first time, I began to fear this group of people and to feel negative
emotion towards a whole group of people. I imagined in my head a long
line of individuals who were never going away—that would always be
with us. They were always going to ask me to help them and give them
things, which I was excited to do, but I didn't know how it was going to
work. And I didn't know what would happen when I ran out of things to
give, especially if the problem was never going away.

In the years following, the other stories I heard about the poor growing up were no more positive. For example, I saw pictures and images
frequently of sadness and suffering. I heard about things that were going
wrong in the lives of the poor. I heard about disease. I heard about war.
They always seemed to be kind of related. And in general, I got this idea
that the poor in the world lived lives that were wrought with suffering
and sadness, devastation, hopelessness.

After a while, I developed what I think many of us do, this predictable response, where I started to feel bad every time I heard about them. I started to feel guilty for my own relative wealth because I wasn't doing more, apparently, to make things better. And I even felt a sense of shame because of that. So, naturally, I started to distance myself. I stopped listening to their stories quite as closely as I had before, and I stopped expecting things to really change.

Now, I still gave. On the outside, it looked like I was still quite involved. I gave of my time and my money. I gave when solutions were on sale. The cost of a cup of coffee can save a child's life, right? I mean who can argue with that? I gave when I was cornered; when it was difficult to avoid; and I gave, in general, when the negative emotions built up enough that I gave to relieve my own suffering, not someone else's. The truth be told, I was giving out of that place, not out of a genuine place of hope and excitement to help and of generosity. It became a transaction for me; it became sort of a trade. I was purchasing something. I was buying my right to go on with my day and not necessarily be bothered by this bad news. And I think the way that we go through that sometimes can, first of all, disembody a group of people, individuals out there in the world. And it can also turn them into a commodity, which is a very scary thing. So as I did this, and as I think many of us do this, we buy our distance, we buy our right to go on with our day. I think that exchange can actually get in the way of the very thing that we want most. It can get in the way of our desire to really be meaningful and useful in another person's life and, in short, to love.

Thankfully, a few years ago, things shifted for me because I heard this gentleman speak, Dr. Muhammad Yunus. I know many in the room probably know exactly who he is, but to give the shorthand version for any who have not heard him speak, Dr. Yunus won the Nobel Peace Prize a few years ago for his work pioneering modern microfinance. When I heard him speak, it was three years before that. But basically, microfinance—if this is new to you as well—think of it as financial services for the poor. Think of all the things you get at your bank and imagine those products and services tailored to the needs of someone living on a few dollars a day. Dr. Yunus shared his story, explaining what that was, and what he had done with his Grameen Bank. He also talked about, in particular, microlending, which is a tiny loan that could help someone start or grow a business.

Now, when I heard him speak, it was exciting for a number of reasons. First and foremost, I learned about this new method of change in the world that, for once, showed me, maybe, a way to interact with someone and to give, to share of a resource in a way that wasn't weird and didn't make me feel bad. That was exciting. But more importantly, he told stories about the poor that were different than any stories I had heard before. The fact that the individuals he talked about were poor was sort of a side note. He was talking about strong, smart, hardworking entrepreneurs who woke up every day and were doing things to make their lives and their families' lives better. All they needed to do that more quickly and to do it better was a little bit of capital. It was an amazing sort of insight for me.

I, in fact, was so deeply moved by this—it's hard to express now how much that affected me—but I was so moved that I actually quit my job a few weeks later, and I moved to East Africa to try to see for myself what this was about. For the first time in a long time, I wanted to meet those individuals. I wanted to meet these entrepreneurs and see for myself what their lives were actually about. So I spent three months in Kenya, Uganda, and Tanzania interviewing entrepreneurs who had received 100 dollars to start or grow a business.

In fact, through those interactions, for the first time, I was starting to get to be friends with some of those people in that big amorphous group out there that was supposed to be far away. I was starting to be friends and to get to know their personal stories. And over and over again, as I interviewed them and spent my days with them, I did hear stories of life change and amazing little details of change. So I would hear from goat herders who had used that money that they had received to buy a few more goats. Their business trajectory would change. They would make a little bit more money. Their standard of living would shift and would get better. And they would make really interesting little adjustments in their lives, like they would start to send their children to school. They might be able to buy mosquito nets. Maybe they could afford a lock for the door and feel secure. Maybe it was just that they could put sugar in their tea and offer that to me when I came as their guest, and that made them feel proud. But there were these beautiful details, even if I talked to 20 goat herders in a row, and some days that's what happened—these beautiful details of life change that were meaningful to them.

That was another thing that really touched me. It was really humbling to see for the first time—to really understand—that even if I could have taken a magic wand and fixed everything, I probably would have gotten a lot wrong. Because the best way for people to change their lives is for them to have control and to do that in a way that they believe is best for them. So I saw that, and it was very humbling.

Anyway, another interesting thing happened while I was there. I never once was asked for a donation, which had kind of been my mode, right? There's poverty, you give money to help. No one asked me for a donation. In fact, no one wanted me to feel bad for them at all. If anything, they just wanted to be able to do more of what they were doing already and to build on their own capabilities. So what I did there, once in a while, was to give people a loan—I thought that sounded very reasonable and really exciting.

And, by the way, I was a philosophy and poetry major in school, so I didn't know the difference between profit and revenue when I went to East Africa. I just got this impression that the money would work. My introduction to business was in these $100 little infuses of capital. I learned about profit and revenue, about leverage, about all sorts of things from farmers, from seamstresses, from goat herders. So this idea that these new stories of business and hope might be shared with my friends and family and, through that, maybe we could get some of the money that they needed to be able to continue their businesses as loans, that's this little idea that turned into Kiva.

A few months later, I went back to Uganda with a digital camera and a basic website that my partner, Matthew, and I had built and took pictures of seven of my new friends; posted their stories—these stories of entrepreneurship—up on the website; spammed friends and family; and said, "We think this is legal. Haven't heard back yet from SEC on all the details, but do you want to help participate in this and provide the money that they need?" The money came in basically overnight. We sent it over to Uganda. Over the next six months, a beautiful thing happened. The entrepreneurs received the money; they were paid; and their businesses, in fact, grew, and they were able to support themselves and change the trajectory of their lives.

In October of '05, after those first seven loans were paid, Matt and I took the word *beta* off of the site. We said, "Our little experiment has been a success. Let's start for real." That was our official launch. And then that first year, October '05 through '06, Kiva facilitated $500,000 in loans. The second year, it was a total of 15 million. The third year, the total was up to around 40. The fourth year, we were just short of 100. And today, less than five years in, Kiva's facilitated more than 150 million dollars, in little 25-dollar bits, from lenders and entrepreneurs—more than a million of those, collectively, in 200 countries.

So that's where Kiva is today, just to bring you right up to the present. And while those numbers and those statistics are really fun to talk about, and they're interesting, to me, Kiva's really about stories. It's about retelling the story of the poor, and it's about giving ourselves an opportunity to engage that validates their dignity, validates a partnership relationship, not a relationship that's based on the traditional sort of donor-beneficiary weirdness that can happen. Instead, it's a relationship that can promote respect and hope and this optimism that, together, we can move forward. So what I hope is that not only can the money keep flowing forth through Kiva—that's a very positive and meaningful thing—but I hope Kiva can blur those lines, like I said, between the traditional rich and poor categories that we're taught to see in the world, this false dichotomy of us and them, have and have not. I hope that Kiva can blur those lines. Because as that happens, I think we can feel free to interact in a way that's more open, more just, and more creative—to engage with each other and to help each other.

Imagine how you feel when you see somebody on the street who is begging, and you're about to approach them. Imagine how you feel. And then imagine the difference when you might see somebody who has a story of entrepreneurship and hard work who wants to tell you about their business. Maybe they're smiling, and they want to talk to you about what they've done. Imagine if you're speaking with somebody who's growing things and making them flourish; somebody who's using their talents to do something productive; somebody who's built their own business from scratch; someone who is surrounded by abundance, not scarcity, who's in fact creating abundance; somebody with full hands with something to offer, not empty hands asking for you to give them something. Imagine if you could hear a story you didn't expect of somebody who wakes up every day and works very, very hard to make their life better. These stories can really change the way that we think about each other. And if we can catalyze a supportive community to come around these individuals and to participate in their story by lending a little bit of money, I think that can change the way we believe in each other and each other's potential.

Now for me, Kiva is just the beginning. As I look forward to what is next, it's been helpful to reflect on the things I've learned so far. The first one is, as I mentioned, entrepreneurship was a new idea to me. Kiva borrowers, as I interviewed them and got to know them over the last few years, have taught me what entrepreneurship is. And I think, at its core, it's deciding that you want your life to be better. You see an opportunity, and you decide what you're going to do to try to seize that. In short, it's deciding that tomorrow can be better than today and going after that. The second thing that I've learned is that loans are a very interesting tool for connectivity. They're not a donation. Yes, maybe it doesn't sound that much different. But, in fact, when you give something to someone and they say, "Thanks," and let you know how things go, that's one thing. When you lend them money and they slowly pay you back over time, you have this excuse to have an ongoing dialogue. This continued attention—this ongoing attention—is a really big deal to build different kinds of relationships among us. And then third, from what I've heard from the entrepreneurs I've gotten to know, when all else is equal, given the option to have just money to do what you need to do or money plus the support and encouragement of a global community, people choose the community plus the money. That's a much more meaningful combination, a more powerful combination.

So with that in mind, this particular incident has led to the things that I'm working on now. I see entrepreneurs everywhere now—now that I'm tuned into this. And one thing that I've seen is there are a lot of supportive communities that already exist in the world. With social networks, it's an amazing way to grow the number of people that we all have around us in our own supportive communities, rapidly. And so, as I have been thinking about this, I've been wondering: How can we engage these supportive communities to catalyze even more entrepreneurial ideas and to catalyze all of us to make tomorrow better than today? As I've researched what's going on in the United States, a few interesting little insights have come up. One is that, of course, as we all might expect, many small businesses in the US and all over the world still need money to grow and to do more of what they want to do, or they might need money during a hard month. But there's always a need for resources close by. Another thing is, it turns out, those resources don't usually come from the places you might expect—banks, venture capitalists, other organizations and support structures. They come from friends and family. Some statistics say 85 percent or more of funding for small businesses comes from friends and family. That's around 130 billion dollars a year. It's a lot. And third, as people are doing this friends-and-family-fundraising process, it's very awkward. People don't know exactly what to ask for, how to ask, and what to promise in return, even though they have the best of intentions and want to thank those people who are supporting them.

So to harness the power of these supportive communities in a new way and to allow entrepreneurs to decide for themselves exactly what that financial exchange should look like, exactly what fits them and the people around them, this week, we're quietly doing a launch of Profounder, which is a crowd-funding platform for small businesses to raise what they need through investments from their friends and family. And it's investments—not donations, not loans—but investments that have a dynamic return. The mapping of participating in the story actually flows with the up and down. In short, it's a do-it-yourself tool for small businesses to raise these funds. And what you can do is go onto the site, create a profile, and create investment terms in a really easy way. We make it really, really simple for me as well as anyone else who wants to use the site. And we allow entrepreneurs to share a percentage of their revenues. They can raise up to a million dollars from an unlimited number of unaccredited, unsophisticated investors—everyday people, heaven forbid—and they can share those returns over time, again, using whatever terms they set. As investors choose to become involved based on those terms, they can either take their rewards back as cash, or they can decide in advance to give those returns away to a nonprofit. So they can be a cash or a cause investor. It's my hope that this kind of tool can show anybody who has an idea a path to go do what they want to do in the world and to gather the people around them that they already have—the people who know them best and who love them and want to support them—to gather them to make this happen.

So that's what I'm working on now. And to close, I just want to say, look, these are tools. Right now, Profounder's right at the very beginning, and it's very palpable—it's very clear to me—that it's just a vessel, it's just a tool. What we need are for people to care, to actually go use it, just like they've cared enough to use Kiva to make those connections. But the good news is I don't think I need to stand here and convince you to care. I'm not even going to try. I don't think, even though we often hear the ethical and moral reasons, the religious reasons, "Here's why caring and giving will make you happier." I don't think we need to be convinced of that. I think we know. In fact, I think we know so much and it's such a reality that we care so deeply that, in fact, what usually stops us is that we're afraid to try and to mess up because we care so very much about helping each other and being meaningful in each other's lives.

I've given you my story today, which is the best I can do. And I think I can remind us that we do care. I think we all already know that. And I think we know that love is resilient enough for us to get out there and try. For me, the best way to be inspired to try is to stop and to listen to someone else's story. I'm grateful that I've gotten to do that here at TED. I'm grateful that, whenever I do that, guaranteed, I am inspired, I am inspired by the person I am listening to. And I believe more and more every time I listen in that person's potential to do great things in the world and in my own potential to maybe help. Forget the tools, forget the moving around of resources—that stuff's easy. Believing in each other—really being sure when push comes to shove that each one of us can do amazing things in the world—that is what can make our stories into love stories and our collective story into one that continually perpetuates hope and good things for all of us. This belief in each other—knowing that without a doubt and practicing that every day in whatever you do—that's what I believe will change the world and make tomorrow better than today.

I Am an American

Hawk Newsome
President, Black Lives Matter, Greater New York

This presentation was given in Washington, DC, on September 26, 2017, at a rally in support of President Donald Trump. Black Lives Matter activists were protesting at the rally, and Tommy Gunn, the rally organizer, gave the group two minutes to address the crowd. Newsome accepted the invitation. Used with permission of Hawk Newsome.

My name is Hawk Newsome. I am the president of Black Lives Matter, New York. I am an American. And the beauty of America is that when you see something broke in your country, you can mobilize to fix it. So you ask why there is a Black Lives Matter. Because you can watch a black man die and be choked to death on television, and nothing happens. We need to address that. We need to fix it. So I say that I am an American. Secondly, I am a Christian. I don't think my Bible is any different from yours when it says, "love they neighbor." It doesn't say that neighbor had to be from the continental United States. I'm sorry. I'm sorry. We love one another.

The reason we fight is to draw attention to issues and to fix it. We are not anti cop. We are anti bad cop. If a cop is bad, he needs to get fired like a bad plumber or a bad lawyer, like a bad fuckin' politician. OK, so if that happens, it needs to be addressed. We don't want handouts. We don't want anything that's yours. We want our God-given right to freedom, liberty, and the pursuit of happiness. When I say I'm African American, I mean both. Get that through your head. Listen. I want to leave you with this, and I'm gone. [Someone in the crowd yells, "all lives matter."] You are right, my brother, you are so right that all lives matter. But when a black life is lost, we get no justice. That's why we say, "black lives matter." Listen, if we really want to make America great, we do it together.

Seeking Adherence

Who Is a True Friend?

Christa C. Porter
Student, Ohio State University

In this presentation, Christa C. Porter assumed the role of a teacher of a Sunday school class for grade-school students. Used with permission of Christa C. Porter.

Good morning, y'all.

Class members: Good morning.

Today, we're going to talk about something you all know a lot about; I hope we'll get some new ideas on the subject that will stay in your heads when you leave and get on the church bus. We're going to talk about friendship. Anybody here have friends?

Class members: Yes.

What is your definition of a true friend? Someone give me a definition of a true friend.

Class member: Somebody who's loyal and who can be trusted.

OK! Somebody else?

Class member: Somebody you can talk with.

All right. Anyone else?

Class member: Someone to do things with and have fun with.

OK. Everyone has their own definition of a friend. I'd like to add mine to the list. One of my definitions is that a friend is someone who will respect what I say. Even if my opinions are different from theirs, they'll still respect me and won't call me stupid. A friend is also someone I can call at 3:00 in the morning and say, "I need somebody to talk to," and she'll talk to me. That's what I consider a friend. Even if she has to wake up at 3:00 in the morning, she's willing to talk to me when I need help.

The Bible has some things to say about friends. Proverbs 18:24 says a friend is closer than any brother. Proverbs 27:10: Far better is the neighbor that is nearer than a brother that is far off. And greater love hath no man than this that a man lay down his life for his friend.

OK, you've given me your definitions of a friend, I've given you my definition, and I've given you some of what the Bible says about friends. We've been looking at friendship from our perspective here—of what friends do for us. How about looking at friendship from the other side? How can we be a good friend? Would I wake up at 3:00 in the morning for my friend—to listen to her? If your friend were stranded 20 miles away, would you go pick her up? So, a lot of times, we think about what we want our friends to do, but we never think about what we would do for our friends.

One of the ways in which we can be good friends to others is by being trustworthy, which Regina mentioned in her definition of a friend. Can I keep a secret? Can I be trusted? Trust. That's a common word that is used in the definition of a friend. You've probably all had the experience of having friends talk about you behind your back, they say bad things about you, they tell your business to everyone. The Bible recognizes this potential problem. Proverbs 18:24 says that he that maketh many friends doeth it to his own destruction. A prime example: If you tell your friend something, your friend could have a friend who has a friend who has a friend. And the next thing you know, your business is around the whole school.

Help me out here—you stand up. Now pick out somebody real quick who's your friend. OK, now you pick out somebody who's your friend, and you stand up. One more time—you pick out someone who is your friend. Now, I could tell her about my conversation with a guy from school, she could tell her something, and she could tell him something, and he then tells it to his friend, over here. And by the time it gets back to me, according to the story, I've had a date with this guy, we've had sex, I got pregnant, and I had an abortion—all that from just telling one person one thing. That's what happens when you have a lot of friends, especially the kind who aren't trustworthy.

The whole point of this is the person you can really have trust in is God. You don't have to worry about Him coming down and saying, "Guess what she did last night?" He's going to be there for you regardless, he's going to listen to you, and he's going to give you the best advice. Our friends can be wonderful, but God is the best friend of all.

Competition, Creativity & Choice in the Classroom

Betsy DeVos
Politician, Businesswoman, Republican Party Fundraiser, and Advocate for Education Reform

This presentation was given in Austin, Texas, on March 11, 2015, at the SXSW EDU conference and festival designed to foster innovation in learning. Betsy DeVos was appointed US Secretary of Education in 2017. Thanks to the American Federation for Children for including DeVos's speech on its website.

I have a confession to make. I'm a Republican.

Humor me for just a few minutes by participating in an informal poll of the audience today, just for fun.

In our system of government, we of course have Republicans, Democrats, and Independents.

By show of hands, how many of you consider yourselves to be Independents?

Now, by show of hands, how many consider yourselves to be Democrats?

And, how many consider yourselves to be Republicans?

Finally, how many of you believe that our education system will ever be fixed by political parties?

If you raised your hand for the last group, I have some bad news for you—you are delusional. I was once in that group though, and there is help for you.

No matter your preconceived notions when you came in the door, I'm going to ask you to open your mind for just a few moments and consider the case I want to make—if I fail to persuade you, then feel free to return to your current thinking.

Here's my thesis for your consideration—*we must revolutionize our education delivery system in America.* That's it—that's all I'm asking for. Open education up; allow for choice, innovation, and freedom.

Now, let me back up and tell you just a little bit about my story. I always enjoy listening to a speaker more if I know a little about him or her.

As a kid, I grew up middle class, but my father was a great innovator with an entrepreneurial spirit, and it wasn't long before my family became part of the infamous 1%.

My husband's family has a similar story, and together my husband and I have also been successful in innovative and entrepreneurial ventures.

So, I am not only a Republican, even worse, I'm a well off Republican.

I spent a number of years working in Republican politics. I was Chairman of the Michigan Republican Party and held a lot of other political positions. I had a lot of success in partisan politics.

And then . . . I quit.

I don't apologize for being involved in politics, but I did become frustrated by them. Why?

Because my real passion in life is education and learning. And I like to think big about education.

I want to convince you in the next 30 minutes to think big about education, too.

The world is full of small thinkers who tinker around the edges, we don't need more of those.

I won't waste your time with a lot of lofty rhetoric. I'll be blunt, and since I got out of politics, I have the freedom to be politically incorrect too.

Let's start by being brutally honest about the status of K–12 education in America today. Not what we wish the status was, not what we want it to be, but what it really is.

I'm going to throw six "inconvenient truths" at you.

The reason for this approach is because we will never solve a problem if we refuse to admit it.

Inconvenient Truth #1. **Our education delivery system in America is antiquated and it is quite frankly embarrassing.** Let's take the example of the Model T. In my home state of Michigan, there was a time when the assembly line for making Model Ts was the envy of the world. There was also a time when the American education delivery system was the envy of the world. But if Detroit had not innovated, if Detroit was still employing the same delivery system for producing automobiles today as they were 90 years ago, American cars would be obsolete. Yet in that same time period, our education delivery system has not innovated or changed at all.

A second example—Kodak. The American education system is fast approaching its Kodak moment—you all remember Kodak, right? . . . well, maybe not all of you do. It likely depends on how old you are if you remember Kodak or not. Like Kodak, our education system is fast approaching its moment to either perish into obsolescence, or to revolutionize and thrive.

Inconvenient Truth #2. **American education has been losing ground to other countries for at least half a century.** The facts here are inarguable. You can see some of them on the screen, but it's really a waste of our time to even slog through this. It's just plain true and everyone knows it.

The one statistic I would call your attention to is this: PISA (*Programme for International Student Assessment*). PISA stats: Arne Duncan called the results, "a picture of education stagnation." U.S. ranked 17th in reading, 21st in science and 26th in math.

Oh, there are always a few people in denial, there are a few who are content, and there are defenders of the status quo, but that is an intellectually indefensible position.

Not only are we falling behind collectively in relationship to other countries, we have far too many children who are straight-up failing. And they are largely concentrated in economically disadvantaged areas.

And we have too many children in middle-class suburban areas that we think are doing well . . . but that are actually seriously underperforming.

The truth is that each and every child deserves the opportunity to fully develop their potential, and collectively, our country will not be competitive unless all kids have opportunity.

Inconvenient Truth #3. **We are stuck in a partisan rut. The political parties are dead enders when it comes to education revolution.** As long as we think political parties might solve the problem, it will never be solved.

Oddly enough—Education choice is very unique in that some conservative Republicans and some liberal Democrats are actually on the same wave length. For instance, John Boehner, Jeb Bush, Condi Rice, and Bobby Jindal are examples of Republican leaders who actually are willing to lead positively on this issue.

And on the Democrat side, Mike McCurry, Diane Feinstein, Cory Booker and Andrew Cuomo . . . are willing to buck their party leaders. And believe it or not, Democrats have led school choice efforts in Arizona, Georgia, Florida, North Carolina, and Oklahoma.

But those are exceptions. The vast majority of the political class is committed to defending and protecting the status quo.

Now, let me get politically incorrect in discussing the political parties.

Let's start with Republicans. Many Republicans in the suburbs like the idea of education choice as a concept . . . right up until it means that poor kids from the inner city might invade their schools. That's when you will hear the sentiment—"well . . . it's not really a great idea to have poor minority kids coming to our good suburban schools." Although they will never actually say those words aloud.

In my home state of Michigan, one of our Republican legislators who everyone assumed was a supporter of education choice in fact came out against even the minor step of "public school choice." His reason was that his district bordered the city of Detroit. Enough said.

And just last year, we saw Republicans in Tennessee, Oklahoma, and Mississippi taking the lead in killing various education-choice measures, all in deep red states.

And now let's talk about Democrats . . . many Democrats love the idea of providing equal opportunity . . . right up until the moment when the teachers union leaders say "no." When that happens, they salute and fall back into formation.

I've had many conversations with Democrat politicians who know in their heart of hearts that education choice is the right thing, but who admit in private that they cannot afford to get crossed up with the teachers unions and the party bosses.

It's a perfect recipe for an intractable political standoff.

Meanwhile, America falls further behind, too many kids are denied an opportunity, too many kids get substandard educations, the status quo remains, change is thwarted, and everyone loses.

Let me give you a real world example of what I'm talking about, and I would like you to think about this as if we were talking about your own children. Here are your two choices.

Alpha School is a high-performing school, with graduation rates ranging from 70–90%, depending on the year.

Beta School is a low-performing school, with graduation rates hovering around 50%.

If you were given the choice between Alpha School and Beta School for your children, which would you choose?

If you chose Alpha School, then in Washington DC, you chose a private or charter school for your kids.

If you chose Beta School, then in Washington DC, you chose the traditional public school.

If you want to risk sending your kids to a failing school, that is certainly your choice, but why would you deny the high-performing Alpha School choice to anyone else?

And yet, our president has tried to terminate these options in Washington DC . . . while, at the same time, he sends his daughters to an elite private school. It's illogical; it's hypocritical; and frankly it's immoral.

Inconvenient Truth # 4. **Government really sucks.** And it doesn't matter which party is in power. Having been around politics and government my entire adult life, I have five observations about government for you:

- Government tends to believe in top-down solutions and government fears of bottom-up solutions.

- Government tends to stifle innovation and it abhors improvisation. Any good military strategist will tell you that a battle plan rarely survives past the first engagement. After that, you have to improvise to survive and to win.

- Government tends to favor one size fits all solutions handed down from central command.

- Government likes committees . . . a lot. Committees kill all the really good ideas and generally all the really bad ideas. They produce middle ground mush.

- Government prefers control and tightly-defined systems. It fears entrepreneurs, open systems, and crowd sourcing. All of which it finds threatening.

Inconvenient Truth #5. **We don't pay teachers enough, and we don't fire teachers enough.** In that one sentence, I've raised the ire of both the Republican and Democrat political establishments.

The Republicans don't want to pay our best teachers enough, and the Democrats don't want to reform tenure laws. It's another partisan standoff.

But I am willing to bet that every one of you had one or more teachers who made a big difference in your life, who opened your eyes to possibilities and to opportunities. You probably recall them in your mind's eye right now.

And likewise, I'm pretty sure that every one of you had one or more teachers who should not have been teaching. That doesn't mean they were bad people, or maybe they were, but regardless, they weren't any good at teaching. You are probably thinking of those teachers right now.

And by the way, teaching is hard. It takes a lot of skill. Not everyone who tries it can do it well. We need to admit that and act accordingly.

We should reward and respect great teachers by paying them more, and we should stop rewarding seniority over effectiveness.

Political parties will not fix this. Republicans don't want to pay teachers enough, and Democrats don't want to reform tenure laws. It's another partisan standoff. The status quo remains.

Lastly, Inconvenient Truth #6. **In America we do NOT provide equal educational opportunity to our kids.** This one is the worst of the worst.

How many here believe that every child deserves an equal opportunity for a quality education?

Good. But that concept is a myth in America today. We don't provide anything of the sort, not even close.

If you live in an area with quality public schools, you can most likely get a reasonable education. In most cases, this means you do not live in an economically depressed area.

If you don't live in an area with good public schools, you can move to a different place if you have the financial means to do so. If you don't, you're screwed.

If your local public schools aren't very good, but you have the cash, you can send your kids to a higher-performing private school. But, if you don't have the financial resources, you are again screwed.

It is not defensible that today you can predict educational outcomes by the zip code in which someone lives.

Defenders of the status quo will tell you to wait and be patient, that things are improving, and that things will really improve if they can just get some more money.

Really? If money was the answer, we would not have a problem. And just think how incredibly arrogant it is to say to the mom of a 3rd grader—just wait, it will get better. No, her 3rd grader will only grow up once. There is no time to wait.

And as we know, too many politicians and too many leaders from within the education system oppose education choice, but they use it for their own families. As my good friend Howard Fuller says—"If choice is so bad, why don't YOU give it up for YOUR family?"

For many defenders of the status quo, it's not their ideology that bothers me, it's their complete hypocrisy that I can't stomach.

We do not have equal educational opportunity in America. This is not just an inconvenient truth, it is immoral.

Don't worry about well-off people, they'll find a way to get a good education for their children. But if "the least of these" are denied an equal opportunity—and they are—then our education industry is failing—and it is.

SO . . . how should equal opportunity in education look?

First, let the education dollars follow each child, instead of forcing the child to follow the dollars. This is pretty straightforward. And it's how you go from a closed system to an open system that encourages innovation. People deserve choices and options.

Let's hear from Denisha Merriweather, a student that got an opportunity through the Florida Tax Credit Scholarship program [video]. So, Denisha's story is compelling—I think we can all agree on that. Thinking about her and millions of others like her, what would an open system of choices look like?

- Traditional public schools
- Public school choice
- Charter schools
- Virtual schools and online learning
- Private and parochial schools
- Home school
- Course choice
- Blended options of all the above
- And perhaps most importantly, new approaches to learning that have yet to be imagined or developed.

Let's talk about a few examples of new thinking and approaches to learning that should be embraced . . . but that the status quo finds terrifying.

- Khan Academy. You can hear more from Sal Khan tomorrow, but his simple approach puts the emphasis on mastery of concepts, and it has far-reaching implications for an open system.
- Hole in the Wall Experiment and School in the Cloud. Dr. Sugata Mitra, winner of the 2013 TED Prize, demonstrates that all children, even those with no formal training, and from some of the most impoverished communities, can self-organize and self-learn.
- José Urbina López Primary School. Teacher Juárez Correa applied some of the principles from Dr. Mitra's research to his classroom in Matamoros, Mexico, and the results were breathtaking—including one student who went from being a bored, uninterested, average student to becoming recognized as a mathematical whiz.

- KIPP Academies, Success Academies in Harlem, Hope Academies in Milwaukee.
- Cristo Rey Schools. The Cristo Rey Network has 28 high schools that serve urban and low-income families. The school partners with local businesses who help pay for tuition through providing real life professional opportunities and training for students.
- West Michigan Aviation Academy. A personal example in that my husband founded this charter high school focused on aviation . . . .and yes, a bunch of those kids are from the inner city, and yes, a number of them get their private pilots license while getting their high school education.
- Acton Academy. I'm looking forward to visiting the Acton Academy later today, an innovative, 21st-century approach to learning here in the Austin community. You can hear Jeff Sandefer, the founder, speak this afternoon.

These are but a few of the new approaches to education and learning, but there is one thing all of these innovative ideas have in common . . . the status quo, in varying degrees, finds them all threatening.

Technology has changed how kids interact with learning, and anyone who doesn't embrace that is kidding themselves. Here's a personal look at how technology is changing the way kids interact with learning. This is a video of my two granddaughters [video].

What can be done about all this?

That's easy—all we need is an *Ed Revolution*.

Change is hard, but change is not difficult. People naturally resist change. But without change and without innovation, everything withers on the vine.

We need an army of big thinkers, of entrepreneurs and innovators, of tech-savvy people who are not afraid of or intimidated by entrenched powers. We need to overcome the political class that keeps us bound to a ridiculously antiquated status quo.

I believe this revolution will be fueled by the younger generation. The older generations are too wedded to political parties, too wedded to romantic memories of what education was like when they were kids, and too wedded to the status-quo group that clings to power.

It really is time for everyone to acknowledge the need to open things up in education and to modernize and innovate. We need to think Big and envision the way things could be, and then move to make it happen.

This is not a battle of left v right, or Democrat v Republican.

It's a battle of Industrial Age v the Digital Age.

It's the Model T vs. the Tesla.

It's old-factory model v the new Internet model.

It's the luddites v the future.

We must open up the education industry—and let's not kid ourselves that it isn't an industry—we must open it up to entrepreneurs and innovators.

This is how families without means will get access to a world-class education. This is how a student who is not learning in their current model can find an individualized learning environment that will meet their needs.

We are the beneficiaries of start-ups, ventures, and innovation in every other area of life, but we don't have that in education because it's a closed system, a closed industry, a closed market. It's a monopoly. It's a dead end. And the best and brightest innovators and risk-takers steer way clear of it.

As long as education remains a closed system, we will never see the education equivalents of Google, Facebook, Amazon, PayPal, Wikipedia, or Uber. We won't see any real innovation that benefits more than a handful of students.

Everyone knows that monopolies suffocate progress. We need to turn our creativity loose and break free from the partisan World War I-style trench warfare that embodies the current debate.

I don't care who the winners or losers are in the current partisan political debate. That is immaterial. If we can manage to break free, to open the system and embrace all choices for education, we will be the first to give politicians awards to hang on their office walls.

But most importantly, the next generations of kids will be the real winners. And collectively, as Americans, we will all benefit from their unleashed horsepower.

If you claim you are for freedom . . . if you claim to be an innovator or you value innovation . . . if you claim to be an entrepreneur, . . . if you claim to believe in equal opportunity . . . if you claim to embrace social justice . . . then you have to embrace educational choice, and you have to embrace opening up our closed education delivery system.

Thank you for your attention. I don't have all the answers, but I'd be glad to take your questions and will do my best to answer them.

Removal of Confederate Monuments

Mitch Landrieu
Mayor, New Orleans, Louisiana

This presentation was given in New Orleans, Louisiana, on May 23, 2017, after Mitch Landrieu had the remaining Confederate monuments removed from the city. These included the Battle of Liberty Place on Canal Street; the Jefferson Davis statue on Jefferson Davis Parkway, the P. G. T. Beauregard equestrian statue on Esplanade Avenue, and the Robert E. Lee statue at Lee Circle. Thanks to the Office of Mayor Mitch Landrieu, City of New Orleans, for making this speech available on YouTube.

Thank you for coming.

The soul of our beloved City is deeply rooted in a history that has evolved over thousands of years; rooted in a diverse people who have been here together every step of the way—for both good and for ill. It is a history that holds in its heart the stories of Native Americans: the Choctaw, Houma Nation, the Chitimacha. Of Hernando de Soto, Robert Cavelier, Sieur de La Salle, the Acadians, the Islenos, the enslaved people from Senegambia, Free People of Color, the Haitians, the Germans, both the empires of France and Spain. The Italians, the Irish, the Cubans, the south and central Americans, the Vietnamese and so many more.

You see: New Orleans is truly a city of many nations, a melting pot, a bubbling cauldron of many cultures. There is no other place quite like it in the world that so eloquently exemplifies the uniquely American motto: *e pluribus unum*—out of many we are one. But there are also other truths about our city that we must confront. New Orleans was America's largest slave market: a port where hundreds of thousands of souls were brought, sold and shipped up the Mississippi River to lives of forced labor, of misery, of rape, of torture. America was the place where nearly 4,000 of our fellow citizens were lynched, 540 alone in Louisiana; where the courts enshrined "separate but equal"; where Freedom riders coming to New Orleans were beaten to a bloody pulp. So, when people say to me that the monuments in question are history, well what I just described is real history as well, and it is the searing truth.

And it immediately begs the questions: why there are no slave ship monuments, no prominent markers on public land to remember the lynchings or the slave blocks; nothing to remember this long chapter of our lives—the pain, the sacrifice, the shame ... all of it happening on the soil of New Orleans. So, for those self-appointed defenders of history and the monuments, they are eerily silent on what amounts to this historical malfeasance, a lie by omission. There is a difference between remembrance of history and reverence of it.

For America and New Orleans, it has been a long, winding road, marked by great tragedy and great triumph. But we cannot be afraid of our truth. As President George W. Bush said at the dedication ceremony for the National Museum of African American History and Culture, "A great nation does not hide its history. It faces its flaws and corrects them." So today I want to speak about why we chose to remove these four monuments to the Lost Cause of the Confederacy—but also how and why this process can move us toward healing and understanding of each other. So, let's start with the facts.

The historic record is clear: the Robert E. Lee, Jefferson Davis, and P. G. T. Beauregard statues were not erected just to honor these men but as part of the movement which became known as *The Cult of the Lost Cause*. This cult had one goal—through monuments and through other means—to rewrite history to hide the truth, which is that the Confederacy was on the wrong side of humanity. First erected over 166 years after the founding of our city and 19 years after the end of the Civil War, the monuments that we took down were meant to rebrand the history of our city and the ideals of a defeated Confederacy. It is self-evident that these men did not fight for the United States of America. They fought against it. They may have been warriors, but in this cause they were not patriots. These statues are not just stone and metal. They are not just innocent remembrances of a benign history. These monuments purposefully celebrate a fictional, sanitized Confederacy; ignoring the death, ignoring the enslavement, and the terror that it actually stood for.

After the Civil War, these statues were a part of that terrorism as much as a burning cross on someone's lawn; they were erected purposefully to send a strong message to all who walked in their shadows about who was still in charge in this city. Should you have further doubt about the true goals of the Confederacy, in the very weeks before the war broke out, the Vice President of the Confederacy, Alexander Stephens, made it clear that the Confederate cause was about maintaining slavery and white supremacy. He said in his now famous "Cornerstone" speech that the Confederacy's "cornerstone rests upon the great truth, that the negro is not equal to the white man; that slavery—subordination to the superior race—is his natural and normal condition. This, our new government, is the first, in the history of the world, based upon this great physical, philosophical, and moral truth."

Now, with these shocking words still ringing in your ears, I want to try to gently peel from your hands the grip on a false narrative of our history that I think weakens us. And make straight a wrong turn we made many years ago—we can more closely connect with integrity to the founding principles of our nation and forge a clearer and straighter path toward a better city and more perfect union.

Last year, President Barack Obama echoed these sentiments about the need to contextualize and remember all of our history. He recalled a

piece of stone, a slave auction block engraved with a marker commemo-
rating a single moment in 1830 when Andrew Jackson and Henry Clay
stood and spoke from it. President Obama said: "Consider what this arti-
fact tells us about history . . . on a stone where day after day for years,
men and women . . . bound and bought and sold and bid like cattle on a
stone worn down by the tragedy of over a thousand bare feet. For a long
time, the only thing we considered important, the singular thing we once
chose to commemorate as history with a plaque were the unmemorable
speeches of two powerful men."

A piece of stone—one stone. Both stories were history. One story
told. One story forgotten or maybe even purposefully ignored. As clear as
it is for me today ? for a long time, even though I grew up in one of New
Orleans's most diverse neighborhoods, even with my family's long proud
history of fighting for civil rights . . . I must have passed by those monuments a million times without giving them a second thought. So I am not
judging anybody, I am not judging people. We all take our own journey
on race.

I just hope people listen like I did when my dear friend Wynton Mar-
salis helped me see the truth. He asked me to think about all the people
who have left New Orleans because of our exclusionary attitudes.
Another friend asked me to consider these four monuments from the
perspective of an African American mother or father trying to explain to
their fifth-grade daughter who Robert E. Lee is and why he stands atop of
our beautiful city. Can you do it? Can you look into that young girl's eyes
and convince her that Robert E. Lee is there to encourage her? Do you
think she will feel inspired and hopeful by that story? Do these monuments help her see a future with limitless potential? Have you ever
thought that if her potential is limited, yours and mine are too? We all
know the answer to these very simple questions. When you look into
this child's eyes is the moment when the searing truth comes into focus
for us. This is the moment when we know what is right and what we
must do. We can't walk away from this truth.

And I knew that taking down the monuments was going to be tough,
but you elected me to do the right thing, not the easy thing and this is
what that looks like. So, relocating these Confederate monuments is not
about taking something away from someone else. This is not about politics, this is not about blame or retaliation. This is not a naïve quest to
solve all our problems at once.

This is, however, about showing the whole world that we as a city
and as a people are able to acknowledge, understand, reconcile and, most
importantly, choose a better future for ourselves, making straight what
has been crooked and making right what was wrong. Otherwise, we will
continue to pay a price with discord, with division, and yes, with violence.

To literally put the confederacy on a pedestal in our most prominent
places of honor is an inaccurate recitation of our full past, it is an affront

to our present, and it is a bad prescription for our future. History cannot be changed. It cannot be moved like a statue. What is done is done. The Civil War is over, and the Confederacy lost, and we are better for it. Surely we are far enough removed from this dark time to acknowledge that the cause of the Confederacy was wrong.

And in the second decade of the 21st century, asking African Americans—or anyone else—to drive by property that they own; occupied by reverential statues of men who fought to destroy the country and deny that person's humanity seems perverse and absurd. Centuries-old wounds are still raw because they never healed right in the first place. Here is the essential truth: we are better together than we are apart.

Indivisibility is our essence. Isn't this the gift that the people of New Orleans have given to the world? We radiate beauty and grace in our food, in our music, in our architecture, in our joy of life, in our celebration of death; in everything that we do. We gave the world this funky thing called *jazz*, the most uniquely American art form that is developed across the ages from different cultures. Think about second lines, think about Mardi Gras, think about muffuletta, think about the Saints, gumbo, red beans and rice. By God, just think.

All we hold dear is created by throwing everything in the pot; creating, producing something better; everything a product of our historic diversity. We are proof that out of many we are one—and better for it! Out of many we are one—and we really do love it! And yet, we still seem to find so many excuses for not doing the right thing. Again, remember President Bush's words, "A great nation does not hide its history. It faces its flaws and corrects them."

We forget, we deny how much we really depend on each other, how much we need each other. We justify our silence and inaction by manufacturing noble causes that marinate in historical denial. We still find a way to say "wait, not so fast." But like Dr. Martin Luther King Jr. said, "wait has almost always meant never." We can't wait any longer. We need to change. And we need to change now.

No more waiting. This is not just about statues, this is about our attitudes and behavior as well. If we take these statues down and don't change to become a more open and inclusive society this would have all been in vain. While some have driven by these monuments every day and either revered their beauty or failed to see them at all, many of our neighbors and fellow Americans see them very clearly. Many are painfully aware of the long shadows their presence casts, not only literally but figuratively. And they clearly receive the message that the Confederacy and the cult of the lost cause intended to deliver.

Earlier this week, as the cult of the lost cause statue of P. G. T Beauregard came down, world renowned musician Terence Blanchard stood watch, his wife Robin and their two beautiful daughters at their side. Terence went to a high school on the edge of City Park named after one of

America's greatest heroes and patriots, John F. Kennedy. But to get there he had to pass by this monument to a man who fought to deny him his humanity. He said, "I've never looked at them as a source of pride. It's always made me feel as if they were put there by people who don't respect us. This is something I never thought I'd see in my lifetime. It's a sign that the world is changing." Yes, Terence, it is, and it is long overdue. Now is the time to send a new message to the next generation of New Orleanians who can follow in Terence and Robin's remarkable footsteps.

A message about the future, about the next 300 years and beyond; let us not miss this opportunity New Orleans and let us help the rest of the country do the same. Because now is the time for choosing. Now is the time to actually make this the City we always should have been, had we gotten it right in the first place.

We should stop for a moment and ask ourselves—at this point in our history, after Katrina, after Rita, after Ike, after Gustav, after the national recession, after the BP oil catastrophe and after the tornado—if presented with the opportunity to build monuments that told our story or to curate these particular spaces . . . would these monuments be what we want the world to see? Is this really our story?

We have not erased history; we are becoming part of the city's history by righting the wrong image these monuments represent and crafting a better, more complete future for all our children and for future generations. And unlike when these Confederate monuments were first erected as symbols of white supremacy, we now have a chance to create not only new symbols, but to do it together, as one people. In our blessed land we all come to the table of democracy as equals. We have to reaffirm our commitment to a future where each citizen is guaranteed the uniquely American gifts of life, liberty, and the pursuit of happiness.

That is what really makes America great and today it is more important than ever to hold fast to these values and together say a self-evident truth that out of many we are one. That is why today we reclaim these spaces for the United States of America. Because we are one nation, not two; indivisible with liberty and justice for all, not some. We all are part of one nation, all pledging allegiance to one flag, the flag of the United States of America. And New Orleanians are in . . . all the way. It is in this union and in this truth that real patriotism is rooted and flourishes. Instead of revering a 4-year brief historical aberration that was called the *Confederacy* we can celebrate all 300 years of our rich, diverse history as a place named *New Orleans* and set the tone for the next 300 years.

After decades of public debate, of anger, of anxiety, of anticipation, of humiliation and of frustration. After public hearings and approvals from three separate community led commissions. After two robust public hearings and a 6-1 vote by the duly elected New Orleans City Council. After review by 13 different federal and state judges. The full weight of the legislative, executive, and judicial branches of government has been brought to bear and the monuments in accordance with the law have been removed. So now is the time to come together and heal and focus on our larger task. Not only building new symbols but making this city a beautiful manifestation of what is possible and what we as a people can become.

Let us remember what the once exiled, imprisoned, and now universally loved Nelson Mandela said after the fall of apartheid. "If the pain has often been unbearable and the revelations shocking to all of us, it is because they indeed bring us the beginnings of a common understanding of what happened and a steady restoration of the nation's humanity."

So, before we part let us again state the truth clearly. The Confederacy was on the wrong side of history and humanity. It sought to tear apart our nation and subjugate our fellow Americans to slavery. This is the history we should never forget and one that we should never again put on a pedestal to be revered. As a community, we must recognize the significance of removing New Orleans's Confederate monuments. It is our acknowledgment that now is the time to take stock of, and then move past, a painful part of our history. Anything less would render generations of courageous struggle and soul-searching a truly lost cause.

Anything less would fall short of the immortal words of our greatest President Abraham Lincoln, who with an open heart and clarity of purpose calls on us today to unite as one people when he said: "With malice toward none, with charity for all, with firmness in the right as God gives us to see the right, let us strive on to finish the work we are in, to bind up the nation's wounds . . . to do all which may achieve and cherish a just and lasting peace among ourselves and with all nations."

Thank you.

University of Colorado Denver as a Pirate Ship

Sonja K. Foss
Professor of Communication,
University of Colorado Denver

This presentation was delivered at the University of Colorado Denver on April 25, 2014, at a fundraising luncheon for professors. Used with permission of Sonja K. Foss.

As you all know, the University of Colorado at Boulder calls itself the *flagship*. But for many years now, I've been calling us the *pirate ship*—because pretty soon, we're going to steal their stuff. We have all the bounty in place to surpass Boulder in terms of quality, resources, and reputation.

I'd like to talk for a few minutes today about why I support this pirate ship called *University of Colorado Denver* and why I encourage you to support it, too. Now I realize that asking you to support something that is generally considered to be illegal and dangerous—piracy—might be a bit unusual. And piracy has resulted in a lot of people ending up in Davy Jones's locker. But I ask you, me mateys, to engage in a bit of "aye, aye"—to weigh anchor with me for a few minutes—while I talk about why we should support the pirate ship that is CU Denver.

So why should we support this pirate ship? Because it's adaptable and innovative. Pirates need ships that are fast, powerful, and have a shallow draft. These features allow them to hide in secluded coves and navigate shallow waters and surprise other ships. CU Denver has these qualities. It's nimble. We can do things with the resources we contribute that are innovative; we aren't bound by as many bureaucratic structures or traditions as flagship institutions are. One of the things I've done is to set up a bequest for the Communication Department that says my money is to be used for research and travel for graduate students and for purchasing things that are difficult for a university department to buy under typical budgetary regulations. I want my treasure chest, so to speak, to help my department be a new kind of department—and I want to help it get there.

Why support the pirate ship that is CU Denver? Because we all share in the results. In the olden days, life on pirate ships could be pretty good compared to life on merchant or naval ships. The crew was treated much better than normal sailors, and prize money was shared equally. I think that's true here. At CU Denver, all of us benefit from what we give. I donate regularly to the Communication Department to help create a pleasing aesthetic environment. For example, I helped purchase a gorgeous quilt made by one of our instructors that fills one wall of our conference room. I purchased an artistic historic photograph of Beijing that hangs on another wall and reminds us of the richness of our Chinese

connections through ICB [International College Beijing]. All of us benefit from the booty we share with all of the hands on this pirate ship of
ours, and it helps make our departments and the university a place where
we all want to be.

Why support the pirate ship that is CU Denver? Because our contributions help arm us so that others surrender to us. The best students,
the best faculty, and the best donors surrender to our creativity, our
excellence, our commitment to students, and the wonderful community
we have created. Maybe our Jolly Roger isn't designed to intimidate passing ships into surrendering without a fight, but all of the things that
make CU Denver a great place certainly attract the attention of those who
are looking for an excellent university. Something else I've done is to
fund an annual undergraduate award for excellence in academic research.

These are the kinds of things, then, that can get people to board the
gangplank and "bring a spring upon the cable"—to come around in a different direction. So, me hearties, heave to. Don't be one of those landlub-
bers who hornswoggles CU Denver. There are many reasons to give. CU
Denver really benefits from our giving because it is nimble and innovative—it can make good use of what we give. We all share in the results of
our giving, and our giving helps others surrender to our excellence.

So let's mutiny against that flagship, let's run a shot across the bow,
and let's engage in some plunder. We deserve it! To quote most of the
pirates we know, "Arrrr!"

Discovering Knowledge and Belief

Focus-Group Discussion of *The Lantern*

Randi Lewis
Student, Ohio State University

In this presentation, Randi Lewis used a focus group to generate feedback for the staff of The Lantern, *the student newspaper at Ohio State University. Her portion of the presentation is included below, although the answers given by her focus-group participants are not. Used with permission of Randi Lewis.*

In public relations, we do a lot of focus groups to find out who our audience is, what they think about a product, or what they like about a product or service. As students at OSU, I'm assuming most of you read *The Lantern*, so that will be the focus of this discussion today. I'd like to begin by welcoming you all to this focus group. Thank you for taking time out of your busy schedules to participate in this session. I will be asking several open-ended questions about *The Lantern* and would like you to be honest in answering them.

There are several goals we are trying to accomplish by conducting this focus group. First, we'd like to find out the aspects you like and dislike about our student newspaper. Second, we want to hear what you think about the stories we've been running the past three quarters. Last, we want to get some suggestions from you—the students who read our paper—on how we can serve you better. The paper is here for you, and we want to do the best job that we can in meeting your needs.

Before we begin the discussion, I would like to give you a little bit of background about *The Lantern*. It is a student-run newspaper that is written and put together entirely by journalism students in the news and public relations tracks. The paper is published every day, Monday through Friday, during autumn, winter, and spring quarters and bi-weekly during the summer quarter. It is funded and supported totally by advertising dollars.

With this background in mind, let's get started with the focus-group questions. You can raise your hand or jump right in, whatever you're most comfortable doing. I'm going to be taking notes while you're talking in order to get your suggestions down.

- How many of you read *The Lantern* on a regular basis?
- How many of you read it more than three times a week?
- How many of you read *The Lantern* as a primary source for your news?
- What are the sections you flip to first or the ones you read most often?

- What about sports? Do you feel we should be including more articles about sports—not just those at OSU but nationally?
- What about the editorial page/letters to the editor? Do you all read that section? What do you think about that section?
- What are some of the stories that stood out for you in *The Lantern* over the past three quarters? Why do you remember those stories in particular?
- What are some of the things you like about *The Lantern*?
- What are some of the things you dislike about *The Lantern*?
- You've given me several valuable suggestions for *The Lantern*. There is one specific question I'd like to ask you. Do you feel we should print Associated Press (or AP) articles in *The Lantern*? There are two schools of thought in journalism. Some think that we should have totally student-written articles—no AP articles whatsoever. Others argue that, for many students, this is their only source of news, so we need to include a balance between AP and student-written articles about campus. What's your feeling on that?

This has been a very productive discussion, but unfortunately, I need to wrap up here. Let me summarize the main ideas you've given me: We need more accurate reporting, more careful attention to grammar and spelling, a more professional look generally, and more in-depth coverage of OSU sports. In terms of AP articles, you believe they are appropriate to include not as major sources of news but to acknowledge certain world events—such as when a prominent person dies. All of these suggestions are extremely valuable.

I want to thank you all for participating in this focus-group discussion. As I said before, you, the students, are the primary audience that we're trying to serve, so your input is greatly appreciated. I want you to know all of your suggestions will be carefully considered by *The Lantern* staff. Thank you all again.

Selecting a Conference Site for ZAPPlication.org®

Anthony J. Radich
Executive Director, Western States Arts Federation (WESTAF)

This discussion among staff at WESTAF was held in Denver, Colorado, on November 10, 2010, to select a city in which to hold the annual conference of artists and arts administrators affiliated with ZAPPlication.org® (ZAPP®). ZAPP® is an online software system that artists can use to enter art fairs. Participants in the discussion, in addition to Anthony Radich, were the members of the ZAPP® project team: Leah Charney, manager; Christina Villa, program assistant; and Adrianne Devereux, finance officer. Used with permission of Anthony J. Radich, Leah Charney, Christina Villa, and Adrianne Devereux.

Anthony: Thank you for taking the time to meet. Our goal at this meeting is to decide where we will hold our ZAPP® conference in 2011. I am going to turn to Leah and ask her to define the problem.

Leah: Okay, we just completed our second annual ZAPP® conference. This is, as you know, a professional development conference for artists and administrators of art fairs. The first conference was in August 2009, and the conference was held in Denver. The second year, it was held in September in St. Louis, so now we are looking to plan our third annual conference. We're searching for another location outside of Denver—a location on the East Coast or in the Southeast—and we want to hold it again in the fall, so August, September, or perhaps October are the months we are looking at.

Anthony: And why are you thinking the East Coast or the Southeast for this conference?

Leah: Sure. We selected Denver for the first year of the conference. Denver is our home city—and when you're launching something, that makes sense. Keep it close to home. Then we moved it to the Midwest for a more central location. So now we're thinking that either the East Coast or the Southeast region makes sense demographically. Moving it there will allow us to attract different folks who may not have been able to join us in the conference's first two years.

Anthony: That makes sense. Thank you. And now shall we turn to brainstorming possible locations for the conference that are in the Southeast or on the East Coast? These also need to be places where we could hold a conference in the fall.

Leah: How about Atlanta or Florida?

Adrianne: Or maybe Pennsylvania?

Christina: I'd like to suggest Virginia.

Anthony: Terry Adams mentioned Kentucky as a possible site when I had lunch with him yesterday. He's the director of the Cherry Creek Arts Festival. Kentucky isn't very far east, but it's east of Denver. Any other suggestions? So far, we have Atlanta, Florida, Pennsylvania, Virginia, and Kentucky on our list.

Christina: I can't think of any others I would propose.

Leah: Me, neither.

Anthony: OK, then, let's turn to evaluating these locations. What criteria do you think we need to use to select a city for the conference?

Leah: We need a city that has either a large artist community or a reputable art fair or arts event. If we held our conference before or after an art fair or other such event, there might be a lot of artists or show administrators who would be interested in coming to that city and staying for the conference. They may even be willing to arrive early for the conference and stay for the art fair. I think we would want to hold the conference before such an event because holding it after a large arts fair probably wouldn't attract the artist population we want.

Anthony: Okay, and why would that be?

Christina: The artists are tired after doing a huge art fair. They would be tired and not inclined to attend a conference right after spending several days at a fair.

Anthony: This is good to know. Anything else for criteria?

Leah: We also would like it to be somewhere that is accessible for many people, so either near a major airport or a major highway.

Anthony: That makes sense. I'm going to now turn to Adrianne. From your work in preparing meetings, are there other criteria you would suggest?

Adrianne: We need to consider whether the location is going to be in a hotel or whether we're going to find a space sponsored by an art fair. In some of the cities on our list, it would be easier to find a space in connection with an art fair, and that could save us some money.

Anthony: Okay.

Adrianne: We also should consider the cost of flying to places. We want something where we can get a good deal even if we're not paying for it. I'm sure more people will come if air fares are not high.

Leah: Not everyone is going to fly to the conference, so we want a site accessible to large numbers of artists traveling by car. We did very well last year attracting local artists—artists in a 300- or 400-mile region—who were willing to drive to the conference.

Anthony: That's an excellent consideration. I want to go back to what Adrianne said and underscore the sponsored space. We had a reception at the St. Louis Artists' Guild that I thought was really lovely and fit us size wise, and I think people really liked it. We can't always come up with something like that for our conference, but I think getting people out in the community beyond the hotel is good. So I would like one of our criteria to be whether we might be able to get a space like this. Christina, are there other criteria you want to add?

Christina: I can't think of any.

Adrianne: Neither can I.

Leah: I think we have the main ones we need to take into account.

Anthony: Our criteria, then, seem to be: The city has an art fair or event that is held in the fall and with which we could coordinate, it is easily accessible by plane or car, it is a city that is cheap to fly to, and it might have a space we could use that is linked to the art event or an arts organization in the city. So now let's go through each site suggested and evaluate it against our criteria.

Leah: I'd like to start with Florida. In talking to the Artists Advisory Committee, it seems like the trend was that the market was really good in Florida, so everyone flocked there, and now artists are trying to stay away from there. So cities in Florida might not meet our criterion of accessibility to artists—at least not to good artists.

Anthony: Okay.

Adrianne: On the other hand, there are definitely more shows in Florida than anywhere else.

Anthony: Really?

Adrianne: Yes, so Florida might give us more opportunities for partnering. We might even be able to sandwich between two prominent events if there is one happening one weekend and another happening the following weekend. If our conference were in the middle, we might attract a different audience. So Florida might meet our criterion of a city where we could link up with arts festivals or events.

Christina: Florida is relatively easy to get to from the Midwest and the East.

Anthony: If we were to hold it in Florida, where in Florida would we do it?

Leah: Miami.

Anthony: Okay.

Leah: Or West Palm Beach, Boca, or Bonita Springs.

Anthony: Okay.

Adrianne: We have some art shows in the Orlando area, but I would say a lot of our shows are in Palm Beach County.

Anthony: So the southern area of Florida.

Adrianne: Yes.

Leah: Yes, Coconut Grove and West Palm Beach.

Anthony: Okay. And how does a site in Florida fit our other criteria? I guess flying there is average in terms of price.

Christina: Getting into Miami is pretty easy, I would say, but accessibility might be an issue if a hurricane comes up. The fall is hurricane season.

Anthony: Yes, between Ft. Lauderdale and Miami, it's pretty inexpensive to get in most of the time, but possible hurricanes could be an issue.

Leah: Yes. Flights are probably cheap, but, yes, we could run into weather issues.

Christina: I like the idea of Coconut Grove or Boca Raton, but many of the significant shows in this area are in the spring, so they don't fit our criterion of being connected to a major art show.

Anthony: Okay.

Adrianne: Like SunFest is in Palm Beach County, but it's in April. Coconut Grove is also in April or May. They do a lot of off-season shows because people go down there in the winter time.

Anthony: Florida, then, seems to meet some criteria, but we're not so sure that it would meet the criterion of being accessible to artists simply because of the unique situation there in terms of perception. Access also might be an issue if there's a hurricane. Does anyone know about spaces in any cities in Florida where we might hold the conference other than a hotel?

Adrianne: No, I don't. I've never been to Florida.

Anthony: How about you, Leah and Christina? Any idea about whether some kind of interesting space might be available to us because of the presence of an arts festival or an arts organization?

Leah: No. This is something we'd have to look into.

Anthony: Yes. Should we move on to another site on our list?

Christina: What about Virginia?

Adrianne: I know there are two major arts festivals in the Virginia Beach and Norfolk area—the Boardwalk Arts Show and the Neptune Festival. The Boardwalk attracts somewhere in the range of 500 to 800 applicants. It's in the summer, though, so we couldn't connect up with that, and it's certainly the major one. Neptune isn't as prominent a show.

Anthony: Okay, so Virginia perhaps doesn't meet our criterion of connecting to a major arts festival because we want our conference to be in the fall.

Christina: It is an accessible location, though—it's sort of in the middle of the area we're trying to reach. People could even fly into Baltimore, which Southwest Airlines serves, and drive down to Virginia Beach. That is about a four-hour drive, though.

Anthony: That's true, so Virginia is somewhat accessible and relatively cheap to reach. I'm familiar with that area, and I think finding an interesting art space in which to hold our conference would be possible. There's a contemporary art center in Virginia

Beach, for example. Virginia seems a possible location, then, in that it meets many of our criteria. If we held it in Virginia Beach, though, the art fair available to us in the fall isn't very large or very renowned, so that might be a problem. Let's turn to Kentucky. I'm the one who mentioned Kentucky. I was thinking of Louisville simply because St. James is a partner, which means we could connect with a large art show and might be able to find a good space in which to hold the conference as a result.

Leah: Yes, and St. James is the main show, but then there are also three other events that happen simultaneously within a mile the first weekend of October. So it might be a great way to capture a lot of artists just because there are four arts events happening simultaneously.

Adrianne: Yes. There are 400 to 600 artists right there.

Christina: Kentucky isn't quite as accessible by plane and car as some other locations, but the fact that there will be so many artists already there helps.

Anthony: Good summary. Shall we take a look at Atlanta?

Leah: Well, I think one thing to note about Atlanta is that you have an easy airport. Many airlines have hubs there, and it's easy to get in and out of the city. It's also often cheap to fly into Atlanta.

Anthony: Okay, so Atlanta meets our criteria of accessibility and cheapness. Atlanta doesn't have hurricanes that might cause problems for accessibility. That's a plus.

Adrianne: They do have a lot of shows in the fall.

Anthony: Okay. Anyone familiar with spaces where we could hold a conference in Atlanta other than in a hotel?

Christina: I'm not that familiar with Atlanta.

Leah: I'm not, either.

Adrianne: It's probably time to turn to Pennsylvania. I suggested it, and I like the idea of Pennsylvania, but I'm thinking now that it probably doesn't meet many of our criteria. There's a great art show affiliated with ZAPP®, but it's out there in central Penn in the middle of nowhere.

Anthony: And I don't think Philly or Pittsburgh would be especially attractive for our target audience.

Leah: Pennsylvania is also pretty far from many areas of the country with large art shows. I'm thinking we should eliminate Pennsylvania from consideration.

Anthony: Okay with everyone?

Adrianne,
Leah, and
Christina: Yes.

Anthony: So let's see where we are. Florida is still in the running, but I think it is lower on our list because, although it's cheap to get to, accessibility might be compromised by the fact that some artists don't want to go there now, and the weather might keep people away. Also, many of the good shows that we'd want to connect with are not in the fall. We don't know enough about possible spaces in the various cities in Florida to tell yet whether we could find someplace to hold the conference that's interesting.

Virginia is still on the list. We could say Virginia Beach is accessible because it's only four hours from D.C. or Baltimore, but it's also not accessible for that reason—some people might balk at that drive. We know there are good spaces there to which we'd have access, but the art show that is held in the fall in Virginia Beach isn't one of the major fairs. So that's a mark against it as a site for the conference.

In Kentucky, we have several arts events held in the same weekend, so we'd already have a lot of potential audience members there, even though accessibility usually wouldn't be quite as easy for many people. Because of the art events going on, we probably could find a good place to hold the conference.

Atlanta is a good contender in that it is accessible by plane or car, is cheap to get to, and we know there are art shows there in the fall. We don't know much about potential spaces there, though.

And we decided to delete Pennsylvania from consideration simply because the major show there is in a remote location and doesn't meet the criterion of accessibility.

Have I accurately summarized your perceptions of where we are in assessing the sites?

Leah: Yes.

Christina: Yes.

Anthony: How about this? We might be able to select from these four options more easily if we had a bit more information.

For our next meeting, Leah, would you come with the names and dates and number of participants in the art shows held in the fall in these four locations?

Christina, would you bring a list of the ZAPP® partners who are located in these cities?

Adrianne, would you do a quick check via Orbitz or Expedia to see how much it tends to cost to fly into these cities? Maybe take two cities in the East or South—places that have a lot of artists—and see how much it would cost to fly into these cities?

We still don't know all that much about interesting spaces in which to hold our conference in these cities, but I'm thinking that's something we can investigate once a site is chosen, especially if we have a partner in the area.

Once we have the information on art shows, partners, and cost of flights, I think we'll be able to select a city pretty easily that we are confident meets our criteria. How does that sound?

Leah: Sounds good.

Adrianne: Yes, I'll bring that information to our next meeting.

Anthony: Shall we plan to meet next Tuesday at this same time?

Christina: That works for me.

Leah: Me, too.

Adrianne: Yes, I'll be here.

Anthony: Great! Thank you for your input and time. I think we'll be able to make our decision at the next meeting.

Endnotes

CHAPTER 1

[1] Thomas L. Friedman, *The World is Flat: A Brief History of the Twenty-first Century* (New York: Farrar, Straus and Giroux, 2005), 49.

[2] Sam Howe Verhovek, *Jet Age: The Comet, the 707, and the Race to Shrink the World* (New York: Avery/Penguin, 2010), 205.

[3] Friedman, *The World is Flat*, 7.

[4] Friedman, *The World is Flat*, 8.

[5] Friedman, *The World is Flat*, 8.

[6] Friedman, *The World is Flat*, 9.

[7] Friedman, *The World is Flat*, 9.

[8] Friedman, *The World is Flat*, 9 [Italics added].

[9] Friedman, *The World is Flat*, 9.

[10] Friedman, *The World is Flat*, 10.

[11] Friedman, *The World is Flat*, 10 [Italics added].

[12] Friedman, *The World is Flat*, 9.

[13] Friedman, *The World is Flat*, 10.

[14] Friedman, *The World is Flat*, 11.

[15] Friedman, *The World is Flat*, 10.

[16] Friedman, *The World is Flat*, 10.

[17] Kati Suominen, "How Digital Protectionism Threatens to Derail 21st Century Businesses," *BRINK*, Global Risk Center, Marsh & McLennan Companies, December 3, 2014; Dominic Eggel and Marc Galvin, "Globalisation Unbound: Transnational Flows in the Digital Era," *Global Challenges*, The Graduate Institute Geneva 3, March 2018.

[18] Pepi Sappal, "Global Tourism Surges +7% to 1.32bn in 2017, Says UNWTO," *TRBusiness*, January 16, 2018.

[19] "Global Digital Population as of April 2018 (in Millions)," The Statistics Portal, Statista, https://www.statista.com/statistics/617136/digital-population-worldwide

[20] Jamake Highwater, *The Primal Mind: Vision and Reality in Indian America* (New York: Meridian, 1981), 65.

[21] The terms *conquest* and *conversion* to describe modes of rhetoric were developed by Sally Miller Gearhart in "The Womanization of Rhetoric," *Women's Studies International Quarterly* 2 (1979): 196. The terms *advisory* and *invitational rhetoric* and the general schema for

the modes of rhetoric were developed by Sonja K. Foss and Cindy L. Griffin in an early draft of "Beyond Persuasion: A Proposal for an Invitational Rhetoric," *Communication Monographs* 62 (1995): 2–18. The term *benevolent rhetoric* was developed by Barbara J. Walkosz in a conversation with Sonja K. Foss, 1999.

22 Suzette Haden Elgin, *How to Disagree Without Being Disagreeable: Getting Your Point Across with the Gentle Art of Verbal Self-Defense* (New York: John Wiley, 1997), 80.

23 Kenneth Burke, *Language as Symbolic Action: Essays on Life, Literature, and Method* (Berkeley: University of California Press, 1966), 44–52.

24 Margaret J. Wheatley, *Leadership and the New Science: Discovering Order in a Chaotic World* (San Francisco: Berrett-Koehler, 1999), 67.

25 Annette Simmons, *A Safe Place for Dangerous Truths: Using Dialogue to Overcome Fear & Distrust at Work* (New York: American Management Association, 1999), 20.

26 Justin Trudeau, Commencement address, New York University, New York, May 26, 2018.

27 Alix Spiegel and Micaela Rodriguez, "Eager to Burst His Own Bubble, A Techie Made Apps to Randomize His Life," National Public Radio, *Invisibilia*, June 15, 2017.

28 Jon Kabat-Zinn, *Full Catastrophe Living*, 15th ed. (New York: Delta/Bantam Dell/Random House, 2009), 9.

29 Dalai Lama and Howard C. Cutler, *The Art of Happiness: A Handbook for Living* (New York: Riverhead, 1998), 173–74.

30 Kabat-Zinn, *Full Catastrophe Living*, 154.

31 John McKnight and Peter Block, *The Abundant Community: Awakening the Power of Families and Neighborhoods* (San Francisco: Berrett-Koehler, 2010); Cormac Russell, *Asset Based Community Development (ABCD): Looking Back to Look Forward* (Cormac Russell, 2015).

32 The ABCD efforts of the Hillside Court neighborhood are described in a video produced by Wendy McCaig, founder of Embrace Richmond, *The Story of Our Shift to ABCD: Making the Shift Series #3*.

33 Ali Bulent Cambel, *Applied Chaos Theory: A Paradigm for Complexity* (New York: Academic/Harcourt Brace, 1993), 1.

34 Edward N. Lorenz, *The Essence of Chaos* (Seattle: University of Washington Press, 1993), 69, 102.

35 Stephen H. Kellert, *In the Wake of Chaos: Unpredictable Order in Dynamical Systems* (Chicago: University of Chicago Press, 1993), 12.

36 Stephen Hawking, *Black Holes and Baby Universes* (New York: Bantam, 1993), 150.

37 Malcolm Gladwell, *The Tipping Point: How Little Things Can Make a Big Difference* (New York: Little, Brown, 2000), 8, 9.

38 Much of this description of invitational rhetoric is from Foss and Griffin, "Beyond Persuasion," 2–18.

39 James S. Baumlin and Tita French Baumlin, "Rogerian and Platonic Dialogue in—and Beyond—the Writing Classroom," in *Rogerian Perspectives: Collaborative Rhetoric for Oral and Written Communication*, ed. Nathaniel Teich (Norwood, NJ: Ablex, 1992), 128.

40 Some of the ideas in this section are from: Sonja K. Foss and Cindy L. Griffin, "The Metatheoretical Foundations of Invitational Rhetoric: An Exploration of Axiological, Epistemological, and Ontological Assumptions," manuscript in preparation for *Inviting Understanding: A Portrait of Invitational Rhetoric*.

41 Carl R. Rogers, *A Way of Being* (Boston: Houghton Mifflin, 1980), 143.

42 Simmons, *A Safe Place for Dangerous Truths*, 99.

43 The conversations about abortion, initiated by the Public Conversations Project, were described in a story on National Public Radio, July 23, 1018.

44 Martha C. Nussbaum, *Cultivating Humanity: A Classical Defense of Reform in Liberal Education* (Cambridge: Harvard University Press, 1997), 10–11.

45 The term *trial empathy* is suggested by Heinz Kohut, *The Restoration of the Self* (New York: International Universities Press, 1977), 168; *trial identification* comes from Stanley L. Olinick, "A Critique of Empathy and Sympathy," in *Empathy I*, eds. Joseph Lichtenberg, Melvin Bornstein, and Donald Silver (Hillsdale, NJ: Lawrence Erlbaum, 1984), 137–66;

and *transient identification* is a label proposed by James H. Spencer Jr., "Discussion," in *Empathy I*, eds. Joseph Lichtenberg, Melvin Bornstein, and Donald Silver (Hillsdale, NJ: Lawrence Erlbaum, 1984), 37–42.

[46] Anatol Rapoport, quoted by Daniel C. Cennett in his book review of *The God Delusion* by Richard Dawkins, *Free Inquiry* 27 (December 2006/January 2007): 66.

[47] Myles Horton with Judith Kohl and Herbert Kohl, *The Long Haul: An Autobiography* (New York: Doubleday, 1990), 16.

[48] Lisbeth Lipari, "Listening, Thinking, Being," *Communication Theory* 20 (2010): 350.

[49] Krista Ratcliffe, "Rhetorical Listening: A Trope for Interpretive Invention and a 'Code of Cross-Cultural Conduct,'" *College Composition and Communication* 51 (1999): 205, 207.

[50] Michael P. Nichols, *The Lost Art of Listening* (New York: Guilford, 1995), 250.

[51] Lipari, "Listening, Thinking, Being," 355.

[52] Lipari, "Listening, Thinking, Being," 350–51.

[53] Abraham Kaplan, "The Life of Dialogue," in *The Reach of Dialogue: Confirmation, Voice, and Community*, eds. Rob Anderson, Kenneth N. Cissna, and Ronald C. Arnett (Cresskill, NJ: Hampton, 1994), 40.

[54] Karen Hellesvig-Gaskell, "The Difference Between Hearing and Listening Skills," June 13, 2017, *Livestrong.com*.

[55] Gearhart, "The Womanization of Rhetoric," 195.

[56] Ursula K. Le Guin, "Bryn Mawr Commencement Address (1986)," *Dancing at the Edge of the World: Thoughts on Words, Women, Places* (New York: Grove, 1989), 150–51.

[57] Sonia Johnson, *The Ship that Sailed into the Living Room: Sex and Intimacy Reconsidered* (Estancia, NM: Wildfire, 1991), 162.

[58] Starhawk, *Truth or Dare: Encounters with Power, Authority, and Mystery* (San Francisco: Harper & Row, 1987), 9–10.

[59] Starhawk, *Truth or Dare*, 11.

[60] Dennis A. Lynch, Diana George, and Marilyn M. Cooper, "Moments of Argument: Agonistic Inquiry and Confrontational Cooperation," *College Composition and Communication* 48 (1997): 80.

[61] Carl R. Rogers, *On Becoming a Person: A Therapist's View of Psychotherapy* (Boston: Houghton Mifflin, 1961), 333.

[62] Martin Buber, *Between Man and Man*, trans. Ronald Gregor Smith (New York: Macmillan, 1965), xiv.

[63] Gearhart, "The Womanization of Rhetoric," 198.

[64] Simmons, *A Safe Place for Dangerous Truths*, 57.

[65] Simmons, *A Safe Place for Dangerous Truths*, 45.

[66] Sally Miller Gearhart, quoted in Eric Mills, "Enriching and Expanding the Animal Movement: Dr. Sally Gearhart Talks about Sexism, Racism and Coalition-Building," *Agenda* 111 (1983): 5.

[67] Deborah Tannen, *The Argument Culture: Stopping America's War of Words* (New York: Ballantine, 1998), 14.

[68] Tannen, *The Argument Culture*, 3.

[69] Suzette Haden Elgin, foreword, *Peacetalk 101* (Maple Shade, NJ: Lethe Press, 2002), 1.

[70] Charles Simic, quoted in Tannen, *The Argument Culture*, 7–8.

[71] Janice Moulton, "A Paradigm of Philosophy: The Adversary Method," in *Discovering Reality: Feminist Perspectives on Epistemology, Metaphysics, Methodology, and Philosophy of Science*, eds. Sandra Harding and Merrill B. Hintikka (Boston: D. Reidel, 1983), 151.

CHAPTER 2

[1] Lloyd F. Bitzer, "The Rhetorical Situation," *Philosophy and Rhetoric* 1 (1968): 1–14.

[2] Kenneth Burke, *The Philosophy of Literary Form: Studies in Symbolic Action* (Berkeley: University of California Press, 1973), 1.

[3] Thomas J. Gallagher, "Native Participation in Land Management Planning in Alaska," *Arctic* 41 (1988): 96.

[4] "How Employers Use Social Media to Screen Applicants," *Undercover Recruiter*, https://theundercoverrecruiter.com/infographic-how-recruiters-use-social-media-screen-applicants

[5] Richard M. Weaver, *Language is Sermonic: Richard M. Weaver on the Nature of Rhetoric*, eds. Richard L. Johannesen, Rennard Strickland, and Ralph T. Eubanks (Baton Rouge: Louisiana State University Press, 1970), 222.

[6] Weaver, *Language is Sermonic*, 224.

[7] Kenneth Burke, *A Rhetoric of Motives* (New York: Prentice-Hall, 1950), 55.

[8] Burke, *The Philosophy of Literary Form*, 146.

[9] Nelle Morton, *The Journey is Home* (Boston: Beacon, 1985), 202–07.

CHAPTER 3

[1] These conditions are derived, in part, from Sonja K. Foss and Cindy L. Griffin, "Beyond Persuasion: A Proposal for an Invitational Rhetoric," *Communication Monographs* 62 (1995): 2–18.

[2] Nancy Signorielli, "Television's Mean and Dangerous World: A Continuation of Cultural Indicators Perspective," in *Cultivation Analysis: New Directions in Media Effects Research*, eds. Nancy Signorielli and Michael Morgan (Newbury Park, CA: Sage, 1990), 85–106.

[3] The theory of spiral of silence offers one explanation for why individuals might conceal their opinions when they believe that their views are in the minority. See Elisabeth Noelle-Neumann, *The Spiral of Silence*, 2nd ed. (Chicago: University of Chicago Press, 1993).

[4] Annette Simmons, *A Safe Place for Dangerous Truths: Using Dialogue to Overcome Fear & Distrust at Work* (New York: American Management Association, 1999), 82.

[5] Simmons, *A Safe Place*, 80–81.

[6] Mary Alice Speke Ferdig, "Exploring the Social Construction of Complex Self-Organizing Change: A Study of Emerging Change in the Regulation of Nuclear Power" (Ph.D. diss., Benedictine University, 2001), 187.

[7] Sally Miller Gearhart, "Womanpower: Energy Re-Sourcement," in *The Politics of Women's Spirituality: Essays on the Rise of Spiritual Power Within the Feminist Movement*, ed. Charlene Spretnak (Garden City, NY: Doubleday, 1982), 95.

[8] Bill Amend, "FoxTrot," *The Albuquerque Journal*, January 12, 2002, F3.

[9] Suzette Haden Elgin, *How to Disagree Without Being Disagreeable: Getting Your Point Across with the Gentle Art of Verbal Self-Defense* (New York: John Wiley, 1997), 145–46.

[10] Adrienne Rich, Audre Lorde, and Alice Walker, "A Statement for Voices Unheard: A Challenge to the National Book Awards," *Ms.*, September 1974, 38.

[11] Barack Obama, eulogy for the Reverend Clementa Pinckney, Charleston, SC, June 26, 2015.

[12] Leopoldina Fortunati, "The Mobile Phone: Towards New Categories and Social Relations 1," *Information, Communication & Society* 5 (2002): 518–19.

[13] Fortunati, "The Mobile Phone," 515.

[14] Jeanine Warisse Turner and Sonja K. Foss, "Options for the Construction of Attentional Social Presence in a Digitally Enhanced Multicommunicative Environment," *Communication Theory* 28 (February 2018): 22–45.

CHAPTER 4

[1] Eli Pariser, *The Filter Bubble: How the New Personalized Web is Changing What We Read and How We Think* (New York: Penguin, 2011); Dominic Spohr, "Fake News and Ideological Polarization: Filter Bubbles and Selective Exposure," *Business Information Review* 34 (2017): 150–60.

[2] Cass R. Sunstein, *Infotopia: How Many Minds Produce Knowledge* (New York: Oxford University Press, 2006), 9.

CHAPTER 5

[1] Ari Seth Cohen and Debra Rapoport, "Better with Age," TEDx, Amsterdam, The Netherlands, December 2, 2014.

[2] Donald J. Trump, speech on Afghanistan, Washington, DC, August 21, 2017.

[3] Nikki Haley, speech on US withdrawal from the United Nations Human Rights Commission, The Heritage Foundation, Washington, DC, July 18, 2018.

[4] David Cameron, speech on immigration, Smethwick, West Midlands, UK, November 28, 2014.

[5] Hans Rosling, "Asia's Rise—How and When," TEDIndia, Mumbai, India, November 2009.

[6] Xi Jinping, speech at opening ceremony of the Nineteenth Congress of the Communist Party, Beijing, China, October 18, 2017.

[7] The motivated sequence was developed by Alan Monroe. See Raymie E. McKerrow, Bruce E. Gronbeck, Douglas Ehninger, and Alan H. Monroe, *Principles and Types of Speech Communication*, 16th ed. (New York: Pearson, 2006).

[8] Ursula K. Le Guin, "The Princess," *Dancing at the Edge of the World: Thoughts on Words, Women, Places* (New York: Harper & Row, 1989), 78–79.

[9] Steve Jobs, "How to Live Before You Die," commencement address, Stanford University, Palo Alto, CA, June 10, 2005.

[10] Rob Portman, speech in support of the "Synthetics Trafficking & Overdose Prevention (STOP) Act," US Senate, Washington, DC, May 24, 2018.

[11] Kevin Durant, acceptance speech, National Basketball Association MVP award ceremony, Edmond, OK, May 6, 2014.

CHAPTER 6

[1] Kendrick Lamar, acceptance speech for best rap album (*Damn*), Grammy Awards ceremony, New York, January 28, 2018.

[2] John Hickenlooper, state of the state address, Denver, CO, January 9, 2014.

[3] Karen Spence, speech to US Conference of Mayors, Washington, DC, January 26, 2018.

[4] J. K. Rowling, "The Fringe Benefits of Failure and the Importance of Imagination," commencement address, Harvard University, Cambridge, MA, June 5, 2008.

[5] Sonia Johnson, *Going Out of Our Minds: The Metaphysics of Liberation* (Freedom, CA: The Crossing Press, 1987), 316.

[6] Martin Luther King Jr., "I Have a Dream," Washington, DC, August 28, 1963.

[7] Serena Williams, speech accepting the *Sports Illustrated* Sportsperson of the Year Award, New York, December 15, 2015.

[8] Melissa Fleming, "A Boat Carrying 500 Refugees Sunk at Sea: The Story of Two Survivors," TEDx Thessaloniki, Thessaloniki, Greece, May 2015.

[9] Donald J. Trump, speech on opioid epidemic, Nashville, TN, May 29, 2018.

[10] Susana Martinez, state of the state address, Santa Fe, NM, January 20, 2015.

[11] Mary Barra, address to employees of General Motors, town hall meeting, Warren, MI, September 17, 2015.

[12] Benjamin Netanyahu, speech to the United Nations, New York, September 19, 2017.

[13] William Jefferson Clinton, presidential nomination acceptance address, Democratic National Convention, New York, July 16, 1992.

[14] Barack Obama, speech at memorial service, Fort Hood military base, Fort Hood, TX, November 10, 2009.

[15] Hillary Clinton, keynote address, Democratic National Convention, Denver, CO, August 26, 2008.

[16] Jane Clare Jones, "Water Baby: A Eulogy for Our Departed Prince," *Popmatters*, June 1, 2016.

[17] Barack Obama, remarks at a town hall meeting, College Park, MD, July 22, 2011.

[18] Pope Francis, speech to the United Nations General Assembly, New York, September 25, 2015.

[19] Fred Rogers, commencement address, Chatham University, Pittsburgh, PA, May 19, 2002.

[20] Walt Bresette, "We Are All Mohawks," *Green Letter* [Winter 1990]: 50.

[21] Bobby Jindal, victory speech upon election as governor of Louisiana, Baton Rouge, LA, October 20, 2007.

[22] Conan O'Brien, commencement address, Harvard University, Cambridge, MA, June 7, 2000.

[23] Chief Weninock, quoted in T. C. McLuhan, ed. *Touch the Earth: A Self-Portrait of Indian Existence* (New York: Touchstone, 1971), 10.

[24] Meghan Markle, speech at United Nations Conference on Women, New York, March 8, 2015.

[25] Frances McDormand, acceptance speech for best actress, Academy Awards, Los Angeles, CA, March 5, 2018.

[26] Tracy K. Smith, "The Good Life," in *Life on Mars* (Minneapolis, MN: Graywolf Press, 2011), 64.

[27] Barack Obama, press conference, White House, Washington, DC, March 3, 2011.

[28] Janet Hughes, "Exhibiting with Pride," presentation at the opening of the Missouri Visual Artists Biennial, University of Missouri, Columbus, MO, March 5, 1993.

[29] Taylor Mali, "What Teachers Make," TED talk, Bowery Poetry Club, New York, November, 2005.

[30] Maddie Poynter, "Anti-Bullying Speech," http://www.thebullyproject.com/anti_bullying_speech.

[31] Alice Walker, "Sent by Earth: A Message from the Grandmother Spirit," in *We are the Ones We Have Been Waiting For: Inner Light in a Time of Darkness* (New York: 2006), 208.

[32] Ruth Bader Ginsburg, speech upon receipt of a lifetime achievement award, Tel Aviv, Israel, July 5, 2018.

[33] Angela Davis, speech at Women's March on Washington, Washington, DC, January 21, 2017.

[34] Drake, "Is There More," *Scorpion*, produced by Promo and Wallis Lane, 2018.

[35] Diane Stein, *Casting the Circle: A Woman's Book of Ritual* (Freedom, CA: Crossing, 1990), 178.

[36] Patrick Modiano, address upon receiving a Nobel Prize in Literature, Swedish Academy, Stockholm, Sweden, December 7, 2014.

[37] Kizley Benedict, "Estimating the Number of Homeless in America: Statistics Show that America's Homeless Problem is Getting Worse," *The DataFace*, January 21, 2018, http://thedataface.com/2018/01/public-health/american-homelessness.

[38] Michelle Obama, keynote address, Democratic National Convention, Denver, CO, August 25, 2008.

[39] Eric Moody, June 24, 1982. For more information, see Betty Tootell, *All Four Engines Have Failed: The True and Triumphant Story of BA Flight 009 and the Jakarta Incident* (London: André Deutsch, 1985).

[40] Lady Gaga, "The Prime Rib of America," Portland, ME, September 20, 2010.

CHAPTER 7

[1] Sonia Sotomayor, opening statement to the Senate Judiciary Committee, Washington, DC, July 13, 2009.

[2] Billy Collins, "Introduction to Poetry," *The Apple that Astonished Paris* (Fayetteville: University of Arkansas Press, 1998), 58.

[3] Jessica Jackley, "Poverty, Money—and Love," TEDGlobal, Oxford, UK, July 2010.

[4] Terry Russell and Renny Russell, *On the Loose* (San Francisco: Sierra Club, 1967), 45.

[5] Nancy Pelosi, "Helen Keller's Statue," Washington, DC, October 7, 2009.

[6] Dan Rather, "CBS Evening News Signoff," New York, March 9, 2005.

[7] Al Sharpton, eulogy for Michael Jackson, Los Angeles, CA, July 7, 2009.

[8] Joe Kennedy III, Democratic rebuttal to the state of the union address, Fall River, MA, January 30, 2018.

[9] Imre Kertész, "Heureka!," Nobel Prize in Literature address, Swedish Academy, Stockholm, Sweden, December 2, 2002.

[10] LeBron James, "We All Have to Do Better," 2016 ESPY Awards, Los Angeles, CA, July 13, 2016.

[11] Barack Obama, farewell speech, Chicago, IL, January 10, 2017.

[12] Shel Silverstein, "Whatif," *A Light in the Attic* (New York: HarperCollins, 1981), 90.

[13] Mark Zuckerberg, commencement address, Harvard University, Cambridge, MA, May 25, 2017.

[14] Jeff Flake, speech announcing decision not to seek reelection, US Senate, Washington, DC, October 24, 2017.

[15] Christine D. Keen, "May You Live in Interesting Times: The Workplace in the '90s," *Vital Speeches of the Day* 58 (November 15, 1991): 83–86.

[16] Quang Nguyen, speech at freedom rally, Prescott, AZ, July 24, 2010.

[17] Mindy Kaling, commencement address, Dartmouth College, Hanover, NH, June 10, 2018.

[18] Pope Francis, address at international peace conference, Al-Azhar University, Cairo, Egypt, April 28, 2017.

[19] Barack Obama, Father's Day address, Washington, DC, June 21, 2010.

[20] Jeff Bezos, commencement address, Princeton University, Princeton, NJ, June 22, 2010.

[21] Barack Obama, eulogy for the Reverend Clementa Pinckney, Charleston, SC, June 26, 2015.

[22] Mo Yan, "Storytellers," address upon receiving a Nobel Prize in Literature, Swedish Academy, Stockholm, Sweden, December 7, 2012.

[23] Lindsay Cook, presentation to conference of the New Zealand Society of Clinical & Applied Hypnotherapy, Hamilton, NZ, September 19, 2009.

CHAPTER 8

[1] Bill Gates, speech at the International Consumer Electronics Show, Las Vegas, NV, January 7, 2002.

[2] Barack Obama, speech on immigration reform, School of International Service, American University, Washington, DC, July 1, 2010.

[3] Naval Adm. William H. McRaven, "To Change the World, Start by Making Your Bed," commencement address, University of Texas at Austin, Austin, TX, May 17, 2014.

[4] Jimmy Fallon, "Remember That It Gets Better," commencement address, Marjorie Stoneman Douglas High School, Parkland, FL, June 4, 2018.

CHAPTER 9

[1] Garr Reynolds, *Presentation Zen: Simple Ideas on Presentation Design and Delivery* (Berkeley, CA: New Riders, 2008), 10.

[2] Elisabeth Bumiller, "We Have Met the Enemy and He Is PowerPoint," *New York Times,* April 27, 2010, www.nytimes.com.

[3] Seth Godin, quoted in Reynolds, *Presentation Zen,* 10.

[4] Franck Frommer, *How PowerPoint Makes You Stupid: The Faulty Causality, Sloppy Logic, Decontextualized Data, and Seductive Showmanship That Have Taken Over Our Thinking,* trans. George Holoch (New York: The New Press, 2012), 227.

[5] David Byrne, "Exegesis," *Envisioning Emotional Epistemological Information* (n.p.: Todomundo, 2003), 1.

[6] Byrne, "Exegesis," 1–2.

[7] Jens E. Kjeldsen, "The Rhetoric of PowerPoint," *Seminar.net* 2 (2006): 2.

[8] Edward R. Tufte, *The Cognitive Style of PowerPoint: Pitching Out Corrupts Within* (Cheshire, CT: Graphics, 2006), 4.

[9] Kjeldsen, "The Rhetoric of PowerPoint," 4.

[10] Tufte, *The Cognitive Style of PowerPoint,* 12.

[11] Ian Parker, "Absolute PowerPoint: Can a Software Package Edit Our Thoughts?," *The New Yorker* 77 (May 28, 2001): 87.

12 Tufte, *The Cognitive Style of PowerPoint*, especially 12, 15, 16, and 24; Gordon Shaw, Robert Brown, and Philip Bromiley, "Strategic Stories: How 3M is Rewriting Business Planning," *Harvard Business Review* 76 (1998): 44.

13 Bumiller, "We Have Met the Enemy."

14 Sebastian Kernbach, Martin J. Eppler, and Sabrina Bresciana, "The Use of Visualization in the Communication of Business Strategies: An Experimental Evaluation," *International Journal of Business Communication* 52 (2015): 164–87.

15 Satoshi Sugahara and Gregory Boland, "The Effectiveness of PowerPoint Presentations in the Accounting Classroom," *Accounting Education* 15 (December 2006): 391–403.

16 Muhlise Cosgun Ögeyik, "The Effectiveness of PowerPoint Presentation and Conventional Lecture on Pedagogical Content Knowledge Attainment," *Innovations in Education and Teaching International* 54 (2017): 503–10.

17 Bent Meier Sørensen, "Let's Ban PowerPoint in Lectures: It Makes Students More Stupid and Professors More Boring," *The Independent*, February 24, 2017, https://www.independent.co.uk/news/education/lets-ban-powerpoint-in-lectures-it-makes-students-more-stupid-and-professors-more-boring-a7597506.html

18 Robin Williams, *The Non-Designer's Presentation Book: Principles for Effective Presentation Design* (Berkeley, CA: Peachpit, 2010), 17.

19 Duarte, quoted in Reynolds, *Presentation Zen*, 90.

20 Kjeldsen, "The Rhetoric of PowerPoint," 12.

21 Reynolds, *Presentation Zen*, 122.

22 Reynolds, *Presentation Zen*, 145.

23 Kjeldsen, "The Rhetoric of PowerPoint," 13.

24 Williams, *The Non-Designer's Presentation Book*, 127.

25 Williams, *The Non-Designer's Presentation Book*, 126.

26 Tufte, *The Cognitive Style of PowerPoint*, 30.

27 Carmine Gallo, "Jeff Bezos Banned PowerPoint in Meetings. His Replacement Is Brilliant," Inc.BrandView, April 25, 2018, https://www.inc.com/carmine-gallo/jeff-bezos-bans-powerpoint-in-meetings-his-replacement-is-brilliant.html

28 Suzette Haden Elgin, *The Last Word on the Gentle Art of Verbal Self-Defense* (New York: Prentice Hall, 1987), 143.

29 Elgin, *The Last Word*, 142.

30 Albert Ellis and Robert A. Harper, *A New Guide to Rational Living* (North Hollywood, CA: Melvin Powers, 1975), 146.

31 This discussion of irrational anxiety is adapted from Ellis and Harper, *A New Guide to Rational Living*, 145–57.

32 Adapted from Elgin, *The Last Word*, 166.

33 For an account of the history of women speakers in the United States, see Karlyn Kohrs Campbell, *Man Cannot Speak for Her: A Critical Study of Early Feminist Rhetoric*, vol. 1 (New York: Greenwood, 1989).

Index